THE SEAT of the ANTICHRIST

Bible Prophecy and The European Union

ERIKA GREY

Pe Danté Press
Danbury, CT

Pe Danté Press

The Seat of the Antichrist: Bible Prophecy and The European Union
Copyright ©2009 Erika Grey
All Rights Reserved. No part of this publication may be reproduced in any form without written permission from Pedante Press.™

Pedante Press™
Suite #4 White Oak
Danbury CT 06810

Library of Congress Control Number: 2010930703
Grey, Erika.
   The Seat of the Antichrist: Bible Prophecy and The European Union/Erika Grey
p.   cm.
Includes endnotes (p.179-192)
Includes Index
ISBN 978-0-9790199-2-0
ISBN 0-9790199-2-3

All Scriptural quotations in this publication are from the New King James Version of the Bible © 1982 by Thomas Nelson, Inc.

Printed in the United States of America

I dedicate this book to the Tribulation Saints. May the teachings in this book help enlighten you, give you knowledge and confirm that which you have been led by the Spirit to know as truth. May our God and the Lord Jesus Christ who you will shortly see coming in the clouds, now be with you as you endure the horrors enacted by the empire of the Beast, and God's judgments onto the earth, which those of us before you have knowledge of, but cannot imagine the magnitude of suffering, pain, distress, trouble, hardship and misery, which you must now endure.

For other works by Erika Grey go to
www.erikagrey.com

TABLE OF CONTENTS

PREFACE 9
INTRODUCTION 11

1   As Were The Days of Noah As Were The Days of Lot 15

As Was the Time of Noah: Violence ....
As Was the Time of Lot: Sexual Immorality................................... 18
False Prophets: The Rise of Cults and the Occult 19
In the Last Days Perilous Times Shall Come.................................. 20

2   The Final World Empire and The Prince That Shall Come 23

The Antichrist ....
The Four Beasts of Daniel.. 25
Tyrus: A Place of Commerce and Trade 29
Babylon... 31
The Final World Empire 33
The Economic Race... 33
The Arrival of the Antichrist... 34
The Antichrist's Reign 35
The Temple Rebuilt... 36
The Abomination of Desolation 38
The Covenant of Death 39
God's Judgments 41
God's Promise 42

3   The Great Whore of Babylon 45

The Mother of Harlots..
False Religion... 46
The Whore's Judgment 47
Religion and the EU's Formation... 49
The Role of the Catholic Church and the European Union....... 52
Social Babylon... 55
Political Babylon's Foretold Destruction 56

4 The Cornerstone for Uniting the World 59

Jean Monnet: The Father of the New Europe 61
The Federalist Movement: Jean Monnet and the EU's Formation 62
Federalist Influence in the EU's Evolution 64
Federalist Ideology 65
Globalization 67
Global Problems 68
World Institutions .....
The Cornerstone for Uniting the World 70
The Coming One-World Government 72

5 The Building of an Empire 73

The First Step to Political Union 74
One Money: The ECU 76
The European Central Bank and the Launch of the Euro 77
The Treaty on Political Union 78
The Amsterdam Treaty 80
The Nice Treaty 81
The Laeken Declaration .....
The Lisbon Treaty 82
The EU Army: The Western European Union .....
The EU and the Nations of the World 86
The Revived Roman Empire 88
The EU Capital 89

6 The Seat of the Antichrist 91

The Ten Horn Federation .....
The Treaty of Rome 92
The Council of Ministers .....
The EU Commission: The Seat of the Antichrist 94
The Vice President of the Commission 104
The European Parliament .....
The Court of Justice 105
The Court of Auditors 106
The European Central Bank 107
Also Within The Institutional Structure .....
The False Prophet .....
DIAGRAM OF EU INSTUTITIONS 110
BIBLICAL DIAGRAM .....

7 Ten Horns Ten Nations 113

27 European Nations? ....
The Three Horns 117
MAP OF EU 120
MAP OF OLD ROMAN EMPIRE ....
STATES ON THE CURRENT AGENDA 121

8 The Mark of the Beast 123

The Technological Race among Nations 124
The Commission's RTD Network 126
Replacing the Cash System 129
The Marriage of Man to Computers 129
The Mark of the Beast 130
The Number of His Name 131

9 The US-EU Partnership 133

The Trans-Atlantic Declaration 135
The Decline of the US 137
The Next Superpower 142
America's Last Stand 146
A View to the Past 148

10 The Peace Treaty 149

Jews Return to Their Own Land ....
Israel's History of Conflict 150
The Peace Process 153
The Oslo Accords ....
The EU and Israel 155
The Conference on Security and Cooperation in the Middle East and the EU . 159
Demands a Leading Role in the Middle East ....
Israel's Covenant of Death 167
The Antichrist? 169

11 It Will Surely Come 171

The Headlines to Watch For 173
The God of the Bible and The Tribulation 174
The Bible's Message of Hope 178
Endnotes 179
Index 193

PREFACE

This work began in the late 1980's as a Bible study to see if our world was in fact in the end times. Disappointed by the conspiracy theories that I learned of in my early years as a Christian, which taught the immediate fulfillment of end time prophecy, I embarked on my own research. If prophecy was to be fulfilled, it would occur through the natural order of events. All previous prophecies came about through the affairs of their day.

Jeremiah predicted the Babylonian invasion of Israel and a conspiracy didn't bring about Babylonia's power. Historical circumstances and events ushered in Babylonian rule. The prophecies of the birth and death of Jesus Christ and the destruction of the second Jewish Temple occurred during Roman rein through its various leaders. Yet when it comes to end time prophecies, conspiracy theories proliferate from the Catholic Church, Illuminati, Masons, Trilateral Commission, Skull and Bones, Rothschild's, Bildeburgers, and Jewish conspiracies which are adopted by some radical Islamic writers and feed the fire of anti-Semitism. These authors always claim to have interviewed insiders who tell all.

The Antichrist steps into his position and forms an alliance with ten rulers. He deceives the world. The Bible does not forecast a group of men as conspiracy theories teach, but one man. A false prophet assists him along with the kings who place their allegiance in him. No conspiracies bring about the final world order.

When examining end time prophecies one discovers gaps. A gap creates a hole from the present to the time of fulfillment and conspiracy theorists fill the gaps with a conspiracy theory. When I began this research over 20 years ago there existed many gaps and in this time they have closed or some have narrowed to the place that one can easily speculate on what will occur next. Conspiracy theories substitute for time consuming research on the part of the author. Many of the authors of prophetic works in relation to current events are theologians and spend little time researching current events. In the end the Devil uses these theories as tools to blind believers from the truth and rob God of glory.

No conspiracy will usher in the final world order. Prophecy will reach fulfillment in the geopolitical system. Viewing it from a geopolitical angle provides a more accurate picture of where our world stands in the prophetic time line in relation to the end times.

My hope is that his book will both educate the reader on the end time prophecies in relation to the European Union and will help to eradicate the conspiracy theories which circulate Evangelical Christian circles. After reading this work the reader will both understand the prophetic forecasts and also gain knowledge of the European Union, which if one eliminated the prophetic writings will alarm anyone. In addition, the reader will stand in awe of a God whose words written several thousand years ago are seeing fulfillment through the events of our day.

INTRODUCTION

After World War II, European leaders proposed the idea of forming the European Steel and Coal Community, which birthed the European Union. Skeptics said the complicated idea will fail. In 1957, European leaders signed the Treaty that marked the birth of the European Union. In the mid 1990's when the EU set out to complete the Common Market and eliminate trade barriers and harmonize laws among the Member States, the skeptics once again said it will fall short.

The prophet Daniel predicted 2600 years ago, the structure of the final world empire that will rule the world in the end of days and launch the Antichrist. He revealed the location of this empire when he forecast that these same people will destroy Jerusalem, and the second Temple. The evil *"prince that shall come"* will arise from these same inhabitants. During the Roman Empire's reign this prophecy saw fulfillment and marked the Roman Empire as the launching pad for the Antichrist. Some Bible eschatologists cited the early European Community as the possible political entity because of its location. With the success of the 1992 Common Market, these scholars were on the mark. When the European Union embarked on its plans for a common currency, experts once again said that the feat will fail. In fact, monetary union achieved such success that the euro is stronger than the US dollar and second in line as a reserve currency to the US dollar.

The Union's next step is to move towards political union and again the skeptics are saying that it will fail for a variety of reasons. Once again they will be wrong as the EU moves to becoming the greatest and most crushing dictatorships ever in existence.

From the start of the research for this work to the completion, this book never became out-dated. Most works that relate Bible prophecy and current events quickly become obsolete as the events turn into history. The Gulf War prompted books as did other historical occurrences. This work from start to finish has not deleted dated information and this book withstands the time test because the European Union continues to evolve into the world power forecast by Daniel and John in the Revelation.

This European Union is a complicated entity and this report takes an academic approach by providing the EU's history, evolution and facts which in many points reveal the EU's wider ambitions and makeup, which parallel with Scripture. This book could have numbered half the pages and with larger print and act as a sensationalized work and leave the reader on the edge of their seat but with many questions. Given the complexity of the EU, less is not more in writing about the EU and prophecy.

The information compiled for this book relied on the European think-tanks that formulate EU Policy and European publications that cover the desks of EU bureaucrats. One can easily find each of the documented works. Several publications that for one reason or another went out of publication such as the newspaper, *The European,* and the journal, *European Affairs* provided excellent information. The Washington Delegation of the European Communities used to publish a magazine called, *Europe: Magazine of the European Communities,* which produced another viable resource. The EU's official publications provide another source. This research began before the advent of the internet when one had to access these periodicals manually. The internet made the research easier because much of the material that one had to order from Brussels or London and subscribe to because US libraries did not carry the information, was now available online. Those publications laid the foundation of knowing where to search online. A good deal of the research for this book does not rely on the American press but rather on the European press and news organizations which offer far greater compressive reporting on the EU and on world news as a whole.

My goal was to leave no stone unturned and provide an analytical work based on quality research. In contrast on the theological end, this work relied on Biblical commentaries from leading commentators in Evangelical circles. Some answers came to me after much prayer, others as I opened the Scriptures and read them in addition to research.

In completing the work came a satisfaction I never experienced with any other work. I came to a place of blessing seeing Scripture literally unfold before my very eyes. Initially, when the first rough draft of this work was completed in the early 1990's, this work was ahead of its time as many people had not even heard of the EU and most could care less. I knew that this would change in time when the EU became more recognized and as the world continued to grow more desperate as the birth pangs that Christ prophesized came upon it. These events occurred this last decade with the horrific hurricane disasters that seemed to occur one after another and the world-wide financial crisis.

At times during the course of this work I felt like a historian, only I was writing about what will take place in the future as if it already happened. I discovered the information that intelligence agency's seek, and questioned why US agencies looked at Japan and China as possible future threats, but never examined the EU, despite its obvious stated ambitions for the global limelight as was in their past, especially considering its undemocratic structure. If I eliminated the Scriptural forecasts out of this report, one will still feel alarmed about the evolving European Union.

As I neared completion of the book, the earthquake in Haiti struck and I felt the urgency to finish the manuscript as soon as possible and get it out to the public because the time of the end is that close.

The EU continues to evolve into the crushing superpower with iron legs forecast by Scripture. Already there are hints of a police state which the British writer and theologian Alan Franklin has reported on concerning various EU laws.

According to prophecy when the Antichrist establishes his dictatorship he will abolish world religion along with any writings that oppose his police state. In that day this book too will be illegal and banned. The timing for this book's message is now while freedom of religion and speech still exists.

CHAPTER 1

AS WAS THE TIME OF NOAH: AS WAS THE TIME OF LOT

As Was the Time of Noah: Violence

One-third of the Bible's message is prophetic. History records the fulfillment of all biblical prophecies except those pertaining to the Tribulation. The "Great Tribulation" occurs within a seven-year time frame (Dan. 9:25-27). It culminates at the battle of Armageddon, which draws the world's armies together in war, which ends with the cataclysmic description of the darkened sun, falling stars and the powers of the heavens shaken (Matt. 24:29). This prompts the second coming of Jesus Christ, who joins the conflict with His heavenly battalion and marks the end of civilization. Daniel 8:23 confirms that the Tribulation begins when society degenerates to such a great degree that God judges the earth. God's purpose is to end sin, fulfill prophecy, and create a new world ruled by Christ.

During Israel's history God utilized the prophets to forecast calamity and judgment on Israeli kings and on the nation for turning against God and following other gods and pagan practices. In some instances, if the king or nation repented, God changed his mind and replaced blessings for judgment. Prior to the Babylonian invasion of Israel the prophet Jeremiah spent his life warning the kings of Israel and the Israelites of the coming Babylonian captivity. In looking at the kingdom period we see that sin progressed from idolatry and worshiping pagan gods to sacrificing children to them. The Israelites torturously murdered their children by burning them in fire to the god Molech. Israel's habitual sin resulted in the Babylonian captivity and the destruction of Solomon's Temple. When God judged Sodom and Gomorrah with fire and brimstone and Noah's civilization with the flood, he rescued Noah and Lot's family and warned each of them of the coming judgment. During the Tribulation God shakes the world with his power and sends his spokespersons. While a few look to Him, the greater number of mankind curses God rather than turn to Him. Today we have God's warning written in the Bible, which contains the books of the Prophets and details the events of the Great Tribulation, which occur during a seven year period of time. Evangelicals believe that just as God spared Noah and Lot's family, he will take believers out of the world in the Rapture just prior to the start of the Tribulation. (Matt.24:30-36, 40-41)

The book of Daniel announces 70 weeks of specific prophetic events which will affect the nation Israel. A Biblical week equals seven secular years. Seventy Biblical weeks total 490 years, which encompass three decrees affecting Jerusalem. Two of these have already happened: from the edict to rebuild Jerusalem under Cyrus, down to the cutting off of the Messiah, was 483 years. The remaining seven years await fulfillment (Dan. 9:24).

During Jesus' ministry, people questioned him about the end of the world. They wanted to know when the end will happen. Jesus provided several signs which include, wars and rumors of wars, famines, pestilences, earthquakes, false prophets, and lawlessness, and all nations will have heard the Gospel. Christ exhorted believers to "watch" for the signs of the times (Mark 13:37). Jesus compared the events leading to His second coming to the labor pains of childbirth (Matt. 24:8, Mark 13:8). These occur closer together, increasing in severity, until the moment of birth.

Events on the international scene, and the escalating rates of violence and natural disasters, happen today at an ever-quickening pace. Hurricanes, tornadoes, and earthquakes break records in their frequency, and strike localities once untouched by the forces of nature. The term tsunami came into our vocabularies after one struck in 2004. According to *National Geographic News*, the tsunami that stuck the Indian Ocean in 2004 became the deadliest tsunami in history. The US Geological Survey estimated that it released the energy of 23,000 Hiroshima-type atomic bombs. After the Haiti earthquake in 2010, *Time Magazine* recorded the "Top 10 Deadliest Earthquakes" in history and three of them occurred within the last six years; the 2004 Indian Ocean Tsunami, the earthquake that struck Kashmir Pakistan in 2005 and the quake in Sichuan Province in China in 2008.[1]

In this past decade, the 2004 and 2005 hurricane seasons were so devastating they made it into *Wikipedia's* "Timeline of US History." In 2004 it records the hurricanes "had numerous unusual occurrences impacting US properties." The 2005 hurricane season is recorded as taking its toll in the Southeast, "most notably, Hurricane Katrina became the costliest hurricane of all time."[2]

The shock waves that rippled through political events and weather patterns hit the global financial markets in late 2007. The financial crash occurred in 2008 after the recession began. The same unpredictable patterns felt in the weather now hit the financial markets, first striking the US and then rippling through the global markets. High level financial managers sat baffled as predictable strategies became unreliable as markets reacted by going in unforeseen directions they had never before moved in history. So great was its impact that the major financial newspapers reported that the world economy came to a literal stop.[3]

Back in 1989, the Berlin Wall collapsed, marking the end of the Cold War and the beginning of the New World Order. The rise of Islamic fundamentalism and the Middle East conflict presented the superpowers with a new focus. In the same period, major American cities experienced in one year's time the doubling of their murder rates. The growth of violent gangs proliferated and killing of rival gang members and innocent victims turned city streets into battlefields. Worldwide crime statistics mounted. National and ethnic conflicts took place in so many nations that civil wars and border disputes became a trend in the New World Order.

Christ, commenting on the end times, foretold in Matthew 24:12: "*lawlessness will abound.*" In two of the Gospels, He compares the days before His coming to the era of Noah and Lot (Matt. 24:37, Luke 17:26). As in the days of Noah, violence becomes an epidemic (Gen. 6:11-12). Wickedness permeates society, and yet people live life as usual. This describes our generation. With prisons filled to capacity, city streets likened to battle grounds, and killings occurring at a record pace, violence has become a social crisis. As a result of the crimes committed by teenagers and grade school children, inner city schools conduct "bullet drills," use metal detectors to scan for weapons, and hire armed security guards.[4] The Economist commented that "it is not condoms that they should be giving out in New York City schools; it is bullet proof vests."[5] In the later years of his life, political commentator and author William F. Buckley remarked that "after two or three more disarmament conferences with the Soviet Union et al., the largest standing army in the world is likely to be New York City school children."[6] Children kill their parents, murder each other, and are basically out of control.

In civil wars, the acts committed on civilian populations by militants surpass the realm of brutality and are nothing short of savage. This past century recorded more mass murder than any other time in history. This does not even include abortions, which, when totaled worldwide in the last two decades, exceed the present US population in number.[7] Yet, violence and lawlessness are only part of the social picture described by Christ in the last days.

As Was the Time of Lot: Sexual Immorality

God destroyed the cities of Sodom and Gomorrah by raining fire and brimstone on them. These cities were renowned for open homosexuality. Young boys accompanied men and engaged in homosexual and violent activities. Sodomites apprehended and raped strange men, and dealt violently with anyone who tried to stop them (Gen. 19:19). These peoples had a distorted sense of right and wrong. Christ compared the days before the Tribulation to the days of Lot, who lived in these cities. Therefore violence, lawlessness, homosexuality, and sexual deviancy (e.g., sex with children) will characterize the end times.

According to Donald E. Wildmon, who wrote *The Case Against Pornography*, "Child pornography has become a $2-3 billion annual business in the US alone." Mr. Wildmon concluded with Charles H. Keathing, Jr., of Citizens for Decency that there exists "a nationwide campaign to normalize sex between adults and young children—to promote incest."[8]

Incidents of men raping men and boys have increased, judging by the number of offenders currently serving time in US prisons. In New York City, a rapist abducted an 11-year old male walking home from school and sodomized him.[9] Grade school children now experiment with sex, and acts of rape occur among them. These incidents will continue to increase as society becomes the civilization God said He would have to judge. Joel 3:3

declares: *"They have cast lots for My people; Have given a boy in exchange for a harlot, and sold a girl for wine, that they may drink."* During the Tribulation, soldiers sell children for sexual purposes, for as little as a bottle of wine. Men will use boys as prostitutes. These acts mirror crimes committed against children today. We have arrived at the end times that Christ foretold in the Gospels.

The rock musician formerly known as Prince toured in the late 1980's with his release of "Signs of The Times." On the CD cover, the peace symbol of the 1960's replaces the "o" in the word "of." In the 1980s, it became the "Cross of Nero." The upside-down cross with the broken cross members signifies the defeat of Christianity among the occultists. Christians view the immorality of the day as signs leading to the Second Coming of Jesus Christ, while Satanists see today's perils as the defeat of Christianity.[10]

False Prophets: The Rise of Cults and the Occult

During the Tribulation, false Christs and prophets perform signs and wonders so great that, if it were possible, they will deceive the very elect (Matthew 24:24). In the present day, weeping and bleeding statues—of Mary and Jesus, and even of Elvis—border on the bizarre, and gain followings. The United States has seen a tremendous rise in cult and sect activities in the past quarter century. Among them, cults that act out murder and mayhem have risen. From Charles Manson, and lesser known criminals who claim to be deities and murder for the cause of their religion, to Jim Jones, who in 1978, incited 918 of his followers to commit mass suicide by drinking poison in Kool Aid. In 1995, the Japanese cult Aleph, released sarin nerve gas into the Tokyo subway system killing twelve people, severely injuring fifty and causing temporary vision problems for nearly a thousand others. They conducted an earlier attack in 1994, that killed seven and injured 500 others in an attempt to hasten the apocalypse. In 1997, there was also the Heaven's Gate UFO cult whose 39 members committed suicide in unison at the appearance of the Comet Hale-Bopp.[11]

In addition to cults Satanism is also on the rise in America. Since 1969, *The Satanic Bible* by Anton Szandor LaVey has gone through 21 printings. The Satanists believe in the coming Antichrist, the son of Satan himself, who will have power and defeat Christianity. Even they hold that Jesus Christ is the Son of God, and prospective members must renounce Him. Satanists know that to get to God, one must go through His Son.[12]

Jesus foretold of false Christs and prophets who will perform great miracles. Falun Gong, founded in the early 1990's by Li Hongzhi in China, provides a prime example of the cult leaders Jesus forecasted will come claiming His deity and able to perform miracles. Li Hongzhi equates himself with a god and claims to have supernatural powers. A Chinese national recalled witnessing a video where Li performed levitation. According to the *New World Encyclopedia*, Li stated, "If I cannot save you, nobody else can do it. *Wikipedia* records Falun Gong as having 70 million practitioners in China and over 100 million Falun Dafa in 114 countries and regions around the world. [13] According to Jesus we will see more false Christs like Li Hongzhi as the end approaches.

In The Last Days Perilous Times Will Come

Violence and sexual perversion mark this decade. Our society is laden with social maladies, and thus has become a replica of Noah's and Lot's. Reports of horrific crimes committed both by children and against them fill our airwaves. In part, the breakdown of the family—evidenced by the rising divorce rate—is to blame for the unruly children who shoot up their schools, and kill their parents and peers. Our homes are in upheaval; people cannot manage to live or work together. Not only must we be aware of the criminals who rob us on the street or invade our homes, but we must also be conscious of the many scams perpetrated by wealthy corporate leaders who rob their employees and investors. It is as if every person is out for themselves. In 2 Timothy 3:1-4, the Bible summarizes the self centered state of man in the last days:

> *But know this, that in the last days perilous times will come:*
> *For men will be lovers of themselves, lovers of money, boasters, proud,*
> *blasphemers, disobedient to parents, unthankful, unholy,*
> *unloving, unforgiving, slanderers, without self control, brutal,*
> *despisers of good, traitors, headstrong, haughty, lovers of pleasure rather*
> *than lovers of God.*

We are, no doubt, at that place of narcissism and lawlessness described in the Scriptures. It is only logical that if events on the social scene point to the Second Coming of Jesus Christ, in the international arena they must come the same distance.

Historical events now happen at such rapid speed that more occurs in a few years than would normally take place over decades. After the fall of the Berlin Wall, Joseph S. Nye, Jr., Director of the Harvard Center for International Affairs noted that: "The world has changed more rapidly in the past two years than at any time since 1945." Mr. Nye suggested that when George Bush launched his New World Order, he never "thought through what it meant by the concept he launched."[14] Politicians grappled with its meaning. Christians recognize the New World Order as the final world order leading up to the Tribulation. This order signifies global government and the launching of the Antichrist as a world leader. To understand how the events of the last few years fit into the prophetic picture, we must first look to what the Bible tells us about the Tribulation period.

CHAPTER 2

THE FINAL WORLD EMPIRE AND THE PRINCE THAT SHALL COME

The Antichrist

The Tribulation is a seven-year period of wars, plagues, famines, earthquakes, and disasters. It ends in the Battle of Armageddon, and the Second Coming of Jesus Christ. Part of the earth's judgments happen through a leader whom the masses empower. The Scriptures profile this dictator's reign of terror. Due to his anti-God, anti-Christ policies, Evangelical circles customarily refer to him as the Antichrist. The Bible mentions this title only once in the Scriptures. The Devil enters this man's body and wreaks havoc on the world. His reign ignites the Battle of Armageddon (Is. 14:12; Ezek. 28:3-4).

Evidencing this leader's significance, over thirty titles relate to him in both the Old and New Testaments. These include:

Ps. 5-6	The Bloody and Deceitful Man
Ps. 10:2-4	The Wicked One
Ps. 10:18	The Man of the Earth
Ps. 52:1	The Mighty Man
Ps. 53:3	The Enemy
Ps. 74:8-10	The Adversary
Ps. 111:6	The Head of Many Countries
Ps. 140:1	The Violent Man
Is. 10:5-12	The Assyrian
Is. 14:2	The King of Babylon
Is. 14:12	The Sun of the Morning

Is. 16:4-5; Jer. 6:26	The Spoiler
Is. 22:25	The Nail
Is. 25:5	The Branch of the Terrible Ones
Ezek. 21:25-27	The Profane Wicked Prince of Israel
Dan. 7:8	The Little Horn
Dan. 9:26	The Prince That Shall Come
Dan. 11:121	The Vile Person
Dan. 11:36	The Willful King
Zech. 11:16-17	The Idol Shepherd
2 Thess. 2:3	The Man of Sin
2 Thess. 2:3	The Son of Perdition
2 Thess. 2:8	The Lawless One
Rev. 9:11	The Angel of the Bottomless Pit
John 5:43	Another Coming in His Own Name
Dan. 8:23	The King of Fierce Countenance
Matt. 24:15	The Abomination of Desolation
Dan. 9:27	The Desolator
Ezek. 28:12	The King of Tyre
Jer. 4:6-7	The Lion
Jer. 4:6-7	The destroyer of the nations
Is. 14:12	Lucifer[15]

1 John 2:18, identifies him as the Antichrist, a liar who denies the Father and the Son. Rev. 13:1 refers to him as "the Beast," and later in the passage names him 666. The number six, translated from the New Testament Greek into English, means "vex," or "curse." Seven represents God's number of perfection. The triple six represents the unholy trinity, with the Devil acting as God. The Antichrist, whom Satanists call the son of Satan, mimics Jesus Christ. The False Prophet who the Bible predicts will comes onto the earth and performs miracles to get the masses to worship the Beast, mocks God's Holy Spirit. The unholy trinity are named in Scriptures as "The Dragon," "The Beast," and "The False Prophet." Unlike previous dictators, Satan himself possesses the Antichrist. He obtains the world's respect by bringing the world prosperity, until the day he declares himself a god and demands worship for himself alone. Once the Antichrist establishes himself as a deity his evil side manifests itself.

Satan provides the Antichrist with a *"great seat of authority,"* i.e., the political position he will hold. Similarly, the Bible presents Jesus sitting on a throne. Daniel refers to the Antichrist as a *"prince,"* with a lower-case p, while capitalizing the Prince of Peace. The Antichrist's *"great seat of authority"* becomes the highest position of the most powerful government to exist. Despite its earthly might, it does not compare to the heavenly kingdom of Jesus Christ. The Antichrist's reign on earth will completely contrast our Lord's. Unlike Christ, whom the masses rejected, the Antichrist they will accept. In John 5:43, Christ affirms: *"I have come in My Father's name, and you do not receive Me; if another comes in his own name, him you will receive."* Jesus came to save, Antichrist comes to destroy. God's kingdom contains numerology such as the numbers 7 and 12 and 40. The final world power contains numerology, numbers 4, 9, 13, 666, which a later chapter discusses.

The Four Beasts of Daniel

Daniel and John, in the Revelation, disclose the area and identity of the final world power. Daniel's vision details the four world empires that ruled the Middle East region throughout history (Daniel 7 and 8). Daniel states in 7:2-7:

> *"I saw in my vision by night, and behold, the four winds of heaven were stirring up the Great Sea.*
> *And four great beasts came up from the sea, each different from the other.*
> *The first was like a lion, and had eagle's wings. I watched till its wings were plucked off; and it was lifted up from the earth and made to stand on two feet like a man, and a man's heart was given to it.*
> *And suddenly another beast, a second, like a bear. It was raised up on one side and had three ribs in its mouth between its teeth. And they said thus to it: Arise, devour much flesh!*
> *After this I looked, and there was another, like a leopard, which had on its back four wings of a bird. The beast also had four heads, and dominion was given to it.*

The Seat of the Antichrist

> *After this I saw in the night visions, and behold, a fourth beast, dreadful and terrible, exceedingly strong. It had huge iron teeth; it was devouring, breaking in pieces, and trampling the residue with its feet.*

Of all of the beastly visions, the fourth beast disturbs Daniel the most, and he inquires of an angel who stood by the vision, and the angel identifies the four beasts as four kingdoms that will rule on the earth. Daniel specifically asks about the fourth beast, which he describes as "*different from all the others, exceedingly dreadful, with its teeth of iron and its nails of bronze, which devoured, broke in pieces, and trampled the residue with its feet*" (Dan. 7:19). In the remainder of the chapter, Daniel continues to describe the fourth beast, including details of the evil leader who commands it. The angel Gabriel further elaborates on the kingdoms and provides their identity. The lion signifies the Babylonian kingdom. The bear represents the second or Medo-Persian empire. The third, the leopard or cheetah, compares to Greece. Daniel describes the fourth beast at the end of its history and, unlike the preceding empires, it conquers the entire world. Dan. 7:23 states: "*The fourth beast shall be a fourth kingdom on earth, which shall be different from all other kingdoms, and shall devour the whole earth, trample it and break it in pieces.*"

The fourth beast possesses the combined strength of all the previous governments, and holds the political seat of the Antichrist. Dwight J. Pentecost, in his book *Things to Come*, quotes Gaebelein, who noted that while the first beast has a man's heart, "it was a beast still," and the three ribs in the bear's mouth are Susiana, Lydia, and Asia Minor, which the Medes and Persians conquered. One paw is upraised because "the Persian element was stronger than that of the Medes." The leopard, which represents Greece, has wings that "denote its swiftness," and its four heads symbolize the division of Greece into the kingdoms of Syria, Egypt, Macedonia, and Asia Minor. He adds: "God tells us that their moral character is beastly. The lion devours, the bear crushes and the leopard springs upon its prey."

While the first three beasts compare to strong, fierce animals that prey on weaker species, the fourth beast appears almost mechanical and monstrous. It possesses great iron teeth, bronze fingernails, and ten horns. Revelation 13, further elaborates on the fourth beast. In addition to his ten horns, he has seven heads, which add to his frightful appearance. The Bible tells us that this beast looks like a leopard with the feet of a bear and it has a lion's mouth (Rev. 13:2).

The Greek and Hebrew word used for leopard includes the various species and specifies the large spots, which also describe the cheetah. Both the lion and bear reign their territories and exist at the top of the food chain because of their power and fierceness. The leopard, though fierce, is no match for a lion. Leopards are stealth predators and of the three big cats they possess adept climbing skills and protect their kills by running them up trees. Today they are more numerous than lions and cheetahs because of their ability to hide and blend in with their environments. The cheetah, though considerably less powerful than a leopard, surpasses all animals in speed; running at speeds up to 70 miles an hour and reaching high speeds in three seconds. Of the three big cats, the cheetah kills more game than the others but does not always get to eat their kill. Tougher opponents such as lions, leopards and hyenas hijack them.

It is this author's view that Scripture refers to the Beast having the body of a cheetah and not a leopard as expositors traditionally teach possibly because they failed to analyze the differences in the species. The cheetah does not have the strength of the lion or leopard because it can out run the fiercest predator. Its speed is its power. The leopard strength lies in its stealth from climbing trees and hiding.

The Beast possesses the mouth of a lion, iron legs, bear's feet and the sleek body of a cheetah which resembles a leopard. The cheetah built for speed has a narrow body, long slender feet and legs, a flexible spine, and bones as light as aluminum. Their paws are less rounded than other cats; their pads are hard, similar to tire treads to help them in fast, sharp turns. Its claws act as cleats for traction when running, its tail moves as a rudder. The cheetah has a powerful heart, oversized liver and large strong arteries. In addition, the tear stripes on inner corner of its eyes act as anti glare device and its small head, flat face and reduced muzzle length allow the eyes to be positioned for maximum binocular vision.

Each of these parts represents the fiercest and strongest attribute of its respective animal. Thus, in possessing the cheetah's (body) speed, the powerful jaws of the lion, and the crushing feet of a bear along with its long sharp nails, he obtains the combined strength and power of all these animals. The final world power will be both strong and fast in the speed at which it conquers other nations vs. conquering through stealth as a leopard.

The straightforward animal nature of the first three beasts symbolizes the notion that these kingdoms possess an earthy element, but the horrifying and dreadful appearance of the fourth—its iron legs and teeth, its bronze nails, and its many heads and horns—makes it appear demonic, as if it emerged from the pits of hell. The iron on the image represents modern weapons of steel. To Daniel, it appeared as a creature out of a dark fantasy, for it was unlike anything he had ever seen.

The contrast of this beast to the others is further seen in Nebuchadnezzar's dream image (Daniel 2: 31-41), which symbolizes the four kingdoms and relates their strength to metals. The golden head of the image is Babylon. Its silver arms and chest are the Medes and Persians. Its bronze thighs represent the Greek empire, and its legs and feet are of iron, but the toes have clay mingled in with the iron. According to Scripture, the fourth beast is made of iron because iron "breaks in pieces and shatters all things." While gold, silver and bronze each possess some esthetic value and pliability, iron's sole value is its strength. This entity does not merely rule and have dominion; it crushes and breaks in pieces all of the other kingdoms, and its purpose is that of a destroyer and crusher rather than a conqueror which is possible using modern weaponry.

The fourth beast encompasses the same area as the ancient Roman Empire. It rises from the midst of the seas, specifically the Mediterranean (Rev. 13:1). When Daniel foretold Jerusalem's destruction in A.D. 70, he simultaneously prophesied that the coming prince would come from the area of the Roman Empire. Daniel 9:26 states: *"The people of the prince that shall come, shall destroy the city and the sanctuary."* The Romans under Titus in A.D. 70 destroyed Jerusalem.

The Antichrist holds his political position in re-empowered Europe. The final world empire represents a second phase in the Old Roman Empire's history. According to Daniel 7:24, the fourth kingdom never passes out of existence, but rather continues in some form until its final condition emerges. The Scriptures view the Roman Empire as continually developing until the second coming of Christ. The final world power will possess similarities to the Old Roman Empire. Dwight Pentecost summarizes the purpose of its revival by concluding: "As the Roman Empire had been the agency through which Satan attacked Christ at His first advent, that empire in its final form will be the agency through which Satan works against the Messiah at His second advent."[16]

Tyrus: A Place of Commerce and Trade

The final world empire is synonymous with international trade. The writings of Ezekiel, Jeremiah, and John in the Revelation evidence this fact. Ezekiel chapters 27 and 28 foretold the destruction of the ancient city of Tyrus, once located on the coast of the Mediterranean Sea. Under Solomon, the Hebrews and the Tyrians had a close alliance. Through trade relations, Solomon obtained supplies from Tyrus for the building of the Temple (I Kings 9:11-14, 26-28; 10:22). This good relationship changed as the Tyrians and neighboring Phoenicians began to buy Hebrew captives from their enemies. They sold them as slaves to the Greeks and Edomites. These acts brought God's judgment upon the City of Tyrus (Joel refers to it as Tyre), as predicted by the prophets.

Throughout Tyrus's history, several conquerors invaded it. From the time of Christ up to the Crusades, it was a flourishing city, renowned for the great wealth it derived from dyes of Tyrian purple—extracted from shellfish on its coast. Its present condition is a fulfillment of Ezekiel 26:5, which describes it as *"a place for the spreading of nets in the midst of the sea."* It contains fifty or sixty poor families, who live in part by fishing, and is a rock where fishers dry their nets. [17]

Ezekiel chapter 26 records Nebuchadnezzar's siege of Tyrus. Chapter 27 describes the city's wealth, and the amount of trade that passed through its borders. Fourteen verses detail the merchandise, and name the many nations that traded with Tyre.

In chapter 28, literal Tyrus, the city of ancient times, changes to illustrate the Antichrist. The Prince of Tyrus is none other than Satan in a man's body. Situated in the midst of the seas, he claims that he is a god sitting in God's seat. He is proud because of his wealth, which he increased through trade. God tells him that he is a man, and not God. Verses 12 to 16, identify the Prince as Satan himself, who was the most prominent angel in all of heaven, and who was cast out by God on the day he sinned.

> *Son of man, take up a lamentation for the king of Tyre, and say to him, Thus says the Lord God; You were the seal of perfection, full of wisdom, and perfect in beauty.*
>
> *You were in Eden the garden of God; every precious stone was your covering, the sardius, topaz and the diamond, beryl, onyx, and jasper. Sapphire, turquoise and emerald, with gold. The workmanship of your timbrels and pipes was prepared for you on the day you were created.*
>
> *You were the anointed cherub who covers; I established you; You were on the holy mountain of God; You walked back and forth in the midst of fiery stones.*
>
> *You were perfect in your ways from the day you were created, till iniquity was found in you.*
>
> *By the abundance of your trading you became filled with violence within, and you sinned; Therefore I cast you as a profane thing out of the mountain of God: and I destroyed you, O covering cherub, from the midst of the fiery stones.*
>
> *Your heart was lifted up because of your beauty; You corrupted your wisdom for the sake of your splendor;: I cast you to the ground, I laid you before kings, that they may gaze at you.*
>
> *You defiled your sanctuaries by the multitude of your iniquities, by the iniquity of your trading; therefore I brought fire from your midst; it devoured you, and I turned you to ashes upon the earth in the sight of all who saw you.*
>
> *All who knew you among the peoples are astonished at you: you have become a horror, and shall be no more forever.*

Verses 18 and 19 describe the Antichrist's and False Prophet's judgment at the Battle of Armageddon. God will cast them alive into the lake of fire (Rev. 19:20-21).

Joel foretells the Battle of Armageddon, and names Tyre as guilty of selling his people and robbing the treasures of Israel (Joel 3:4-6). The Antichrist, like Tyre's king, invades Israel, takes spoil, and persecutes the

Jews. Tyrus, as the final world power, obtains its wealth through trade, and its king claims to be God.

To better understand prophecy in Scripture one must consider that the prophetic writings retain continuity from author to author and time does not count as we measure it. In the forecasts events take place all in the same time period. The Scriptures note that certain events will take place in the latter or end of days because the Bible describes ancient and future locations in the present tense. Their beginning, era of notoriety and their end are relayed as if in the same time frame. Although these places have passed out of existence the Bible views them in existence. There exists no differentiation from their end and the people and nations that arrived in their stead as exampled by Tyrus and Babylon.

Babylon

While the prophet Daniel establishes Babylon as parallel with the final world power and provides many details of its structure; Jeremiah 51 predicts Babylon's judgment. He prophesizes against the literal land that once existed, as well as its latter-day counterpart. As with Tyrus, whose king God identifies as Satan, God refers to the king of Babylon as Lucifer. The Antichrist is *"the King of Babylon."* Isaiah 14:4-6 records his evil rule and conquest:

> *That you will take up this proverb against the King of Babylon, and say, How the oppressor has ceased! The golden city ceased!*
> *The Lord has broken the staff of the wicked, the scepter of the rulers. He who struck the people in wrath with a continual stroke, He who ruled the nations in anger, is persecuted and no one hinders.*

The passage later identifies Satan as the King of Babylon, and describes Satan's fall from heaven. Isaiah 14:12-17 continues:

> *How you are fallen from heaven, O Lucifer, son of the morning! How you are cut down to the ground, you who weakened the nations!*

> *For you have said in your heart, I will ascend into heaven, I will exalt my throne above the stars of God: I will also sit on the mount of the congregation, on the farthest sides of the North:*
>
> *I will ascend above the heights of the clouds; I will be like the most high.*
>
> *You will be brought down to Sheol, to the depths of the pit.*
>
> *Those who see you will gaze at you, and consider you saying, Is this the man who made the earth tremble, who shook kingdoms;*
>
> *Who made the world as a wilderness, and destroyed its cities who did not open the house of his prisoners?*

Babylon was the commercial hub of the Near East. Trade and commerce increased its wealth. The invention of wheeled carts allowed trade to expand from local to foreign commerce. Nebuchadnezzar helped Babylonian businesses by improving the highways. Countless caravans brought to Babylon's shops half the world's products. Under Nebuchadnezzar, Babylon became a thriving and prosperous marketplace. Babylon, referred to in ancient times as "a great city," drew the nations of the Mediterranean world into closer contact.[18]

Like Tyrus, ancient Babylon was renowned for trade. Revelation records Babylon's fall in the end times. The merchants lament its destruction. The verse reads: *"And the merchants of the earth will weep and mourn over her; for no one buys their merchandise anymore"* (Rev. 18:11). Revelation 18:15 reiterates: *"The merchants of these things, who became rich by her, will stand at a distance for fear of her torment, weeping and wailing."* The world's nations will prosper from trading with this political power, which acts as a hub for trade. Ezekiel 27:33 confirms: *"When your wares went out by sea, you satisfied many people; you enriched the kings of the earth with your many luxury goods and your merchandise."*

The Medes and Persians conquered Babylon. The Greeks followed and the Roman Empire came next. The Antichrist emerges from the revived Roman Empire, which becomes powerful through trade and commerce. It makes itself and the world's merchants rich. Its prosperity extends to the earth's rulers. Nations will gain wealth by trading with this world power. This prophecy is beginning to see fulfillment with the emergence of the European Union.

The Final World Empire

The European Union is a group of Western European nations that eliminated their trade barriers to form a Common Market. Trade among the Member States moves about freely. As the world's largest market, the EU is virtually synonymous with international trade and commerce. The Union coordinates more than economic policy; it has instituted a governing body to which the member nations are accountable in certain areas. Many refer to the EU as "the United States of Europe." The EU has its own currency, flag, and national anthem. The EU's founding fathers viewed the achievement of economic strength as a prerequisite for attaining political power—the Union's ultimate aim. The EU aims to become a powerful political player on the world stage.

The Economic Race

Tyrus and Babylon provide age-old lessons in economics. Trade accelerates the economic growth of nations, increasing their wealth and power. Today's superpowers realize that military might alone will not make a nation great and powerful. Economic strength is key to a nation's prosperity. At the end of the Cold War, economic wealth replaced military might as the primary goal of the superpowers. The stake is what Helmut Schmidt once called the struggle for the world product, rather than for traditional power—wealth and power have become more closely tied together.[19] For this reason, nations are uniting with one another to become regional trading blocks, to guarantee economic success. This premise underlined the US's free trade agreement with Canada and Mexico, as well as the formation of the European Union.

Today the EU is an economic powerhouse, with almost 500 million citizens. The EU generated an estimated nominal gross domestic product (GDP) of 18.39 trillion dollars based on purchasing power parity in 2008, accounting to over 22% of the world's total economic output in terms of purchasing power parity which makes it the largest economy in the world and the second largest trade bloc economy. It is also the largest exporter and largest importer of goods and services and the biggest trading partner to several large countries such as India and China. Of the 500 largest corporations measured by revenue, 178 have their headquarters in the EU.

In addition to becoming the leading place of trade and commerce—a major characteristic of the final world empire—the European Union will become a political power as well. The completion of the 1992 Common Market acted as a first step toward political union. The EU's objective is to obtain superpower status, as many of its member nations had in their individual histories. According to the Scriptures, this new world power becomes the most powerful political entity the world has ever known.

The European Union's borders lie within the realm of the Holy Roman Empire of old. Like Babylon and Tyrus, it is renowned for international trade, except it holds the political seat of the Antichrist.

The Arrival of the Antichrist

The Antichrist arrives in the right place at the most opportune time. His astute abilities in national and international finance help him to direct the EU into great prosperity. His genius leads them into superpower status. Ezekiel 28:3-5 deems him *"wiser than Daniel"* for *"there is no secret"* hidden from him. By *"wisdom"* and *"understanding,"* he accumulates *"riches and gold and silver"* into his treasuries. Ezekiel concludes: *"By your great wisdom in trade you have increased your riches, and your heart is lifted up because of your riches."*

Daniel 8:23 describes the Antichrist's understanding of sinister schemes and his fierce features, and states that he deifies himself (Dan. 11:37). Isaiah 10:13 confirms the Antichrist's estimation of his wisdom. *"For he says, By the strength of my hand I have done it, and by my wisdom, for I am prudent; Also I have removed the boundaries of the people, and have robbed their treasuries; So I have put down the inhabitants like a valiant man."*

The Antichrist's genius is greater than Daniel's, whose intelligence surpassed that of all the other prophets and Old Testament patriarchs. Daniel was skillful in all learning, knowledge, and wisdom. He understood science and comprehended the most difficult concepts. Daniel also possessed the ability to interpret dreams and visions (Dan. 1:4,17, 5:11-12). In addition to having wisdom like Solomon, he possessed the mind of a scholar, scientist, and mathematician. Recognized for his brilliant mind, Daniel served in Nebuchadnezzar's court as Master over all of the wise men, the consultants to the king. When Darius the Median (the Medo-Persian Empire succeeded the Babylonian) took over Babylon, he appointed 120 princes to rule over the whole kingdom. Presiding over the princes were three presidents, of whom Daniel was first. All of the officials were accountable to him (Dan. 6:1-3). When Cyrus the Persian succeeded Darius, Daniel served and prospered during his reign as well. Daniel acted as chief consultant to kings who ruled two of the four world empires that once existed. The Antichrist's abilities will enable him to rise to world leadership.

The Antichrist's Reign

The Tribulation begins when the Antichrist makes a covenant of peace with Israel (Dan. 9:27). His government will agree to act as the guarantor of the nation's peace. Prosperity follows the first three and a half years after the agreement. The Antichrist raises the EU into a great economic and political world power. Nations prosper through trade and association with him. The Antichrist wins the favor of the masses because he leads the European Union into great prosperity, and all associated nations will prosper.

The Antichrist gains popularity through deceit. The seeming people's president tells the people what they wish to hear, while pursuing his own diabolical plans. Midway through the Tribulation, the Antichrist changes his pro-peace policy. He receives a deadly head wound, possibly from an assassination attempt. Miraculously, he comes back to life (Rev. 13:3). A terrorist group may murder him due to his pro-Israeli policies. For one reason or another, certain individuals will oppose him.

Zechariah elaborates upon his wound. He describes: *"The sword shall be against his arm, and against his right eye: his arm shall completely wither, and his right eye shall be totally blinded"* (Zech. 11:17). He will remain blinded in his right eye, and paralyzed in his right arm. The Antichrist's return from the dead—or near death—instantly increases his notoriety. The Antichrist allies himself with "the False Prophet," (Rev. 19:20) a member of the unholy trinity. A renowned religious leader able to perform miracles he campaigns for the Antichrist. In this time frame, the Antichrist institutes the Mark of the Beast worldwide. No person can buy or sell unless he wears it.

The Temple Rebuilt

During the first half of the Tribulation, the Jews rebuild the Temple of Solomon according to the exact dimensions described in I Kings, chapter 6. Christ warns the Jews of the *"abomination of desolation: spoken of by the prophet Daniel,"* indicating the Jewish Temple's restoration. The abominable act takes place inside the Temple. This desecration prompts the beginning of God's severe wrath and judgments upon the earth.

Currently, the Dome of the Rock, an Islamic Shrine which houses the foundation stone and a major landmark built in 691 a.d. making it the oldest Islamic building in the world was constructed over the site of the second Jewish Temple destroyed in AD. 70. At present, in Israel a Fundamentalist Jewish movement exists that aims to rebuild the Temple. Within the Israeli government, the right-wing political party, the Temple Mount Faithful, also known as Temple Mount and Eretz Yisrael Faithful Movement wish to relocate the Dome to Mecca and replace it with a third Temple. They intend on constructing the third Temple on the Dome of the Rock and also suggest building a new Temple on the site, in a place that will not interfere with existing buildings. They openly declare that their ultimate goal is the demolition of the al-Aqsa Mosque and the Dome of the Rock, and the reconstruction on their site of King Solomon's Temple. The Temple Mount is the holiest site in Jerusalem. [20]

Jeremiah foretold the Temple's destruction by the Babylonians (26:6-12). Daniel predicted the Temple's desecration by the Syrian king Antichious Euphrates (Dan. 8:8-12). He also foretold Jerusalem's restoration and rebuilding by Herod and the Temple's destruction by the Romans in A.D. 70 (Dan. 9:25). Hosea 3:4-5 foretells the long time the Jews remain without the symbols used in their worship, and without the Temple and how they will return to their God in the latter days.

For the children of Israel shall abide many days without king or prince, without sacrifice or sacred pillar, without ephod or teraphim.

THE FINAL WORLD EMPIRE AND THE PRINCE THAT SHALL COME

Afterward shall the children of Israel return, and seek the Lord their God, and David their king; and shall fear the Lord and his goodness in the latter days.

Daniel also foretells the desecration of a future third Temple, and the persecution of the Jews by the Antichrist (Dan. 9:25-26)

Before this prophecy will see fulfillment the Jews will erect a new Temple which means that some future event will destroy the mosque and the Dome of the Rock that are on the site. This destruction will either happen from a natural disaster such as an earthquake or by war. Earthquakes have rumbled through the area in the past causing damage to the al-Aqsa mosque.

The Russian and Arab invasion predicted in Ezekiel may destroy the Dome of the Rock located on Mount Moriah. Bible scholars debate the timing of the battle. Some argue the war occurs prior to the Tribulation and others that this conflict takes place during the millennial reign of Christ. Either way we know some event will destroy the existing buildings which will clear the area for the building of the third Temple.

Temple Mount History

- 950 B.C. Solomon completes building the first Temple.
- 587 B.C. Nebuchadnezzar of Babylon destroys Solomon's Temple.
- 515 B.C. The book of Ezra records the building of the second modest Temple.
- 161 B.C. A Syrian ruler pillages this second Temple.
- 164 B.C. The Maccabees (an Israeli priest and his five sons) recapture the Temple. (The Jewish holiday Hanukkah celebrates this restoration.)
- 37 B.C. to 4 B.C. Herod, King of Judea, triples the area of the Temple Mount in expanse to accommodate an enlarged Temple and other buildings.
- A.D. 70 Roman armies, in a quest to end Jewish rebellion, storm and dismantle the Temple, and hurl its stones over the parapets of the mount. (Today, a remnant of the Temple complex is a portion of the western retaining wall, named the Wailing Wall.) The Romans forbid Jews from entering the old city of Jerusalem, but eventually permit them to enter once a year "to wail over its stones."
- A.D. 687 A mosque, the Dome of the Rock, is built there, and remains today. At the southern rim of the platform stands the silver-domed al-Aqsa Mosque. For Muslims, the same place, Haram-al-Sharif, which means Noble Sanctuary, is the third holiest site, after Mecca and Medina. Muslims believe that the prophet Mohammed made a miraculous night journey from Mecca to this place, and from there ascended to heaven.

The Abomination of Desolation: *Matthew 24:15, Mark 13:14, Daniel 8:11-14, 12:11-13, 9:26, 11:31, Joel 1:6*

Within Solomon's Temple, the "most holy place" (I Kings 6:16-36) housed the Ark of the Covenant. This sanctuary was the place God dwelt among the Israelites (Exodus 25). The Ark (made of shittim wood overlaid with gold) housed the two tablets of the Ten Commandments, Aaron's rod, and manna. Upon the Ark's mercy seat, the sprinkled blood of sacrificed animals atoned for all of Israel. It stood as a symbol of the blood of Jesus Christ, which would one day be shed and remit the sins of the world. The priests abided by many details of dress, conduct, and worship. When the priests performed these rituals, God met with the children of Israel and sanctified the Temple by His glory (Ex. 29:43). All of these details and acts symbolized the Messiah, who was to come and be the propitiation for sin. In that most holy place, God reaffirmed His promise to His people.

Today's Jews fundamentally reject Jesus Christ as their Messiah, and do not recognize the New Testament. They abide by the regulations of the Old Testament's Law of Moses and the rabbinical traditions of the Talmud. The Levitical priests performed the rituals and rites within the Temple. Animal sacrifice was necessary for the remission of sin. Without a Temple, no Orthodox Jewish person living today can practice his faith to the letter of the law. This explains the desire of some Jewish sects to rebuild the Temple, which is as great a part of Judaism as possessing the land which God gave to the Israelites.

Three and a half years after the Antichrist agrees to his covenant (i.e., peace treaty) with Israel, he invades Jerusalem with an army (Joel 1:6, Dan. 11:31, 9:26). He then enters the most holy place, sits in the Temple and declares himself a god (II Thes. 2:4). The Antichrist terminates the worship and sacrifice, and commits sacrilegious acts, desecrating the Temple. He places some abominable thing in the Holy Place. His true character reveals itself as he lays siege to Israel, occupies its territory, and wages war against Christians and Jews, undertaking their annihilation (Dan. 11:33-35, 12:10, Rev. 6:10-11, Jer. 50:33, Joel 1:6, Matt. 24:9, Mark 13:9-13). Only a third of the Israelites will survive. Zechariah 13:8 declares: *"And it shall come to pass, in all the land, says the Lord, two in it shall be cut off and die; but one third shall be left in it."*

THE FINAL WORLD EMPIRE AND THE PRINCE THAT SHALL COME

Concurrently, he and his federation of kings abolish the Catholic Church, and destroy the Vatican (Rev.11). The Antichrist will not tolerate any religion other than the worship of, and devotion to, himself and his empire. Daniel 11:37 affirms that the Antichrist regards no man, and thus has no regard for human life or suffering. He epitomizes man's inhumanity to man.

Christ solemnly warns the Jews in Judea at the time to flee to the mountains. He commands them to run and leave their jackets behind. He notes the additional suffering for pregnant and nursing mothers who must flee. In Matthew 24:21, Christ declares: *"For then there will be great Tribulation, such as has not been since the beginning of the world until this time, no, nor ever shall be."*

The Covenant of Death

In Isaiah 28:18, God refers to the treaty as a *"covenant with death,"* an *"agreement with hell."* In Ezekiel chapter 13, God is angry at the prophets and prophetesses who speak from their hearts and tell the Israelites of peace. Verse 16 reads: *"That is, the prophets of Israel who prophesy concerning Jerusalem, and who see visions of peace for her, when there is no peace, says the Lord God."* Psalm 55:20-21 describes the Antichrist's aims by stating:
"He has put forth his hands against those who were at peace with him: he has broken his covenant. The words of his mouth were smoother than butter, but war was in his heart: his words were softer than oil, yet they were drawn swords." Isaiah 33:7-9 adds: *"Surely their valiant ones shall cry outside, the ambassadors of peace shall weep bitterly. The highways lie waste, the wayfaring man ceases. He has broken the covenant, He has despised the cities He regards no man."*

The four horsemen of Revelation 6:1-8 symbolize the Antichrist's reign of terror. Entering the world on a white horse in the name of peace, he comes to conquer. The red horse signifies the bloodshed wrought by him in war. The black horse depicts famine. The pale horse, a mixture of all the colors, represents the death of one-fourth of the world's population—a result of his conquest.

Coincidentally, the Nazi flag was red, white, and black, and both the swastika and the circle are satanic symbols. Hitler declared that these colors formed "the most brilliant harmony in existence."²¹ Red and black are also the symbolic colors for Satanism.

When the Antichrist enters power, he acts deceptively, and exalts himself above all, and speaks against the God of gods. He honors a strange god of fortresses by acknowledging and glorifying it and causing it to rule over many (Dan. 11:23, 36-39). This might possibly be a weapon system, or computer infrastructure. The Antichrist changes times and laws (Dan. 7:25), and has a statue made of himself, which the False Prophet will cause to speak. Those who refuse to honor his image, he murders. He demands worship from the masses, and the crowds worship him (Rev. 13:8, 14-16). He prospers by accomplishing his aims. His dreadful and terrible empire devours the world, and breaks it in pieces, with the speed of a cheetah. (Dan. 7:7, 8:24; Rev. 13:2).

The final world power is the equal of all the previous world powers combined, and its authority extends worldwide (Rev. 13:2). Revelation 13:7-8 confirms that *"authority was given him over every tribe, tongue and nation and all who dwell on the earth will worship him."* The Antichrist initially gains the masses' admiration through his eloquence, financial solutions and his ingenious peace proposals. He invades and conquers those nations that oppose him. Isaiah 10:14 records the power of the Antichrist's conquest in his own words. He declares: *"My hand has found like a nest the riches of the people: and as one gathers eggs that are left, I have gathered all the earth; and there was no one who moved his wing, nor opened his mouth, with even a peep."* This lines up with Daniels description of a demonic, animal, metal beast, which rises to great power.

Russia, the kings of the East, and a great nation from the coast of the earth attack and destroy his kingdom, possibly by a nuclear attack. Hearing of this, he goes out with great fury to destroy and annihilate many people, and flees to his sanctuary in Jerusalem. Invading armies attack him in Israel, and the remaining troops of the nations join them at the battle of Armageddon (Rev. 16:16, 18; Ezek. 38; Jer. 4, 5, 50; Dan. 11:40-45).

All of the Old Testament prophets refer to Armageddon as *"The Day of the Lord."* Jeremiah 46:10 records it as *"a day of vengeance, a great slaughter, north of the river Euphrates."* The greatest earthquake in history levels and divides cities around the globe. Mountains cease to be, and islands sink under water. The sun darkens, stars fall from the sky, and the moon turns to blood (Is. 2:12; Ezek. 30:3; Zech. 14:1-9; Zeph. 1; Joel 2:1-2, 10, 3:1, 15; Rev. 6:12, 16:9; Mark 13:24-25; Matt. 24:29).

At the Tribulation's end, Jesus Christ, shining bright as the sun, appears in the clouds with the saints and legions of angels (Rev. 19; Mark 13:26-27; Matt. 24:30). John Walvord records in his book *Daniel: The Key to Prophetic Revelation* that: "The description of the time of the end confirms Daniel's revelation that it will be a period of trouble such as the world has never known, trouble of such character that it would result in the extermination of the human race if it were not cut short by the consummation, the second coming of Jesus Christ."[22]

God's Judgments

The Antichrist's reign and the final cataclysmic earthquakes and radical changes in the solar system are only part of the Tribulation that befalls mankind.

- Nation rises against nation in war (Matt. 24:7).
- An army of 200 million men (possibly China) slays a third of the earth's population (Rev. 9:13-21).
- A great volcanic eruption destroys a third of all sea life.
- Hail and fire mingled with blood burns a third of all trees and grass (Rev. 8:7).
- A great star falls from heaven, poisoning a third of the earth's waters (Rev. 8:10-11).
- Day and night reverse (Rev. 8:12).
- A five-month plague of locusts stinging like scorpions leave men in agonizing pain (Rev. 13:21).
- Large hailstones rain down on the earth (Rev. 16:21).
- Rivers, seas, and lakes become as blood, and all sea and aquatic life disappear (Rev. 16:3-4).
- The sun becomes extremely hot, and scorches men with great fear and fire (Rev. 16:18).
- Darkness fills the seat of the kingdom of the Beast, and grievous sores torment the individuals who bear the Mark of the Beast (Rev. 16:2,10).

- The river Euphrates dries up, making way for the kings of the East (Rev. 16:12).

After all of these events occur, the world's armies surround Jerusalem for the battle of Armageddon. Christ returns in the clouds with His legions of angels. The Antichrist and the world's armies attempt to make war against him. Christ casts the Beast and the False Prophet into the lake of fire, and slays the remainder of his forces by the sword of His word (Rev. 19:19-21). The earth returns to its pre-flood state, and God judges the nations (Matt. 25). Christ himself rules the earth for a thousand years, and binds Satan. At the millennium's end, God looses Satan, and he causes men to rebel against God. They surround the holy city, and God sends fire from heaven to devour them. God casts Satan into the lake of fire for eternity. At this time the judgment seat of God takes place. Those whose names are not in the book of life, God casts into the lake of fire (Rev. 20:15).

God creates a new heaven and earth. The New Jerusalem descends from heaven, with streets of gold and walls of precious stones. The glory of God and the light of Christ illuminate the new heaven, and those who placed their faith in Jesus Christ live on for eternity (Rev. 21).

God's Promise

God provides man the opportunity to seek Him during the Tribulation. "Two witnesses" prophesy for almost three and a half years. Men try to hurt them, and they smite the earth with plagues that cause rain to stop, and water to turn into blood. The beast that ascends out of the bottomless pit makes war against them and kills them. The nations rejoice at their death. God raises them from the dead and lifts them into heaven (Rev. 11:3-13). Tradition identifies these men as Moses and Elijah (Rev. 11:16) because God gave Elijah and Moses the ability to perform miracles and because they both appeared with Jesus on the mount of transfiguration (Matt.17:1-3). Elijah and Elisha together as a team might also be the two witnesses because of all the prophets they performed powerful miracles which included raising a person from the dead.

In addition, during the Tribulation 144,000 witnesses, consisting of 12,000 from each of 12 tribes of Israel, preach the Gospel to the four corners of the earth (Rev. 7:1-9, 14:1-7). Despite the outpouring of God's anger and judgments, He still desires that men turn to Him. Revelation 9:20-21 declares: *"after all of these plagues, man will not repent of his evil ways. Instead, he curses God."* This phrase repeats throughout the entire book of Revelation with each plague issued.

Today we have the Gospel and the Bible which teaches us about Jesus Christ and forewarns the world about the horrific events that are yet to come. Those who have accepted Jesus Christ as their personal savior will not go through the Tribulation. God takes them out of the world in the Rapture just prior to the earth's final seven years. II Thessalonians 4:14-18 tells us:

> *For if we believe that Jesus died and rose again, even so God will bring with Him those who sleep in Jesus.*
>
> *For this we say to you by the word of the Lord, that we who are alive and remain until the coming of the Lord will by no means precede those who are asleep.*
>
> *For the Lord himself will descend from heaven with a shout, with the voice of an archangel, and with the trumpet of God: and the dead in Christ will rise first:*
>
> *Then we who are alive and remain shall be caught up together with them in the clouds, to meet the Lord in the air: and thus we shall always be with the Lord.*
>
> *Therefore comfort one another with these words.*

In John's vision on the Isle of Patmos, he saw an innumerable multitude of people dressed in white robes, praising God. John asked who these people were. The angel answered him and said: *"These are the ones who come out of the great Tribulation, and washed their robes, and made them white in the blood of the Lamb"* (Rev. 7:9,13,14). Christians will come out of the Tribulation. The blood of Jesus Christ makes them perfect in God's sight.

God ushered Lot and his family out of Sodom and Gomorrah before destroying the city. He commanded Noah to build the ark, rescuing his family from the flood. God brings those who have placed their faith in his Son out of the Great Tribulation. The rapture occurs just prior to and after the sealing of the 144,000. This disappearance of people will go virtually unnoticed amid the tumultuous events of the times. Some may regard it as a rare occurrence of individuals disappearing into another dimension. Others may claim that aliens abducted the missing. Various experts will offer their explanations of how the disappearance of these people could have occurred. On the whole, though, with paranormal incidents occurring with increasing frequency, and stories of alien abductions filling the airwaves, the Rapture will seem unremarkable to most of the world's inhabitants. After the Rapture, the Tribulation will usher in signs and wonders performed by false Christs, the False Prophet and those performed by God Himself through the two witnesses.

CHAPTER 3

THE GREAT WHORE OF BABYLON

The Mother of Harlots

Revelation, Chapter 17, describes the Great Whore of Babylon, who represents false religion. Babylon's political and religious aspects bring down God's judgment. While political Babylon's judgment occurs just prior to the battle at Armageddon and results from the Antichrist's reign, religious Babylon's annihilation comes through the Antichrist and his federation of kings. The Antichrist abolishes religion, and persecutes its followers for not worshipping him alone. In Dwight Pentecost's *Things To Come: A Study of Bible Escatology*, Pentecost quotes Scofield, who confirms: "Two 'Babylons' are to be distinguished in the Revelation...Ecclesiastical Babylon is 'the great whore'(Rev. 17:1), and is destroyed by political Babylon (Rev. 17:15-18), that the beast may be the alone object of worship (II Thess. 2:3, 4; Rev. 13:15)."[23]

As one reviews history, one realizes the identity of the woman in Revelation Chapter 17. She sits upon many waters, and is arrayed in purple and scarlet, and adorned with gold, precious stones, and pearls. Her hand holds a golden cup full of abominations and the filthiness of her fornication. Upon her head one sees words written in capital letters: "MYSTERY, BABYLON THE GREAT, THE MOTHER OF HARLOTS AND ABOMINATIONS OF THE EARTH." Drunk with the blood of the saints (martyrs) she sits upon seven hills (Rev. 17:4-5, 9).

Harlotry, in the Bible, equals idolatry. When Israel worshipped other gods, God compared the nation to a harlot. The book of Hosea elaborates on this precept by its description of an adulterous wife and a faithful husband, symbolic of the unfaithfulness of Israel to God through idolatry.

The bride of Christ is pure and holy, and she embraces truth. The harlot symbolizes all false teaching. She leads individuals away from the true God, to herself. The mother of harlots encompasses all doctrine, beliefs, practices, and ideology that diametrically opposes the truth of Jesus Christ.

Immorality, sorcery, and idolatry imprinted Babylonian society. The nation was famous throughout the ancient world for astronomy. They were astrologers first and foremost. Sorcerers and necromancers were more popular than physicians. Divination and the interpretation of dreams were common practice. Hepatoscopy, a favorite Babylonian method of divination, involved examining the livers of animals. Ezekiel confirms these Babylonian practices in declaring: *"For the king of Babylon stands at the parting of the road, at the fork of the two roads, to use divination: he shakes the arrows, he consults the images, he looks at the liver"* (Ezek.21:21). Heavily superstitious; the Babylonians were idolatrous, with innumerable gods. Historian Will Durant numbered their gods around 65,000.

The Babylonians worshipped one woman in particular. This woman is Ishtar, whom the Babylonians worshipped for being the mother of God. Her titles include "The Virgin," "The Holy Virgin," and "The Virgin Mother." Ishtar represented the divinity of bounteous motherhood. Those who worshiped her considered her a goddess of war as well as love. She stood over prostitutes as well as mothers. She called herself a caring courtesan. Babylonians represented Ishtar sometimes as a bearded bisexual deity, and sometimes as a nude female offering her breasts to suck. Though Babylonians referred to her as "The Virgin," this merely meant that her illicit lovers were free from all bonds of wedlock.

Revelation 18:7 states: *"She says in her heart, I sit as queen, and am no widow, and will not see sorrow."* Ancient Babylonian prayers referred to her as "Queen of all cities, Queen of Heaven and Earth,...Ishtar is great! Ishtar is Queen! My lady is exalted; my Lady is Queen." Revelation 17:16 names her *"the whore."* In later centuries, among Babylon's enemies, the upper classes called her the "whore of Babylon."[24]

False Religion

False religion led the Israelites from the true God to its teachings. Babylon's religious symbols and doctrines bore many similarities to those taught in the Scriptures, in part because the Jews lived within Babylonia and Jewish doctrine influenced their myths. Ancient Jews embraced the Babylonian religion, and God rebuked the Jews for following its practices. During Ahab's reign in Israel's northern kingdom, Jezebel, the Phoenician princess, instituted Baal worship and murdered the prophets of God. Baal was the Sun-god, the Life-Giving One, equivalent to Tammuz. Baal worship was part of Babylonian society, and caused the Babylonian invasion of Israel. In Jeremiah 44:17-20, the Jews acknowledged to Jeremiah that they burned incense, and gave drink offerings to the Queen of Heaven. This passage mentions the "Queen of Heaven" four times. Four in the Bible represents the number of man, and man invented religion. From Babylon this mystery-religion spread to all the surrounding nations, and the symbols remained similar, including the image of the Queen of Heaven with a baby in her arms. Astoreth and Tammuz became Isis and Horus in Egypt, Aphrodite and Eros in Greece, Venus and Cupid in Italy, and bore many other names.[25]

The Babylonian religion merged with Christianity during the reign of the Roman emperor Constantine. These combined beliefs became part of the Catholic Church. Historians Will and Ariel Durant recorded that, "Babylonian altars frequently sacrificed a lamb, as the substitute for man who gave it in exchange for his life... priests carried from sanctuary to sanctuary the image of Mardak, and performed the sacred drama of his death and resurrection. They anointed the idols with sweet-scented oils, burned incense before them, and clothed them with rich vestments."[26]

The woman in Revelation 17 sits dressed as a harlot leading to herself the hearts of men. Revelation 17:2 tells us that the world's kings commit fornication with the Great Whore. The fornication committed is not merely physical, but spiritual adultery. As men deny the true Church of Jesus Christ by embracing the harlot's false teaching, they become corrupt in unholy union.

The Whore's Judgment

In the end times, the Great Whore sits upon the Beast-joined to his Kingdom—and later the Antichrist and his federation of kings destroy her. They carry her off, leaving her naked and burned. Her presence indicates political influence. Her destruction by the Beast reveals that she exercises limited power over the Antichrist and his federation of kings. Though present in the kingdom's early stages, she does not remain long after the entity becomes powerful. Her destruction occurs when the Antichrist claims to be god and demands worship of him alone. His ideology diametrically opposes her precepts. All religions threaten his imposed laws.

Revelation 17 and Isaiah 47 describe the Great Whore's judgment by God. In verse 6, the Scriptures describe her as "*drunk with the blood of the saints and with the blood of the martyrs.*" Verse 7 describes the Beast "carrying her." Initially the Bible pictures the woman sitting on the Beast—joined to his kingdom—which reveals that she has influence over the Beast. Later they carry her, indicating that she grows into a burden, and in verses 16 and 17 the Bible tells us: "*And the ten horns which you saw on he beast, these will hate the harlot, make her desolate and naked, eat her flesh and burn her with fire.*"

The Whore's judgment comes from God. Making her desolate and naked, eating her flesh, and burning her with fire indicate that violence will be committed against her—such as spoiling the treasures of her churches, taking possession of her land, burning her Bibles, religious literature, statues, religious paraphernalia, and buildings, and persecuting her followers so that the Antichrist alone can be the sole object of worship. While she initially has influence over the Beast's kingdom, she does not remain long after his government becomes powerful. Her destruction occurs when the Antichrist claims to be a god and demands worship of him alone. All religions then become a threat to him, and he sets out to remove them from the face of the earth.

In the past century many dictatorships arose and each of them eliminated freedom of religion and speech as the state and the dictator act as the objects of one's sole dedication. The Antichrist will limit these freedoms on a worldwide scale and the nations which do not willingly go along he will conquer.

Several Bible scholars teach that "*the Whore*" represents a one-world religion, which operates along with a one-world government. These writers cite the ecumenical movement that embraced many religions and supported left wing revolutionary groups as the forecasted one world religion. The movement endorsed liberation theology, which taught that Jesus was the first Marxist. Liberation theology used the Scripture to prove that the Bible provided the basis for Communism. The Catholic Church, one of the largest churches in the world, refused to join the Ecumenical Church.

Some expositors teach that the Antichrist heads the one world religion which launches the False Prophet. This author holds the view that the Whore of Babylon and the Beast operate separately and the Whore's location, religious teachings and influence over the area of the Beast intertwines them. Revelation 17:7 states that the beast "*carries*" the woman. The verse uses bastazo, the Greek word for carries which according to Strong's Lexicon means: 1) to take up with the hands, 2) to take up in order to carry or bear, to put upon one's self (something) to be carried, a) to bear what is burdensome, 3) to bear, to carry, a) to carry on one's person, b) to sustain, i.e. uphold, support, 4) to bear away, carry off.

This woman clearly becomes a burden to these kings and the Scripture tells us "*these shall hate the Whore.*" Verse 17 explains that they give their allegiance to the Beast who deifies himself and establishes his own religion (Dan. 11:39). The Revelation chapter specifies that the woman sits on the Beast because she shares the same location. Her teachings influence the leaders and people of the land.

Religion and The EU's Formation

The Bible depicts the Whore sitting on the Beast, signifying that she plays a principal role. Religion does play a part in European politics. Its precepts provided the ideology that prompted the European Union's formation. Religion has a voice in European politics through the Christian Democratic and Socialist political parties, which elect statesmen who share their beliefs. The leaders of these parties become the political representatives of their churches. During the French Revolution, as Democracy spread through Europe, so did Christian political parties. Most of these parties were Catholic. The Christian Democratic political movement would defend the Church's ultimate interests. This political party assumed responsibility for the social services that the Church was no longer in a position to provide. The Whore in part sits on the Beast through the Christian political parties that are responsible for the European

Union's formation and evolution. While Christian doctrine founded America, the Whore's precepts provide the ideological basis for the formation of the final world power's government.

Catholic ideals influenced the European Union's founders. During World War II, French Foreign Minister Robert Schuman, German Chancellor Konrad Adenauer, and Alcide de Gasperi, each man exemplary Catholics, had been hunted by Nazis and Fascists. De Gasperi—the founder of the Christian Democratic Party in Italy, and a militant Catholic activist and anti-fascist—became premier of Italy in 1945. He believed that the party man remained linked with his spiritual mother, the Church. His theological convictions influenced his public and private actions.[27]

German Chancellor Konrad Adenaeur helped found the Christian Democratic Union (CDU) in Germany in 1945. He "typified a Catholic Germany in contrast to a pagan Germany." In 1949, the Frenchman Robert Schuman became France's foreign minister. He had wanted to become a priest, but gave the idea up to serve his faith in other ways. For him, politics was a priestly duty. All three men were politicians with high ideals. Pope Pius XII, who held strong political beliefs, sought to aid the cause of peace with the help of fellow Catholics. He and the leaders of the Christian Democratic parties formulated a plan. For the first time, leaders of the Catholic Church headed the French, Italian, and German governments. The Christian Democratic political parties aroused hopes of a new Christianity. The movement arranged religious gatherings where they planned political action. Vatican Europe became part of the political scene.

Europe, devastated by two world wars, directly felt the threat of two atheistic ideologies—communism and fascism. The European political leaders believed that the only way to have peace among nations would be if the nations aligned themselves in economic and political pursuits. Schuman proposed that France and Germany create a Coal and Steel Community, encompassing the two nation's production. Konrad Adenauer welcomed the idea as a way to prevent war among these two nations. They invited other nations to join as well.

• On May 9, 1950, the Schuman Declaration led to the first European Union.

THE GREAT WHORE OF BABYLON

- On April 18, 1951, European leaders signed the European Coal and Steel Community (ECSC) Treaty in Paris.

The entire Franco-German production of coal and steel resided under a higher authority. Its decisions bound France, Germany, and other member countries. A Council represented the interests of the Member States. The common assembly later became the Court of Justice. In their view, this foundation of a European federation was vital to the preservation of peace. The union would prevent war. The French and German heavy industries urgently needed rebuilding. The ECSC would spur growth. This agreement marked the birth of the European Union. Ratified by the governments of France, the Federal Republic of Germany, Italy, Belgium, the Netherlands, and Luxembourg, the ECSC began functioning in 1952. It represented a revolutionary approach to international relations, as the first international organization with a federal governing body.[28] This led to the drafting of the EURATOM (European Atomic Energy Community) and Common Market Treaties.

- On March 25, 1957, European founders signed the EURATOM (European Atomic Energy Community) and the Common Market Treaties in Rome on one of its seven hills—Capitoline Hill.

Religion influenced the European Union's formation through political leaders who embraced its precepts. These men acted as key players in the Union's formation. They held the highest positions in its newly established organizations. Robert Schuman became the first president of the European Commission in 1958. Alcide de Gasperi held the presidential post of the ECSC Common Assembly in 1954. Monsignor Pierre Raffin, the Bishop of Metz, in Schuman's native Lorraine, launched a campaign for his beatification; the first step on the way to sainthood. Some Christian Democratic members of the European Parliament backed the initiative.[29] Of Jacques Delors, the former EU Commission president, Stanley Hoffman, who writes on European Union affairs, wrote: "A former official of the French labor union inspired by progressive Catholic thought, he exemplifies the synthesis of Christian democracy and socialism on which the Community was built."[30] One's religious convictions greatly affect one's political beliefs.

In the summer of 1998, the *United Methodist News Service* issued a press release stating that European churches were preparing to play a major role in the continued development of the European Union. The European Ecumenical Commission for Church and Society merged with the Conference of European Churches into the Commission on Church and Society. Members of this new commission included Methodists, Lutherans, Baptists, Anglicans, and the Orthodox. The Conference of European Churches comprised 123 different church bodies, and also cooperated with the Roman Catholic Church. Keith Clements, the conference's general secretary, commented: "For the first time in centuries, there's the possibility of creating a Europe without barriers, the challenge to the churches is whether they themselves can contribute to the unity."[31]

The Role of the Catholic Church and the European Union

Catholic thought provides the ideological basis for a united Europe, and presents itself as a political point of reference. The Church along with the unification of Europe, is simultaneously attempting to unify and strengthen itself. It aims to become the spiritual backbone of the evolving European Union. According to *See Change*, a publication for Catholic organizations, which reports on how the hierarchy of the Catholic Church involves itself in public policy debates:

> It seems that the bishops want the European Union to become an extension of the church, by confirming that European civilization, in the words of the pope, "emerged because the seed of Christianity was planted deep in Europe's soil." (Zenit, "Popes, proposals for European Charter of human rights, "September 24, 2000.)
> Few democracies in Europe mention God in their constitutions but this did not deter the bishops from demanding that the European Union should do so.[32]

On January 13, 2003, Pope John Paul II gave his State of the World address to representatives of 177 countries in Vatican City. Concerning the

THE GREAT WHORE OF BABYLON

European Union he stated: "The Holy See and all the Christian Churches have urged those drawing up the future Constitutional Treaty of the European Union to include a reference to Churches and religious institutions." He added: " A Europe which disavowed its past, which denied the fact of religion, and which had no spiritual dimension would be extremely impoverished in the face of the ambitious project which calls upon all its energies: constructing a Europe for all." [33]

Within two weeks of the Pope's address, *United Press International* reported that the Pope was "lobbying European governments to officially recognize the European Union's Christian roots," and they reported on the Catholic Church's efforts to work a strong Christian reference into the preamble of the EU Constitution. The Vatican argues that "Christianity's fundamental role in shaping European culture should be acknowledged in what is destined to become the European Union's key document." Convention delegates are reluctant to involve religion in the new constitution, for fear that it might create additional problems for the Union.[34]

Dr. Ian Paisley of the Institute of Protestant Studies, whose web site (http://www.ianpaisley.org/about.asp) promotes, defends, and maintains Bible Protestantism in Europe, exposes the papacy as the Beast of Revelation and offers some enlightening facts. His article "The Vacant Seat Number 666 in the European Union Parliament," records:

> The prophetic significance of the European Union has been revealed as the saga unfolds. First, the sign which it chose as its symbol was the woman riding the Beast. This comes from a prophecy in Revelation 17. The depiction of the harlot woman was reproduced on the centenary stamp of the European Union, in a huge painting in the Parliament's new building in Brussels, and by a huge sculpture outside the new EU Council of Ministers Office in Brussels. The new European coinage, the euro, bears the same insignia. The Tower of Babel has been used on the posters emanating from Europe – a truly suggestive prophetic sign.
>
> Now, a massive Crystal Palace tower (officially called the Tower Building) houses the Fifth Parliament of Europe...The

seats... there are 679 of them – but wait for it! While these seats are allocated to Members, one seat remains unallocated and unoccupied. The number of that seat is 666.

The web site also exposes the Catholic Church's immorality and its political role within the European Union, and alerts its readers to EU legislation that infringes on the freedoms of European citizens.[35]

In November of 2008, the Catholic Church demanded that the EU enshrine Sunday observance into law. In October of 2009, the Catholic News Service reported Pope Benedict XVI asserting:

> If European unity is based only on geography and economics, it cannot succeed in promoting the common good of all Europe's citizens and in helping the rest of the world. The recognition of the dignity of the human person and the obligation to work for the common good ~ values Christianity fostered on the continent ~ are what inspired the movement toward European unity and are the only guarantee of its success.
>
> The European Union did not bring those values to the 27 member countries, but rather it is these shared values that have given birth to and were like a gravitational force that drew the countries together and inspired them to form a union.
>
> When the church recalls the Christian roots of Europe, it is not seeking a special status for itself, instead, it is calling Europeans to remember that the values that brought peace to the continent and freedom and dignity to its people must be allowed to continue nourishing it...Europe will not truly be herself if she cannot keep the originality that made her great.[36]

In the Pope's own words we see the image of the woman sitting on the Beast and her influence is clearly evident. So much so that contributors have devoted a page to *Wikipedia*, the online encyclopedia entitled "European Union- Holy See Relations," and another entry titled, "The European Union and the Catholic Church." [37]

A few years back there was a web site dedicated to exposing the meaning of the EU flag. The site called itself "The EU Flag's True Symbolism Revealed." The writer presented the idea that the symbol derived from the Virgin Mary, and is a tribute to her. The EU's flag, a circle of twelve stars on a blue background, depicts Judeo-Christian symbolism. The twelve stars symbolize the twelve tribes of Israel, the twelve apostles, along with the twelve months in a year, and the Greek myth that speaks of the twelve labors Hercules performed to gain immortality.

The European Union bases many of its symbols on pagan myths; the very name Europe is from the Greek mythological Europa, a Phoenician noble woman kidnapped by Zeus who came to her as a bull and took her to the island of Crete where she became queen. Ian Paisley pointed out the similarity of Revelation Chapter 17 depiction of the harlot riding the beast and the EU's woman seated on the bull which are outside several of the European Union's institutions, as well as on the Greek euro coin.

Europa's name appeared on postage stamps commemorating the Council of Europe, issued in 1956. Furthermore, the dome of the European Parliament's Paul-Henri Spaak building contains a large mosaic by Aligi Sassu portraying the abduction of Europa with other elements of Greek mythology. Europa also serves as the national personification for Europe.[38]

Social Babylon

God condemned all three aspects of Babylonian society—political, religious, and social. Besides being a hub for international trade, and religiously devoted to the Queen of Heaven, Babylonian society was immortal, steeped in superstition, divination, idolatry, and sexual promiscuity. The morals of Babylon shocked Alexander the Great, himself a drunkard. Temple prostitutes practiced sacred prostitution in Babylon until abolished by Constantine. Babylonians engaged in considerable premarital experience. Poor men prostituted their daughters for money. The indulgence in fleshly pleasures abounded.

Babylonian men acted effeminate. They wore their hair as long as the women did, dyed and curled it, perfumed their flesh, rouged their cheeks, and adorned themselves with necklaces, bangles, earrings, and pendants.[39] This also describes many of today's rock groups, transvestites, transsexuals, and homosexual drag queens.

In Europe today, materialism and superstition abound. Italian housewives practice forms of divination such as divining oil to read a migraine headache, or determining the sex of a baby by reading the movements of a needle over a pregnant woman's womb.

French society is one of the best educated in the world. Yet, in 1990, ten million French citizens consulted clairvoyants and astrologers. They spent three times as much on faith healers as they spent on family doctors. Almost half of the French population believes in faith healing. One in four believes in clairvoyants, and one in three believes in astrology. Many believe in the power of faith healers, astrologers, and palmists.[40] In France, as many as sixty corporations use an organization called Divinitel, which employs astrology and tarot card reading for the recruitment of executives.[41]

In European society, extramarital affairs are so common that spouses expect each other to have lovers. Europeans view Americans' disdain for infidelity as being out of touch with the facts of life. Germany has legalized prostitution. Hard rock, punk, and new wave all originated in Europe, and their dress and music have influenced groups in the US and around the world.

The Green parties in Europe have revived a form of idolatry that originated with the Greeks: earth worship. To the Greeks, she was a goddess; earth as mother. Green policies for the preservation of the earth began in West Germany, spread through Europe and then into America. Ironically, the earth that these groups take such pains to preserve for future generations God will destroy. Mother Earth cannot save anyone from the coming Tribulation.

Political Babylon's Foretold Destruction

The book of Revelation foretells the destruction of Babylon. The Scriptures refer to Babylon as a "she." International trade characterizes her. God cites her as a deceiver of nations, and the means by which the merchants and great men of the earth trade (Revelation 18:7,23). The European Union's political ideology derives from the Whore's teachings. The act of uniting Europe to prevent war among its nations finds its roots in religious conviction. Nations will not wage war against one another while united in economic alliance. If nations align with one another they will eliminate war and achieve peace. The deception exists in the premise that worldwide democracy will ensure peace, justice, and human rights. Revelation 18:11-15 lists twenty-seven exported goods combined with categories of products. The 28th phrase lists *"souls of men."* Verse 23 concludes with: *"For by thy sorceries were all the nations deceived."* The Scriptures teach that man is sinful, and because of his nature there will be no peace on earth until the second coming of Jesus Christ.

During Nebuchadnezzar's reign, Jeremiah foretold Babylon's judgment in the latter days. Just as Nebuchadnezzar laid siege to Jerusalem and oppressed the Jews (Jeremiah 50:30), the Antichrist will do the same. When the Antichrist treads down the nations, the nations become angry. Jeremiah 51:7 states: *"Babylon was a golden cup in the Lord's hand that made all the earth drunk: The nations drank her wine; therefore the nations are deranged."* Revelation 17:4 tells us that abominations and filthiness of fornication fill the gold cup in her hand. The kings of the earth commit fornication with her and become drunk with the wine of her fornication. Revelation 18:3 adds that *"the merchants of the earth have become rich through the abundance of her luxury."* The rest of the chapter predicts her destruction. The remaining passages refer to her as the hub for trade for the earth's merchants. Upon her destruction, these merchants mourn, for they can no longer trade with her.

After the Antichrist wreaks his havoc upon the earth, armies will go to fight against the European Union. Jeremiah 50:41 states: *"Behold, a people shall come from the North, and a great nation and many kings shall be raised up from the ends of the earth."* In the Bible, North always refers to the area of the Soviet Union. "A great nation" may be the US. "At the noise of the taking of Babylon the earth trembles, and the cry is heard among the nations" (Jeremiah 50:46).

God destroys political Babylon i.e. the final world empire. As Hitler was the spark for World War II, when he invaded and conquered nations in Europe; the Antichrist's swift and fast conquest will prompt powerful nations to wage war against him. Daniel 11:40 states that *"at the time of the end, the King of the South shall attack him: and the King of the North shall come against him like a whirlwind, with chariots, horsemen, and with many ships."*

When armies invade his land, the Antichrist enters into the attacking countries and defeats them. He conquers Egypt and North Africa. Hearing reports from the North and East, he goes forth with great fury to destroy. He ends up at a place prepared for him in Jerusalem (Daniel 11:42-45). Israel and the Middle East become part of Antichrist's conquered territory, according him the exact borders of the Roman Empire at the time of Christ. Jeremiah 4:6-7 tells us: "*Set up the standard toward Zion: take refuge! Do not delay!: For I will bring disaster from the North, and great destruction. The lion has come up from his thicket, and the destroyer of the nations is on his way; he has gone forth from his place to make your land desolate; your cities will be laid waste without inhabitant.*"

The Antichrist's armies, the Soviet Union, the Eastern nations, and the US surround Jerusalem. The river Euphrates dries up, and prepares the way for the kings of the East. God draws the world's armies to the place called, in the Hebrew tongue, Armageddon (Rev. 16:12-16).

CHAPTER 4

THE CORNERSTONE FOR UNITING THE WORLD

Bible Scholars agree that the final world power will rule globally. The Scripture states that the entire world worships the Beast and he institutes his Mark worldwide. End time watchers follow developments in globalization and the New World Order. Unfortunately, around this premise many conspiracy theories have arisen teaching that secret societies are planning for world dominion. The Masons, the Illuminati, the Trilateral Commission, the Catholic Church, the Jewish elite, the Bildeburgers are among the groups planning the takeover. Each theory claims to document their facts on insider's revelations and sound research.

While looking for the secret society, these end-time watchers have failed to discover a European think-tank whose members belong to a political ideological movement which do not operate in secret but out in the open and have influenced the European Union's evolution. Their teachings provide a blueprint for global rule. These individuals believe in European "federalism"—the ideological term for one-worldism.

The movement began in the late 1930's in Britain, as a solution to the World War. In this proposed solution, the US federal government's model would govern on a worldwide scale. The "federalist papers," which drew their inspiration from English federal thought, inspired many writers and works on the topic from 1910 onward. *The Round Table*, a well-known political publication, advocated federalizing the British Empire.

In 1929, a New Europe Group proposed a European federation with a common currency, and foreign and defense policies. In 1939, the federalists published the Federalist Union Manifesto. They sought out activists by sending letters to those in the Who's Who interested in world affairs. Federalists believe that a nation's sovereignty is artificial, and that there can be no hope for international order while nations act independently. A writer stated that "unless we destroy the sovereign state, the sovereign state will destroy us," and they envision a world order which limits national sovereignty. They insist that federal union will take the globe's governments from the nation-state to the world-state, which would be an evolutionary advance.

The ultimate aim of federalism is world government, for they view federalism as the antithesis of totalitarianism. Supporters of federalism proposed that "the long-term aim of Federal Union remains the establishment of a world federation." Their more immediate aim was "the promotion of a democratic federation of Europe as part of the post-war settlement."

During these early years, author and lecturer Lionel Robbins sketched the outline of a new world order. He suggested that Europe become a federation of states, consenting to limited sovereignty while pursuing a common trade policy. His proposals foreshadowed what the European Union later accomplished. The formation of the European Community occurred in line with federalist thinking. Although these policies duplicate what occurred in the historical account of the European Union's formation, the federalists did not initiate its creation.[42] Jean Monnet is responsible for the EU's formation.

In 1944, the group established the European Union of Federalists (EUF). They associated themselves with the worldwide movement for world federal government. Today in Washington exists the headquarters of the World Federalist Association which in 2004 became the Democratic World Federalists. This group enlists the Hollywood crowd, and is a branch of the liberal left. They embrace Mother Earth rhetoric. Environmental issues, which leaders view as a global crisis, support their argument for international law.

Federalist slogans include "Peace Through World Law," "One Planet—One People," and "One Earth Needs World Federation." World Federalists seek to strengthen the UN as a prospect for world government. They applaud the EU's endeavors.[43] The European federalists lead the movement by enlisting political leaders and intelligentsia; in addition, they publish sophisticated journals propagating their ideology.

THE CORNERSTONE FOR UNITING THE WORLD

The Federalist Movement, Jean Monnet and the EU's Formation

When nuclear bombs fell on Hiroshima and Nagasaki in 1945, the urgency of the federalists' desire for action became more intense than ever. For many, this meant action on a world scale. Federalist groups now existed throughout the world. The Federal Trust for Education and Research formed in 1945 in London. The Trust's activity involved itself with the European Union, as a route to its wider agenda.

Stalin ordered a total blockade of Berlin in 1948, impelling Europeans to unite. That summer, World Federalists held their second congress in Luxembourg. Emery Reves, one of the speakers, began to see European federation as a possible step toward world federation, in line with federalist policy. Federalists endorsed regional integration as "an approach to world federation." The long-term goal of "world government" seemed less immediate and practical than action on a smaller, more limited front, either in Europe or across the Atlantic.

The federalists sought to improve and strengthen world institutions such as the United Nations, the International Monetary Fund, and the World Bank. These globalists ranked first in undertaking the work of turning the UN into an effective world authority. While these efforts failed, Jean Monnet reiterated their vision for the European Union. Federalists viewed the EU as an indirect route to achieve their end.

On April 18, 1951, European leaders signed the European Coal and Steel Treaty in Paris. The treaty's members included France, Germany, Italy, Belgium, Luxembourg, and the Netherlands. That same year, an editorial in *Federal News* declared: "Just as European Federalists have rightly said that it will be impossible to build a world federation without first federating Europe, it is now becoming clear that it may not be possible to federate Europe without doing so as part of a wider scheme of federation."

Federalists declared that Federal Union should not advocate the setting up of any specific federation, but should encourage the establishment of any federations and international organizations that would tend to lead to ultimate world federation.

Monnet, with the Benelux statesman Paul-Henri Spaak and Jean Beyen, worked on a plan for the reformation of Europe, which took clear form in 1955. The foreign ministers of the six member countries met in

Messina, Sicily. They launched the process that ended with the establishment of the European Community and EURATOM (European Atomic Energy Community) on January 1, 1958. The six decided to create a specialized community based on the ECSC, (European Coal and Steel Community) for the peaceful development of nuclear energy. At the same time, they decided to remove trade barriers and create a common market in which goods, persons, and capital could move freely. On March 25, 1957, European leaders signed the EURATOM (European Atomic Agency) Treaty and the European Economic Community (EEC) or Common Market Treaty in Rome on Capitoline Hill. The EU's founders viewed economic union as the prerequisite for eventual political integration.

The EEC's institutional structure, laid out in the Treaty of Rome, was federalist in character. The resemblance was not coincidental; Altiero Spinelli, an Italian federalist, influenced de Gasperi in the writing of the treaty. He wrote Monnet's speech for his inaugural address as the first president of the EEC's High Authority. The widespread acceptance of federalist thinking in the six ECSC countries in the early 1950's ensured the approval of their logic by politicians and the public.

In 1957, with the signing of the Rome Treaties, the Trust's European activities expanded. Membership grew, and a wide range of expert speakers became available to the Trust including people from the EU Commission and the member countries. The subjects soon covered such specialized fields as agriculture, financial investment, transport, labor law, and tax. The Trust developed the reputation as a significant organization. One of the speakers, Fernard Braun, a young commission official, later became the Director-General in charge of the program to complete the international market by the end of 1992. [44]

Jean Monnet: The Father of the New Europe

Europeans historically regard Jean Monnet as the father of Europe, the father of the common market. Born in 1888 to a family of wine growers, Jean Monnet long remained anonymous despite his accomplishments. He was neither a politician nor a technocrat. He had no particular expertise in any field, although some experts listed him as an economist.

In 1919, the Treaty of Versailles established the League of Nations. Monnet became the League's Deputy Secretary General. Europe experienced the devastation of two world wars and faced the dictatorships of Hitler and Mussolini. Economic crisis and unemployment marked postwar Europe, while both the United States and the Soviet Union emerged in much stronger positions. Monnet believed that the countries of Europe should unite to bring freedom and prosperity to their continent. He argued that national sovereignty was outmoded if it prevented Europe from keeping pace with the times in the age of the superpowers.

During the Kennedy era, growth in the EU slackened due to de Gaulle's nationalism and anti-American sentiments. He called the US, "the unwanted federator of an integrated Europe." To refute this, Kennedy called for a joint interdependence. In 1963, Kennedy's speech in St. Paul's Church of Frankfurt expressed satisfaction with a United Europe. He stated: "It would be a world power, capable of dealing with the US on equal footing in every domain."[45]

After de Gaulle's departure, Jean Monnet's idea of building up the European Union as a partner of the United States gained popularity. European federalists began to consider how a federal Europe might help to build a wider union of democracies, as a step on the long road to world federation. David Barton, in an article in *World Affairs*, gave a more exact meaning to the term "Atlantic Community." Essentially, he saw it "as linking militarily, politically and economically large trading blocs or regional groupings." He believed these would serve as an example for other regions, and could finally lead to a world community.[46]

Although the Federalist Trust focused on the EU, Jean Monnet, its true founder, did not follow a federalist blue-print. In 1976, the European Council made Jean Monnet an "Honorary Citizen of Europe." In March of 1979, Monnet died. As the European Document entitled "Jean Monnet, a Grand Design For Europe," states:

> His message has the force of all simple ideas. Instead of wasting time and energy in trying to apportion blame for a horrific war, the countries of Europe should combine to bring freedom and prosperity to their continent. The imperative of the age was to bring economies together, to merge interests, to

make the means of production more efficient in a world dominated by competitiveness and progress. Monnet's message went to the root of national sovereignty which he argued was outmoded if it prevented Europe from keeping pace with the times in the age of superpowers.[47]

Federalist Influence in the EU's Evolution

By 1966, the Trust's focus shifted toward the Community's economic, institutional, and political development. Those attending its conferences began to include a wider range of policy-makers and Community watchers. By the late 1960s, the Trust studied ways to improve Community institutions and policy. Federalists began thinking in terms of a common set of foreign, security, defense, and monetary policies.

Many of the staff members of Federal Union regarded European federalism as the first step in establishing a new world system. Most of them later became prominent in their various occupations. Some became members of the EU Commission, some became editors for European affairs journals, and still others held other influential posts. Former French President Valéry Giscard d'Estaing spoke at Federal Trust conferences before his presidency.

• In 1973, Britain, Denmark, and Ireland joined the Community, bringing the number of Member States to nine.
• On January 1, 1981, Greece became the community's tenth member.
On January 1, 1986, Spain and Portugal became the Community's next two members, bringing the number of Member States to twelve.

EU countries in the early 1980s suffered high unemployment and low growth. Europe barely recovered from the 1982 recession, unlike the US this sparked renewed commitment. European leaders felt it imperative to reconstruct their economies, to provide a large base for their companies to compete in the global marketplace. Two major decisions helped them to accomplish this goal. First, in June 1985, the Community published a white paper entitled, "Completing the Internal Market." It contained 285 directives and specific regulations, and assigned each directive an expected date of adoption ranging from 1985 to 1991. The directives removed fiscal, technical, and physical barriers and harmonized product standards, diplomas, insurance and credit regulations, as well as differences in taxation from country to country throughout the Community.

The second major decision, the European Single Act, came into force on January 1, 1987. Under the Act, a yes vote by the Council of Ministers only called for a weighted majority, except in cases involving health and environmental issues. In the past, all decisions made by the Council required voting by unanimous decision. This method slowed the EU's growth. The EU could now move forward.

In 1987, the Trust examined the idea of a European Security Community. The group's report proposed that the Union pool their defense forces. The European Union would become the partner of the United States as the European pillar of the Atlantic Alliance. It would seek a common security relationship with the Soviet Union while reforming the United Nations into a more effective peacekeeper. The report views the Union as a kind of world community made up of regional communities, as a stage in the progression toward the more distant prospect of a world government. The Trust produced a set of proposals on how the Community might develop into a Union with federal institutions. They suggested instituting a European federal bank to underpin economic and monetary union. The Trust also proposed a common security and foreign policy. The Union adopted all of these proposals, and they are now Union policy. The European Central Bank under the Lisbon Treaty became an official EU institution.

In 1995, Austria, Sweden and Finland became members of the Union bringing the number of Member States to 15.
In 2004, 10 new countries, the Czech Republic, Estonia, Hungary, Latvia, Lithuania, Poland, Slovakia, and Slovenia, plus the Mediterranean islands of Malta and Cyprus joined the Union.
In 2007, Romania and Bulgari followed bringing the number of EU Member States to 27.

Federalist Ideology

Federalists believe that sovereign nations are no longer able to solve the world's problems. They regard national sovereignty as a traditional governmental precept of the past. Former NATO General Secretary Manfred Worner stated: "If Europe is to measure up to its new responsibilities—and it has no choice—it must—then it will have to pull itself together rapidly and free itself of outmoded notions of sovereignty."[48] The Belmont European Policy Centre in Brussels, a European think-tank made this statement: "On May 1950, the Schuman Declaration proclaimed that the so-called sovereign nation state no longer constituted a satisfactory model for organizing relations between European states. Only through pooling specific elements of sovereignty could they prevent further catastrophes and regain their ability positively to influence their nations' destinies."[49]

Franz Anderiessen, former Vice President of the EU Commission, declared: "Europe, and the world at large have suffered immeasurably, not least in this enlightened century, from exaggerated ideas of the role of the sovereign states."[50] The European Commission in part funds the *New Federalist*, the newsletter of the Young European Federalists. An eminent member of the World Federalists in the United States commented in an essay, which appeared in the newsletter:

> The current nation-state system is impractical and, in many ways, a global anarchy...Presently, blind, idolatrous nationalism is the primary force in opposition to world federation. Children at a young age must be taught the importance of loyalty to one's family, community and homeland... loyalty to one's planet must also be emphasized. Is there a better way than war and economic coercion to solve the world conflict? Yes, a better alternative is through system of equitable and enforceable world law.

Federalists aim for a new world based on the rule of international law, thus achieving *Pax Universalis*. To the federalist, one's loyalty belongs to planet Earth. Urgency accompanies their cause, with the slogan "mankind must unite or perish." Some members believe federalism is a force that will be unleashed throughout the whole world. They view global unity as the utopian solution to end all wars. Federalists believe that with the collapse of communism, their goal for world government has become a concrete and political aim.

In this age when threats can be global in nature, nations will find no other alternative but to align with one another. Federalism's precepts have humanistic aims. *The New Federalist* summed up the ideology for international law in stating that:

> Federalism overcomes the cause of war: the division of the world into sovereign states with the world federation, that final stronghold of violence between men, war, will be eliminated: international anarchy will be replaced by the rule of law between states. The world federation will, as Kant taught us, open up a world in which man can consider other men as ends in themselves and in which he can fully and autonomously develop all the capacities that are within him. The world federation will open the history of the human race. [51]

We know from Scripture that the world federation will not open the history of the human race but rather end it. The Antichrist will use this ideology to gain dictatorial control over the world.

Globalization

Along with the one-world government movement, social, economic, and political trends are bringing about the unification of the globe. Even religion follows the global path through organizations such as the World-Wide Council of Churches.

With today's technology, no one nation remains isolated. Television satellites, fax machines, and data banks bring many countries together in the transference of information. Technology has made the world a smaller, more unified place. While Globalization is a process, technological developments act as the catalyst that speeds it along. Payment systems of major countries closely interlink. Banks around the globe communicate electronically. *The Economist* stated: "Today's economies are interdependent and interconnected. Flows of trade and capital tie countries more closely together than at any time since the 19th century. A recession in one country slows growth elsewhere. One government's budget deficit draws resources not just from domestic savings but from a global pool of capital that all have to share."

In addition to economic and financial interdependence, the world is breaking up into regional groupings of nations that act as trade blocs. As twenty to thirty nations form one of these blocs, they become a section of the globe. As the world coalesces into sections, unification becomes a simpler process. Five or six parts of a pie join easily, compared to over 160 pieces of a puzzle. The Great Recession showed the impact of globalization the day the American financial markets plummeted. The European markets followed and caused a ripple effect hitting every major market around the globe. Within days major financial papers reported that the world economy had literally come to a stop.

Global Problems

National problems that have a worldwide impact such as the Great Recession, nuclear arms buildup, the environment, and drugs, have prompted nations to intensify their efforts to work together in their common causes. Banks even unite internationally to fight computer crime and money laundering.

The Earth Summit of 1992 brought together nations from around the globe to coordinate global environmental policy. This Summit involved nearly four times as many countries as founded the United Nations. Maurice Strong, the Secretary General for the United Nations Conference on Environment and Development, felt that environmental problems such as global warming, the ozone hole, acid rain, soil degradation, and deforestation jeopardized all nations, and because of this he stated that "the world has now moved beyond economic interdependence to ecological interdependence—and even beyond that to an intermeshing of the two. The world's economic and earth's ecology are now interlocked—'unto death do them part,' to quote one of Canada's industrial leaders. This is the new reality of the century, with profound implications for the shape of our institutions of governance, national and international."[52]

World Institutions

During World War II, world leaders recognized the need for international economic institutions. In 1944, political leaders established the International Monetary Fund and the World Bank. The General Agreement of Tariffs and Trade (GATT) followed in 1948, along with a new wave of regional organizations. It instituted a code of rules by which countries could trade, as well as a forum for resolving disputes among trading partners. It aimed to liberalize world trade through the reduction of trade barriers, for free trade ensures peace among nations. Nations coordinate their trade policies through the GATT. The European Union advocated an international currency to replace the dollar and the yen, and a new international monetary system to underpin the GATT trade system. The Union stated that the GATT's ultimate objective is "a single world market." The European Union proposed the idea of a one-world monetary system in 1986, as an amendment to the GATT.[53]

At the conclusion of the Uruguay Round in April 1994, over 120 countries signed an agreement in Marrakesh, Morocco, that created the World Trade Organization (WTO). The successor to the GATT, it acts as the United Nations of world trade, and continues to liberalize the global market. It began operation in January of 1995.

The UN, founded with 51 Member States, now includes 192. The UN's peacekeeping role has broadened considerably in recent years. Since the end of the Cold War, the UN has involved itself in the settling of conflicts across the globe. Commenting on this development, *The Economist* stated: "For the first time the nations of the world, rich and poor, are beginning to cooperate for agreed ends on a scale that hitherto only idealists have even dreamed about."[54]

Federalists aim to transform the United Nations into a democratic world federation. In 1991, a year before the Earth Summit, thirty-six respected world leaders put forth a document calling for a World Summit on Global Governance. The Stockholm Initiative aims to strengthen the UN so that it can better handle the global challenges of the future. It seeks to adopt a new approach to maintaining and developing international law. The proposed Commission on Global Governance seeks to strengthen the UN or form a new institution for the same purpose. Former European Commission President Jacques Delors suggested that the UN develop a "Council for Economic Security" to rewrite the rules for the global village. Delors saw it as unacceptable that single nations attempt to solve problems that have a worldwide scope.

The idea of having international rules echoes in many foreign affairs journals. Dennis Healy, Britain's former Defense Minister and Chancellor of the Exchequer, stated: "If we are talking about a new world order, I can only see a role for the UN. We can no longer tackle the great problems like environmental pollution, migration and global arms control, on a regional basis. International rules are required, especially when we remember that the population of the world is doubling every 50 years."[55]

The International Monetary Fund (IMF), founded at the Bretton Woods Conference in 1944, secures global monetary joint action. It enlists 184 member nations. The Conference on Security and Cooperation, created in 1975, enlists 56 nations. Established as a regional organization of the UN Charter, it deals with security, human rights, and trade. Its job includes giving early warning of potential conflicts, improving crisis management, and developing military confidence-building mechanisms. Besides the CSCE, other regional organizations have sprung up since World War II.

End time watchers often look at the UN and various world institutions as the possible launching pad for the Antichrist. These institutions have no governmental powers. No single world institution has the power or capacity to govern the world. When one notes how the EU utilizes these institutions, and its future plans for them, one sees Scripture unfold before their very eyes.

The EU bases its policy and laws on those of global institutions. For areas of policy not covered by any of these organizations, the EU establishes its own regional ones. The Council of Europe deals with human rights, health, migration, law, culture, and the environment. All of these organizations use abbreviated letters or acronyms which are synonymous with the EU. Political leaders are negotiating and signing so many of these treaties that it would require an entire book to list and explain them all. These treaties form a web over the entire globe. With each new treaty, one more additional strand links nation to nation. Technological advances and infrastructures act as the bonding material holding them all together.

The Cornerstone for Uniting the World

Within the EU, federalists hold key positions, and impact upon the

THE CORNERSTONE FOR UNITING THE WORLD

EU's future direction and policies toward global governance. EU bureaucrats have adopted a federalist blueprint. With EU laws based on those of world institutions, once the EU becomes the world's leading power, it will lead other nations into global governance. In its mega superpower status, its policies will take precedence on the world stage.

Lucio Levi, the editor of *The Federalist Debate*, published in Torino, Italy, stated in the July 2001 issue: "A center of power must emerge with the capability of supporting the plan for a world democratic order. The European Union could be such a power....It is reasonable to believe that Europe will hold sufficient power to relieve the United States of some of their overwhelming world responsibilities, and thus have the authority to persuade them to support the democratic reform of the United Nations."[56]

Federalists have already mapped out the route the EU will take to achieve world government. A powerful EU will have the greatest voice in world organizations. Most nations will hand over their sovereignty to these institutions. When the EU has sufficient power, it will write the rules for the world. Italy has proposed that in the future the European Union might seek a single permanent seat at the UN Security Council. Germany's defense minister also supports the EU's having a single seat on the UN Security Council. These proposals are the first stage of what has yet to occur. The 1999 issue of *The Federalist*, published in Pavia, Italy, states:

> It is as indicated, a question of predicting what type of world equilibrium the birth of the European federation will help to create, and what new forces it will help to unleash. We are all federalists because of our conviction that the founding of a European federation will be an important step forwards on the road towards the creation of a world federation, that it will allow the establishment of more stable, peaceful and open relations between peoples, that it will give the United Nations a more solid basis for action, that it will, through the example which its own birth will set the world, favor the development of new trends toward regional unification and give considerable impulse to the diffusion of the culture of the unity of mankind. And it will do this by mere virtue of its mere existence, and regardless of its governments' inclinations over foreign policy.[57]

Federalist thought provides the ideological backbone for the European Union. These ideals based on both religious and humanistic thinking or the teachings in the cup of the Whore, provide the Antichrist with a perfect platform for world rule.

The Coming One-World Government

A single world system is not new to man. Genesis records the historical account of the Tower of Babel. Mankind in ancient times united their efforts to build a tower to reach into the heavens. God declared that *"now nothing that they propose to do will be withheld from them,"* and confounded their language. Give man too much power, and he becomes dangerous. A unified world with a single world government will be a modern-day Tower of Babel.

It is paradoxical that as the world grows more populated, it becomes more of a single unit. To date, we see the skeletal form of a one-world system, and can speculate on its continuing evolution. The world is breaking up into regional economic groupings. Pat Buchanan commented that "in the New World Order, rules are set by west and east globalists."[58] These policy makers think in terms of international law as evidenced by the European Union federalists. World institutions will gain more power, and govern in their respective areas with the Antichrist as head of the European Union leading the world into oneness.

A one-world government will become man's final attempt at creating a utopian society that excludes God and deifies man. The one individual who will advocate and pursue this ideology will be man's greatest enemy. The world federation will not "open the history of the human race," but rather end it.

The process of globalization is occurring through the natural order of events. At present, the world is fragmented. The European Union will act as the cornerstone for uniting the world, in the same way Jesus is the "chief cornerstone" of the church. None of this is coincidental; we know that the Antichrist's empire here on earth mimics the Kingdom of God.

CHAPTER 5

THE BUILDING OF AN EMPIRE

Former Harvard Professor Samuel Huntington speculated in the 1990's that "the EC if it were to become politically cohesive, would have the population, resources, economic wealth, technology and actual potential military strength to be the preeminent power of the 21st century." Cornelius van der Klugt, while he chaired Philips, affirmed: "If we organize ourselves, Europe will grow faster than the US and Japan combined." The EU is in the process of building its empire. According to Scripture, the EU will become the most powerful empire the world has ever known. EU bureaucrats purpose to transform the EU into a political world power. Former French President François Mitterrand stated: "From now until the turn of the millennium, we have ten years to win the race for Europeans. No institution should escape this critical examination, not the European Community, NATO, the Council of Europe or the CSCE. All should play their part." Former German Chancellor Helmut Kohl declared: "I am convinced this is going to be the decade of the Europeans."[59]

One motive for European unity is to reclaim the limelight that virtually all of its member countries enjoyed during earlier periods of history. At the start of the Cold War, the US and Soviet Union became the leading world powers. Europe suffered the greatest share of the war's destruction. America aided in the rebuilding of Europe and provided for its defense through the North Atlantic Treaty Organization. Although Europe and America stood alongside each other as strong allies, Europeans harbored ill feelings concerning certain American policies. Some

Europeans desired a significant place on the world stage.

At the end of World War II, the European dream was reborn, and during the Cold War it crept along. Charles de Gaulle stated in his *Memoirs* that "Europe by confederation of its nations, can and must be for the well-being of its people, become the greatest political, economic and military and cultural power that ever existed."[60] From the mid- to late 1980s, a spark rekindled, and the fall of the Berlin Wall added fuel to the fire. The end of the Cold War and the beginning of the New World Order marked a new era for Europe.

The First Step to Political Union

The completion of the 1992 Common Market acted as the first step toward political union. The EU aimed to become an economic power on equal footing with the US and Japan. This proclamation underscores their ambition for attaining superpower status, as many of the member nations had in their history. With the completion of the 1992 program, an economically united Europe became the world's largest market and largest trader. Edward Heath, former British Prime Minister and an ardent federalist, affirmed: "All history tells us that economic reform is followed by political reform and that political power follows economic power." The Soviet Union and the United States demonstrated this. It will be the same with the European Community."[61]

Many individuals view the EU as a solely economic venture among European nations. Skeptics doubted that the EU would ever work together on an economic scale, let alone a political one. Peter Linton, a Brussels-based American consultant, warned that: "You [had] better be ready for the integration process that is moving ahead faster and farther than anyone has realized."[62] He added that many Americans have yet to grasp the political significance of the process, and to take it very seriously. As evidence of the magnitude of the EU's potential for superpower status, Lester C. Thurow, MIT's best known economist, declared: "In the past half century, the world played by rules written mostly by Americans; in the next half century, the world will play by rules written mostly by Europeans.[63]"

While natural disasters are occurring with greater frequency, events on the international scene have experienced more dramatic changes in a shorter span of time than at any previous time in history. As a result, some experts now say that *"a year is a long time in history."* In three years' time, the Berlin Wall and the Soviet Empire collapsed, and Germany reunited, marking the end of Communism and the Cold War, and the beginning of the New World Order. For the first time, an international coalition fought a war in the Middle East. The Israeli-Arab Peace Conference began. Islamic Fundamentalism, resurgent nationalism, and many internal conflicts around the globe emerged. During this time, the European Union signed its treaty on political union.

With the rapid changes sweeping Europe, the Union decided it was time to "renew their vows, the marriage contract of the twelve." The EU's response to these changes was to accelerate integration within the EU itself. The revolutions in Eastern Europe turned 1992 from a time of economic reform into the beginning of a political transformation. The European Union would remain the stable, solid core around which Europe would rebuild itself. During an EU summit meeting in 1989, EU leaders declared that "at this time of profound and rapid change, the Community is and must remain a point of reference and influence. It remains the cornerstone of a new European Architecture."

In 1990, former European Commission President Jacques Delors told the European Parliament that the Community would move fast toward full political union, a full fledged EU foreign policy, and deep institutional reform.[64] He felt that events in the East and the danger of resurgent nationalism underscored the need for closer EU political integration. Delors believed that these events made it "impossible...to separate the Community's economic role from its political one."[65]

Those in the Union feel that the EU is "now perceived as a major power and is expected to be a big-league player." During Jacques Delors, EU Commission presidency, he took advantage of every opportunity to strive for the unification of Europe. Concerning the Gulf Crisis, he commented, "It is a unique change for this Community to make the new qualitative leap which will make (it) the cornerstone of the greater Europe of tomorrow and...an actor of stature equal to its responsibilities on the world stage."[66]

It seemed that whatever the event, European Union leaders called for the EU to take a greater political role in the world. These proclamations underscored their ambitions and role within the Union to help it evolve into a leading superpower. This was after all their intentions from early on in the Union's formation.

One Money: The ECU

To be a truly single market with political clout in the world, Europe needed a single currency. The single most political act that the EU embarked on in addition to forming the Common Market was the decision to have its own currency. Political ambitions prompted the adoption of a single currency. Unionists viewed monetary union as the catalyst that would transform Europe's economic union into its political union.

Valéry Giscard d'Estaing, former president of France and founder of the annual G7 summits, stated in an interview that the creation of the single currency would "be seen by people as a major political advance." He believed that monetary union would "induce a move toward a more organized political Europe."[67]

Former German Chancellor Helmut Kohl asserted that the accords signed in Rome would ultimately lead the continent to political union. He went on to state: "One thing is certain, when this Europe ... has a common currency from Copenhagen to Madrid and from The Hague to Rome, when more than 350 million people live in a common space without border controls, then no bureaucrat in Europe is going to be able to stop the process of political unification."[68] Former French President François Mitterrand declared: "With a single currency (and other factors), Europe will have the means to affirm itself as the world's main power...It is not that we have ambitions to dominate, but together, we are already nearly the main commercial power in the world...together, on all markets in the world we will be at least as strong as the United States or Japan." [69]

In 1979, the European Monetary System began to function. The EMS kept EEC currencies within a fixed exchange rate structure. At the same time, the twelve member nations strengthened and coordinated their economic and monetary policies. European leaders decided in 1989 that all currencies will join the exchange rate mechanism (ERM) of the European Monetary System (EMS) on July 1, 1990.

The EU bears striking similarities to the Old Roman Empire and added one more by having their own currency. *The Economist* even noted:

"So Europe's future lies with monetary union? Perhaps, but this also a step back to the past. The Roman Empire remember had a single currency."[70]

In 1987, the Belgians minted the first silver coins, aimed at the collectors' market only. Imprinted on the coins were twelve stars, symbolizing the nations of the European Union, and the bust of Emperor Charles V. He was born in the Belgian town of Ghent, and was crowned head of the Holy Roman Empire in 1519. Europeans chose Charles V for the first ever European Currency Unit (ECU) because of the striking geographical similarity between the Common Market and the Holy Roman Empire.[71]

Former Commission President Jacques Santer made monetary union a priority while he was president-elect in 1994. Despite the skeptics' negative views, Santer showed no signs of wavering. He firmly stated: "EMU is coming as decided and planned." Santer affirmed:"The euro would be a strong currency." He summed up the purpose for the single currency when he stressed that "European countries can only be sure of making themselves heard on world monetary affairs if they have a single currency as powerful as the dollar and the yen." Santer believed that the "euro will be a counterweight to the US dollar in the international financial system." Santer was convinced that the euro will give the Union political status; he stated that "in the years ahead it will be interesting to see how the euro will reinforce the European Union externally."[72]

The European Central Bank and the Launch of the Euro

EU leaders determined that the launch of the euro would occur in three stages. The first stage occurred in 1990 when currencies joined the exchange rate mechanism (ERM) of the European Monetary System (EMS) in, 1990. The second stage two called for the creation of the European Central Bank. Based on the German Bundesbank, it is now one of the most important central banks and is responsible for monetary policy covering the 16 Member States of the Eurozone. The EU established it in 1998.

On January 1, 1999, the euro became legal tender. On July 1, 2002, national currencies ceased to be legal tender. Euro bills and coins became the traded currency. Andrew Crockett, while he was general manager of the

Bank for International Settlements (BIS) in Basel, stated: "Monetary union in Europe holds the promise of profound change in international finance. The economies sharing the euro could face the world as the largest single currency area and the largest trading bloc." Fred Bergsten, a leading US international economist who heads the Washington-based Institute for International Economics, believes that the "single currency in monetary union will become a fully equal partner of the United States in all economic terms." US finance officials are beginning to worry about how the single currency will affect the dollar's role as the world's dominant currency. Bergsten predicted that because the euro belongs to the world's second largest economy, "it will thus immediately become the world's second key currency."[73]

In 2002 China's finance minister Xiang Huaicheng, commented that his government should consider buying more euros as soon as possible, so as to not be overly reliant on the US dollar in its foreign exchange reserves. China considers the euro important, and believes that it will someday be on equal footing with the US dollar. Xiang Huaicheng stated that "it is inevitable that the euro will become some countries' reserve currency." The euro has already become a key currency for trade.[74] The euro will increase the Union's clout in world markets. The euro will develop into a global reserve currency, and will alter the power relationship between the US and Europe on monetary and fiscal issues. It will challenge the dollar's role as the world's key currency eventually overtaking it. A later chapter covers this in detail.

The Treaty on Political Union

In April 1990, France and Germany launched the idea of a new Treaty on Political Union that would include foreign policy. That month, after a one-day summit meeting in Dublin, "The Community firmly, decisively, and categorically committed itself to political union," stated Charles Haughey, the Irish Prime Minister at the time. On December 15, 1990, the Council of Ministers met in Rome at an Intergovernmental Conference on Political Union (IGC).[75] One year later in December 1991, at Maastricht, the Netherlands, the conference convened.

Maastricht's most solid achievement was the firm commitment to establish economic and monetary union (EMU) involving a single currency governed by a European Central Bank by 1999, which it accomplished. Along with monetary union, the treaty established the beginnings of a common defense component which would evolve with later treaties. Article J.4 of the Treaty on European Union added: "The common foreign and security of the Union, including the eventual framing of a common defense policy, which might in time lead to a common defense." It paved the way to the creation of a distinct political identity. The Maastricht agreement marked the first step in adding a political dimension to the EU, and transforming it from an economic venture into a political reality. An objective of the Maastricht Treaty was for the EU to "assert its identity on the international scene...through the implementation of a common foreign and security policy." The Maastricht Treaty, a 189-page document, allowed the EU to forge common foreign and defense policies for the first time. Former French President Mitterrand affirmed: "For the first time in their history, the Union will act together in foreign policy."[76]

Prior to Maastricht, the EU acted in the area of foreign policy through European Political Cooperation (EPC). This was the EU's process of consultation and common action among its members in the field of foreign policy. An EPC meeting brought together the Member States' highest officials, their foreign ministers, and the EU Commission. The confidential telex system (coreu) linked the twelve foreign ministries of the Member States, the EPC secretariat, and the Commission. It provided rapid and secure communications, and reduced the need for holding special ministerial meetings. Through its single, coherent approach, EPC aimed to maximize its influence in international affairs.[77] Maastricht turned EPC into something more than a consultation club; it laid the foundation for a real government. The 1992 Maastricht Treaty changed the name of the European Communities to the European Union and gave the EU the formal title of "Union."

The Economist, commenting on the treaty, stated: "Believers in a federal Europe insist that the treaty lays down the main elements, if only in embryo, of a future European government, a single currency, common foreign and defense policy, a common citizenship and a parliament with teeth. It is just a matter of waiting they believe, for history to take its course."[78]

Alan Sked, who chaired the Anti-Federalist League, made similar observations and brought out additional points. He stated in *The European*, a European newspaper that existed during the 1990s and provided excellent coverage of the evolving European Union, that after Maastricht:

> The Commission is preparing to become the government of Europe, with Jacques Delors or his successor as executive president. He himself proposed such a scheme to the European Parliament in January 1990, and on June 4, 1992 the former Italian Foreign Minister, Emilio Columbo, introduced ... an outline Constitution for the European Union, drawn up by four professors. Chapter 4 of this simply stated: The Commission is the government of the Union....The Community is almost a state already. It has its own flag, its own anthem, its own driving license, its own diplomatic service, its own parliament, and its own supreme court. Maastricht will give it its own bank, currency, police force, data bases and army. A Committee of the Regions will be set up to help suppress nation states. ... All of Europe's leaders...know exactly what is being planned: the creation of a centralized superstate. [79]

The EU leaders agreed to meet again in 1996, to work out a second treaty on political union. They hoped that the next treaty would complete the process that Maastricht started.

The Amsterdam Treaty

In the summer of 1996, EU leaders met and concluded the intergovernmental conference that led to the signing of the Amsterdam Treaty. The treaty did not accomplish what many had hoped. US leaders could not agree on the issues that needed reorganization. This treaty was supposed to make many internal changes so that the Union could enlarge to include new members. The treaty created a representative to speak for the Union on foreign policy issues; the High Representative for Common Foreign and Security Policy which acted as a junior foreign minister. The Treaty of Amsterdam, signed on October 2, 1997, entered into force on

May 1, 1999. It amended and renumbered the EU and EC Treaties, and EU leaders looked forward to meeting again immediately after the turn of the millennium. The Amsterdam Treaty strengthened Union's powers in foreign policy and judicial cooperation.

The Nice Treaty

EU leaders met and negotiated the Treaty of Nice and signed it on February 26, 2001, as an amendment to the existing treaties. The Nice Treaty overhauled the institutions of the European Union in preparation for a union of twenty-seven Member States rather than fifteen. This treaty also provided the EU with a military structure and staff. Most of the changes agreed upon at Nice concerned power sharing within the European institutions as the Union expands. The treaty, capped the number of seats in the European Parliament and the size of the commission, two of the European Union's leading institutions. The next chapter discusses them in further detail. The Treaty of Nice prepared for enlargement and added more competencies for the EU including employment policy and a common foreign and security policy to cement the Union's political union.

The Laeken Declaration

On December 14 and 15, 2001, the European Council met in Laeken with the purpose of providing impetus to increase the momentum of integration. They adopted a declaration of their intention to achieve a simpler union, and one that would have more presence in the world. They initiated a convention run by Federalists V. Giscard d'Estaing, G. Amato, and Jean-Luc Dehaene to write the Constitution of the Union—which, unlike the US Constitution, would become the final treaty, encompassing all of the previous treaties. By October of 2002, the convention presented a draft treaty for the Union. Laeken addressed the transition to euro coins, enlargement, internal market issues, the September 11 attacks, and the Union's policies on combating terrorism, including their actions in Afghanistan and a declaration of their position in the Middle East. The Laeken Declaration asked: "What is Europe's role in this changed world? Does Europe not, now that it is finally unified, have a leading role to play in the new world order, that of a power able both to play a stabilizing role worldwide and to point the way ahead for many countries and peoples?" Laeken also issued its "Declaration on the Operational Capability of the Common European and Security and Defense Policy," and provided teeth to the military structure organized at Nice.

Former British Prime Minister Margaret Thatcher referred to the decisions made at Nice and Laeken as "one of the most ambitious political projects of our times."[80] It should be noted that this "ambitious political project" began at the moment of the EU"s inception, for the primary aim of EU leaders has always been a political one, and those who viewed the EU as nothing more than an economic bloc are uninformed.

The Lisbon Treaty

In 2003, the EU drafted its Constitution and in 2004-2005, the EU Council approved the European Constitution (Treaty) and the Member States voted on it and rejected it. The European Council met in Lisbon for a new EU reform treaty (instead of a European constitution.) In 2007, EU leaders signed the Lisbon Treaty, which entered into force on December 1, 2009. The European Constitution merged into the Lisbon Treaty. The Lisbon Treaty amended previous EU treaties and is more modest than the previous constitutional project. The Charter of Fundamental Rights, which covers freedom and speech and religion, will legally bind 25 of the 27 EU Members. Britain and Poland obtained an opt-out.

Lisbon made changes to the EU institutions. The European Central Bank gained official status of being an EU institution along with the Council of Europe and the euro became the official currency of the Union. The Lisbon Treaty also renamed leading institutions. The High Representative for Common Foreign and Security Policy created by the Amsterdam Treaty was promoted to Vice President and Foreign Minister of the Union along with other changes to help the 27 member union run smoothly, efficiently and to move it forward politically.[81]

The EU Army

In order for the EU to become the powerful world empire outlined in the Scriptures, it must have a militia. The Antichrist's army conquers and treads down parts of the world. It lays siege to Israel, and assists in killing all who do not pay homage to the Antichrist.

Since 1946, several European nations have attempted to create military alliances. In 1948, the Brussels Treaty Organization (BTO) formed, but was absorbed by NATO in late 1950. In 1952, the newly established European Defense Community (EDC) attempted too much too soon, and it collapsed. In 1948, European leaders signed the Brussels Treaty—a modification of the EDC. It resulted in the Western European Union, which came into being in Paris on October 23, 1954, and ratified by all members in London on May 6, 1955. Its members included Britain and the six members of the EU. The WEU underwent significant changes.

In 1984 the European defense and foreign affairs ministers agreed to "reactivate" the WEU and harmonize the members' views on key issues. In 1987, the WEU Council adopted a "Platform on European Security Issues" and declared its intention to develop a "more cohesive European defense identity." During the 1987 oil shipping crisis in the Gulf, the WEU dispatched military forces—a sign that its vision of a cohesive identity had, in fact, become reality, due to the speed of world events, the WEU gained renewed interest. The end of the Cold War caused German unification, the end of the Warsaw pact, and uncertainty regarding NATO's role. Prompted by the crisis in the Gulf and by German unification, which meant a larger, more powerful Germany and an uncertain NATO, the EU members decided that their union should include defense. Other potential threats include international terrorism, political instability in North Africa, and threats from the USSR, China, and the Middle East. Some suggested that the WEU merge with the EU.

At the time, Luxembourg's Foreign Minister Jacques Poos argued that the Gulf Crisis illustrated the urgent necessity of establishing a common European foreign and security policy. A spokesman for former French president Mitterrand advocated: "Whatever the problem, our answer is the same, more Europe."[82] The WEU admitted a host of new members in the mid 1990's. These included Greece and the non-EU, NATO member countries of Iceland, Norway, Turkey, Hungary, Poland, the Czech Republic, Austria, Finland, and Sweden. The European Council met in Cologne in June of 1999 and decided on a common policy on Russia which was the first use of the Common Foreign and Security Policy and adopted the declaration on Kosovo. In relation to the European Security and Defense Policy, the Council declared that the EU must have the capacity for autonomous action, backed up by credible military forces, the means to decide to use them, and a readiness to do so, in order to respond to international crises without prejudice to actions by NATO." In 2000, the European Council at Nice established the decision making bodies (Political and Security Committee and a Military Committee reinforced by a Military Staff) and a crisis reaction force of sixty thousand soldiers.

In May of 2001, leading members of the EU's newly established military organizations, high-ranking officials and military personnel from the various Member States, and members of several European military and political think-tanks met in Berlin for a colloquy where they established the EU's security concepts and risks. Over four hundred participants from over thirty countries attended and all discussed security issues that would affect Europe and the EU's development of its own military. Professor de Wijk of the Royal Military Academy in Breda summed up the colloquy's purpose when he stated:

> At the same time, the US must accept the EU as an equal partner. We may have different views, but in the final analysis we share the same historical and cultural background and seek to protect the same values and interests. Moreover, only a military capable EU can help defend common EU-US interests.
>
> Indeed, as the EU has global interests, the EU should develop capabilities with a truly global reach. I am very much against a division of labour where Europe sees to Europe and the USA sees to the rest of the world. For that reason, the security concept of the European Union must contain guidance for the development of power projection capabilities which can be deployed worldwide. In practice, a EU security concept should deal with the following questions: how to link the EU's military capabilities to its political objectives? Where and when the EU will make use of its military capabilities? What kind of operations will be conducted? How these operations will be conducted? What kind of military forces are required to conduct these operations?[83]

Although the Amsterdam Treaty gave the WEU an integral role in giving the EU an independent defense capability, playing a major role in the Petersberg tasks in November 2000, WEU Ministers met in Marseille and agreed to begin transferring the organization's capabilities and functions to the European Union, under its developing Common Foreign and Security Policy (CFSP) and European Security and Defense Policy (ESDP).

In January 2002, the WEU's Security Studies Institute and the Satellite Centre transferred to the EU and became the European Union Institute for Security Studies and the European Union Satellite Centre. The Nice Treaty removed the role given to the WEU in the Amsterdam Treaty.

The European Defense Agency is a continuation of the work of the Western European Armaments Organization (WEAO) and the Western European Armaments Group (WEAG). It represents the transference of their functions from the WEU and to the EU framework, and thus continues the decommissioning of the WEU.

The European Defense Agency (EDA) is an agency of the European Union headquartered in Brussels. Set up in July 2004, it is a Common Foreign and Security Policy (CFSP) body set which reports to the Council of the European Union.

The Lisbon Treaty scrapped the WEU and kept the mutual defense clause of the Treaty of Brussels as a basis for EU mutual defense arrangement. The Treaty of Lisbon states the following: "The common security and defense policy shall include the progressive framing of a common defense policy. This will lead to a common defense, when the European Council, acting unanimously, so decides."

In February of 2009, the European Parliament voted in favor of the creation of Synchronized Armed Forces Europe (SAFE) as a first step towards a true military force. An EU directorate will direct SAFE with training standards and operational doctrine. SAFE created an EU "Council of Defense Ministers" and a European statute for soldiers governing training standards, operational doctrine and freedom of operational action. SAFE is based on voluntary participation and will lead to the synchronization of the European forces. SAFE aims to develop an integrated European security structure. There will be civil and military capabilities in the member countries' reach.

According to the November 17, 2009, *Times Online*, Italy will push for the creation of a European Army after the adoption of the Lisbon Treaty. According to the article, Franco Frattini, the Italian Foreign Minister, said that the Lisbon Treaty established "that if some countries want to enter into reinforced co-operation between themselves they can do so." This agreement existed with the euro and the Schengen accords on frontier-free travel, and a "common European defense" will take the same approach. Mr. Frattini suggested that if there was a European army one nation can send planes, another tanks and another armored cars. He said this is the idea of a European army. [84]

The EU's army continues to evolve and will evolve into the eventual powerful military the Scripture's forecast. The Lisbon Treaty added the necessary foundation for the EU's military evolution.

The EU and the Nations of the World

The common market is having such a colossal effect on the continent of Europe that all European nations want some form of associate status with the European Union. Even Russia expressed a desire to join. The Union is forming association agreements with the remaining European nations that do not hold EU membership. These nations will enact common market legislation. Some have linked their currencies to the ECU without having any say in EU laws. As this occurs, the EU's sphere of influence broadens beyond its existing members. The EU is like a giant octopus; its long tentacles reach into the rest of Europe and beyond.

European leaders established the EFTA, or European Free Trade Association, whose members included Austria, Finland, Iceland, Norway, Sweden, and Switzerland, in 1959. In 1984, the Luxembourg Declaration created a free trade area embracing the eighteen nations of both the EU and the EFTA. In 1990, the EFTA and EU foreign ministers opened formal negotiations to create a "European Economic Space," where goods, services, capital, and people would flow freely between the countries of both groupings. The EEA represented the world's biggest free trade area, with 380 million consumers. It accounts for 46 percent of world trade. In 1994, European leaders established the European Economic Area. It allows the EFTA countries to participate in the European single market without joining the EU. Since Austria, Finland and Sweden jointed the EU in 1995, Iceland, Liechtenstein and Norway are its remaining members.

On May 7, 2009 the EU inaugurated in Prague the Eastern Partnership. It provides an institutionalized forum for discussing visa agreements, free trade deals and strategic partnership agreements with the EU's eastern neighbors. Controlled directly by the EU Commission, its geographical scope consists of Belarus, Armenia, Azerbaijan, Georgia, Moldova and Ukraine. Russia accused the EU of trying to carve out a new sphere of influence. An EU official retorted by stating: "We're responding to the demands of these countries...and the economic reality is that most of their trade is done with the EU."

The EU negotiated these various pacts to increase its stature and position in the world. According to Stanley Hoffman, Chairman of the Center of European Studies at Harvard: "Clearly the purpose of the whole effort is not merely to increase wealth by removing obstacles to production and technological progress, but also to increase Europe's power in a world in which economic and financial clout is as important as military might."[85] In addition, as EU legislation extends into these countries, they will come under the EU's sphere of influence. They will have to adopt EU laws without any voice in EU government. The Antichrist will easily institute his political policies throughout these nations.

The EEA exists as a regional grouping of nations in a common pact. With the fall of the Berlin Wall, Eastern European countries voiced their desire to join the EU. This event marked the beginning of a political identity for the European Union. Eastern Europe looked to the EU for aid and investment, as opposed to looking towards the US and they wanted associate status with the EU which they more than obtained.

The Euro-Mediterranean Free Trade Area (EMFTA) is a free trade zone still evolving based on the Barcelona Declaration, a framework plan adopted in 1995 through association agreements between Brussels and each state bordering the Mediterranean. The countries participating include Algeria, Egypt, Israel, Jordan, Lebanon, Morocco, Syria, Turkey, Tunisia and the Palestinian Authority. The agreement involves trade, investment, and deep political reform which Brussels calls "approximation" of other countries' legal and political institutions with its own. The aim is a "genuine free trade area as soon as possible."[86]

The fall of Communism ushered in a New World Order, and thereby paved the way for the revival of the Roman Empire and the fulfillment of the prophecies for the "latter days." An EU report on Eastern Europe in 1991 affirmed: "The map is being redrawn with the Community firmly at the heart of the new Europe. This Europe is to emerge as a new force in the balance of world power, a fact already recognized by the US of America, Japan, and the Soviet Union.

The Revived Roman Empire

The EU bears many similarities to the Old Roman Empire. European Union leaders such as Former Belgian Prime Minister and candidate for Presidency of the EU Commission, Guy Verhofstadt classify the Union as an Empire. [87]

In September 2007, a reporter asked Commission President Jose Manuel Barroso what type of political entity the Union will be after the Lisbon Treaty is enforced. Barroso responded that the European Union will not be a superstate, that it is a unique organization of free countries that are united, that started to work together in cooperation. He said that the national level is not enough for today's problems such as climate change. "We are not forming a superstate, there is not such a risk, on the contrary what we are seeing is the formation of something different. The rationale for the reform is keeping the great vision of the founding fathers." He then called the EU "an unidentified political object, a very successful experiment. In the history of institutions' we never had such a thing. Sometimes I like to compare the European Union to the creation of empires, because we have the dimension of empires, but there is a great difference from the empires that were created through force, we are the first non imperial empire, we have 27 countries that decided to work together and pool their sovereignty." [88]

Geographically, the majority of the EU lies within the Roman Empire's old borders. The Roman Empire had its own currency and army. It used two languages for everyday communication: Latin and Greek. In the same way, the European Union recognizes French and English. The Roman Empire built roads throughout the whole of its empire. The Channel Tunnel, which links Britain to the rest of the continent, is "the first truly integrated pan-European transport system since the Roman roads."[89]

The EU's has its own national anthem, which coincidentally is Beethoven's "Ode to Joy," and the melody for the Christian hymn "Faithful, Faithful We Adore Thee." The EU has a motto," united in diversity," and even its own holidays. EU citizens celebrate May 9 as Shuman Day the date that marked the birth of the EU in the same way Americans celebrate the 4th of July.

The EU's flag mentioned in an earlier chapter, a circle of twelve stars on a blue background, depicts Judeo-Christian symbolism. The stars symbolize the twelve tribes of Israel and the twelve apostles, along with the twelve months in a year, and the Greek myth that speaks of the twelve labors Hercules performed to gain immortality.[90]

The EU Capital

Some Bible scholars believe that Rome will become the headquarters of the final world empire. Although Rome is the city where the EU was established, and was the location of the conference on political union, it is not the capital of the new Europe. The capital is Brussels, Belgium, headquarters of the European Commission. Luxembourg is the financial and legal capital of the Union. The European Parliament meets in Strasbourg, France.

Around the time of Christ, Belgium lay just within the Roman Empire's northern border. It divided the conquered territory from the unconquered Germanic and Russian lands. In modern times, Brussels is centrally located between the EU, and eastern bloc nations. During the first advent of Christ, the world's population lived primarily around the Middle East and Mediterranean regions, and Rome was central to the Empire. The final world empire will have a sphere of influence over many more nations.

The Antichrist's headquarters change after the middle of the Tribulation. Daniel 11:45 attests: *"and he shall plant the tabernacles of his palace between the seas in the glorious holy mountain; yet he shall come to his end, and none shall help him."* Near the time of the end, the Antichrist will move his headquarters to Jerusalem, which, besides being the Holy City, is more central to the world at large. The Antichrist will, at this time, be in control of the Middle East region.

Revelation 13:2 tells us that the Dragon gives Antichrist "his power, his throne, and great authority." The European Union is evolving into a world power that will act as the launching pad for the devices of Satan. The Antichrist's reign here on earth will mimic that of Jesus Christ. While society grows more in line with Christ's warnings and natural disasters increase, the European Union evolves into the final world empire. Former US Senate Majority leader George Mitchell called "the economic integration of Western Europe...the most important event of our times." The idea of reuniting Europe has existed since the fall of the Roman Empire. The formation of the European Union will end up becoming the single most important attempt in world history.

The Scriptures specifically state that the Antichrist will raise the Community to its pinnacle of power. The Union will not be as powerful at the time of his appointment. From the signing of the treaty, the Antichrist will have three years to bring the Union to its height of power. This does not include his efforts before the start of the Tribulation. The lust for power that presently exists among Unionists provides the Antichrist with an opportune climate to pursue his demoniac ambitions.

CHAPTER 6

THE SEAT OF THE ANTICHRIST

We do not want another committee. We have too many already. What we want is a man of sufficient stature to head the allegiance of all people and to lift us out of the economic morass in which we are sinking. Send us such a man and be he god or the Devil we will receive him.
      Former Belgian Prime Minister, 1ˢᵗ President of the EU Parliament: **Paul-Henri Spaak**

Daniel's visions of the final world empire, describe a distinct political government, and provide a view to its institutional and structural make-up. Under the Antichrist's authority, it reaches its zenith of power. Daniel describes it as *"dreadful and terrible and exceedingly strong."* The Beast devours and breaks in pieces its enemies to the point of crushing their remains (Dan. 7:7). John likewise sees it in its final form *"rising up out of the sea"*—a figurative illustration of its rise to power (Rev. 13:1). This political power possesses the combined strength of all the empires before it. Unlike them, it devours and treads down the entire earth (Dan. 7:23, Rev. 13:2).

The Ten Horn Federation

The Beast has ten horns, and among them comes up a little horn who is the Antichrist (Dan. 7:7-8). Daniel 7:24 states that *"the ten horns are ten kings who shall arise from this kingdom: and another shall rise after them."* Revelation 13:1 depicts the horns as wearing crowns. Both, the book of Daniel and the Revelation identify the horns as kings (Rev. 17:12). The prophets add that these kingdoms do not in exist at the time of the writings. European nations did not come into being until over a millennium later. Only in this last couple of centuries have these nations reigned as separate, sovereign kingdoms. The horns wearing crowns signify established kingdoms or nations. The little horn appears after the kings, and *"comes up"* among them. His small horn represents a relatively new political seat on the world stage when he takes power. Horns grow with age, but this one grows extremely large, quickly. Daniel tells us, "*And out of one of them came a little horn, which grew exceedingly great, toward the south, toward the east, and toward the glorious land*" (Dan. 8:9-10).

Despite the EU's newness in the international arena, it has the potential to create a dictatorship that could obtain world rule. Satan himself provides the Antichrist with a political position by which he rises to greatness and conquers the world. He wears no crown because he is not the king of any one nation, yet he leads the federation.

The Antichrist exists in a symbiotic relationship with the kings. Revelation 17:13 tells us: "*These are of one mind and they will give their power and authority to the beast.*" The Antichrist partners with the Kings. Some label the Union a confederation. The Union considers itself a federation. In a confederation, nations or states share governmental tasks. In a federation, the members relinquish some of their sovereignty to a higher authority, which makes the laws and regulations for the signing states. The Scriptures describe the federation's members as actual nations, not provinces or states. The Bible's federation acts as a dictatorship.

The Treaty of Rome

Seven main institutions (based on the Treaty of Rome) make up the European Union: the Commission, the European Parliament, the Council of Ministers, the Court of Justice, and the Court of Auditors. Nine additional treaties amended the Treaty of Rome, which established the European Union on March 1, 1957. The recent Lisbon Treaty added two more institutions: the European Central Bank, and the Council of Europe which the EU previously regarded as governing bodies but not official institutions. The Treaties provide the format for the EU's institutional structure and the agreements by which the signing nations are to abide. The member nations surrender parts of their national sovereignty to the higher authority.

The Council of The European Union

The Antichrist will be in a federation with ten kings. These kings are the Council of The European Union formerly named the Council of Ministers. They are the governmental heads of each of the Member States. Each nation addresses them by a different title, but the Bible refers to them as kings. "Prime ministers" and "presidents" have essentially the same meaning. The Council represents the highest decision-making authority in the EU, and holds the preeminent position in the institutional power balance. Although the Council does not initiate EU laws, it must approve all Community legislation. Its secretariat is located in Brussels. The Council also concludes, on behalf of the EU, all international agreements; makes the decisions necessary for framing and implementing the Common Foreign and Security Policy; and adopts measures in the field of police and judicial cooperation.

The Bible always refers to the word "council" in a negative context. In Mark 13:9, Christ warns the Jews during the Tribulation to *"watch out for yourselves: for they will deliver you up to councils; and you will be beaten in the synagogues. And you will be brought before rulers and kings for My sake, for a testimony to them."* The EU's Council of Ministers may be one of the councils Christ mentioned in Scripture. The scriptures specifically mention councils and two councils exist within the EU's institutional structure.

It is common knowledge among journalists covering the EU that the Council of Ministers meets in secret. The Belmont European Policy Center stated, in a report on the Maastricht Treaty, that the "EC Council of Ministers remains the most secretive of Community institutions."[91] On this subject, *The Economist* commented that the ministers are "The EC's real legislature and the only one in the world that does not let in the public."[92]

In 2009 when EU leaders met to nominate the first president of the Council and foreign affairs minister, the Former Lavian president Vaira Vike-Freiberga, said that EU leaders conducted the nomination process with Soviet-style secrecy and contempt for the public. He attacked the EU for operating in "darkness and behind closed doors" and said it should "stop working like the former Soviet Union."[93] The Council of Ministers already acts in an undemocratic fashion. The previous chapter discussed the ambition that reigns among these leaders for leading superpower status which creates the climate for a powerful leader.

Revelation 17:12 describes the ten horns as ten kings who *"receive authority for one hour as kings with the beast."* During the Tribulation, the

Council promotes the Antichrist's agenda and essentially acts in a marriage type of relationship with him. They act together as if joined with the Antichrist leading. As Jesus led his disciples, the Antichrist will lead the Prime Ministers or Presidents.

The EU Commission: The Seat of the Antichrist

When the European member nations signed the Treaty of Rome, they agreed to hand over some of their powers to a higher authority called the Commission. As the EU's executive arm, it acts as an overseer of the EU Treaties, and upholds them. Members of the Commission represent the interests of the Union as a whole. The size of its staff is comparable to the US Department of Commerce.

The Commission, a non-elected body, is comprised of representatives from each of the member nations. The Commission has a president who sits among the Council of the European Union (or "kings"). He is responsible for the major decisions and laws that move the EU forward into the international arena as a single political and economic entity. Former Belgian Prime Minister Guy Verhofstadt suggested changing its name to the "European Government", calling the present name of Commission: "ridiculous" because of its governmental powers. Coincidentally, the Commission's headquarters are located in Brussels with the President's office and the Commission's meeting room based on the 13th floor of the Berlaymont building.[94]

The Commission President's position fits the description of the "*little horn*" in Daniel for he stands among the ten horns or prime ministers and unlike the kings which head nations, he has no nation beneath him, he heads the federation. The horn signifies a relatively new position on the world stage which fits the EU Commission. The Scriptures provide specific details concerning the Antichrist's authorities. The political seat he holds must allow him the powers cited in the prophetic writings.

THE EU COMMISSON PRESIDENCY PROVIDES THE ANTICHRIST WITH THE POWERS OUTLINED IN SCRIPTURE— HIS POSITION MUST ALLOW HIM A MINIMUM OF A SEVEN-YEAR TERM

Daniel 9:27 states: *"Then he shall confirm a covenant with many for one week,"* i.e., seven years. The seven-year Tribulation begins with the signing of a peace treaty with Israel. The Antichrist is in power before the Tribulation begins. No leader signs a treaty on the day of his election. The Council of Ministers appoints the Commission President to a five-year renewable term. They make these appointments in years ending in four and nine.

HE WILL BECOME STRONG WITH A SMALL NUMBER OF PEOPLE

Daniel 11:21, 23, states: *"And in his place shall arise a vile person, to whom they will not give the honor of royalty; but he shall come in peaceably and seize the kingdom by intrigue. And after the league is made with him he shall act deceitfully; for he shall come up and become strong with a small number of people."* Some say these passages refer to Antiochus IV Epiphanes, a ruler of ancient Greece, reputed as a famous persecutor of the Jews. While he represents a prototype of the final world ruler; this prediction describes how the Antichrist comes into power. [95]

The people do not elect the Commission President. The Council of Ministers consults with the European Parliament, and nominates the person they intend to appoint to the Commission presidency. This nomination, subject to a vote and the approval of the European Parliament, concludes by the Council of Ministers' appointment. The "small number of people" refers to this close-knit group of EU bureaucrats who place him in power. It may also signify his being a prime minister from one of the smaller EU countries. To date, European Commission Presidents have held prior EU posts such as officials from one of the Member States and even former prime ministers.

During the 2009 nomination of the first EU Council President, journalists noted that EU leaders strategized picking someone from a small country with little international power instead of a charismatic heavyweight. As the EU chose former Belgian Prime Minister Herman van Rompuy as the new Council President and Britain's Catherine Ashton for the post of EU High Representative a headline reported, "Unknown duo chosen as new faces of Europe." The idea is that a low key leader will be more effective in achieving consensus among so many leaders of the various nations than a well known charismatic one. According to the *Associated Press*: "for EU leaders to pick a boss they can all live with, they must strike the right balance between big countries and small, east and west, socialists and conservatives, perhaps male and female. They must manoeuvre between proponents of a strong Europe and those who fear it—eurocentric's and euroskeptics, in the local parlance."[96] The EU will select the leader who the Bible deems as the Antichrist in the same manner.

HE WILL BE IN A FEDERATION WITH TEN KINGS

Revelation 17:12-13 tells us: *"And the ten horns which you saw are ten kings who have received no kingdom as yet; but they receive authority for one hour as kings with the beast, these are of one mind, and they will give their power and authority to the beast."* This verse describes the relationship of the ten kings to the Antichrist. They both strive for the same goals. One entity does not exist without the other. The Council of The European (formerly Council of Ministers) give their strength and power to the Commission. Without the member nations that hand over their authority to the Commission, there would be no European Union. Several articles in the EU Treaty reflect their having one mind. Article 162 states: "The Council and the Commission shall consult each other and settle by common accord their methods of cooperation."

The Scriptures are unprecedented in their accuracy and detail. Although written 1,900 years ago, one Bible verse epitomizes the contents of two treaties in just 14 words. *"These shall have one mind and shall give their power and strength unto the Beast."* Over and over, one reads of the Commission's and Council Ministers' simultaneous role. Peter Ludlow, the founding director of the Centre For European Policy Studies think-tank in Brussels, referred to the Commission-Council relationship as a "partnership."[97] Of the EU's institutions, the Commission and the Council (of Ministers) represent the leading authorities. The Court enforces EU laws, and the Parliament acts as a forum with some legislative powers.

HE WILL BE BOTH PRESIDENT AND FOREIGN MINISTER SIGNING TREATIES WITH OTHER NATIONS

The Commission negotiates treaties, making agreements with other nations and with world organizations. It makes recommendations to the Council of the European Union i.e. the Council of Ministers, which authorizes the opening of negotiations and conducts them. Special committees formed by the Council assist the Commission. The Commission proposes agreements to the Council, which votes by a qualified majority, consults with the European Parliament, and then concludes the agreements. The Commission President thus negotiates and signs treaties with other nations. The Commission can impose sanctions on third world countries. It maintains EU relations with the UN, WTO and all other world institutions. The Council and the Commission take responsibility for ensuring the consistency of all EU policies.

THE ANTICHRIST WILL HAVE A DIVERSE ROLE FROM THAT OF THE TEN KINGS

Daniel 7:24 states: *"The ten horns are ten kings who shall arise; from this kingdom and another shall rise after them; he shall be different from the first ones."* As the EU's executive arm, the Commission's major responsibility is to oversee EU treaties. It initiates EU laws and policy. Thus, the Higher Authority acts as the lawmaker while the Council of the European Union approves the laws.

HIS POSITION WILL GIVE HIM THE POWER TO EXPEL THREE OF THE KINGS

Daniel 7:24 continues, *"...and shall subdue three kings."* Regarded as the "Guardian of the Treaties," the Commission can take action against member governments that it believes have violated their treaty obligations. It proposes to the Court of Justice the fines imposed on Member States proven in default under the treaty. Presently, the Union cannot expel a Member, but allowing this action has come under discussion. The Lisbon Treaty amended articles to allow a nation to withdraw from the Union.[98]

HE WILL HAVE AUTHORITY TO DETERMINE WHO WILL BUY AND SELL WITH HIS GOVERNMENT

Revelation 13:17 tells us: *"...and that no one may buy or sell, except one who has the mark, or the name of the beast, or the number of his name."* This passage deals with individuals living under the Antichrist's dictatorship, and extends to persons worldwide. The Commission initiates the Union's internal market policy and external trade, including that with the US. It determines the guidelines for trade with other countries, as well as for its members within the Union. Thus, the Commission determines with whom it will buy and sell, and how. The Commission also negotiates international trade agreements.

THE ANTICHRIST WILL CHANGE TIMES AND LAWS

Daniel 7:25 reports: *"He shall speak pompous words against the Most High, shall persecute the saints of the Most High, and shall intend to change times and laws."* The Commission introduces EU legislation, carries out decisions, and oversees the enforcement of European laws. With this authority, the Antichrist can easily implement his laws and change existing ones.

HE WILL HAVE DIRECT ACCESS TO RECENT TECHNOLOGICAL ACHIEVEMENTS, AND CONTROL OVER THE DEVELOPMENT OF NEW TECHNOLOGIES

Revelation 13:16-17 states: *"And he causes all, both small and great, rich and poor, free and slave, to receive a mark on their foreheads; And that no one may buy or sell, except one who has the mark, or the name of the beast, or the number of his name."* The Commission oversees the research and development of new technologies. It determines which programs and projects will receive funding. The development of new technologies remains an EU priority. The Antichrist will have access to those new technological systems, and the power to authorize their implementation.

HIS GOVERNMENT MUST GIVE RISE TO A DICTATORSHIP

Revelation 13:15 tells us that *"he was granted power to give breath to the image of the beast, that the image of the beast should both speak, and cause that as many as would not worship the image of the beast to be killed."* The Antichrist kills those who do not worship him—a common trait of most dictatorships. Dictators reign from political positions that provide them with complete authority. The Commission's authorities are not balanced by either the Court of Justice or the Parliament. The European people do not elect its members, although it is the EU's executive arm, making it a non-democratic institution.

Former British Prime Minister Margaret Thatcher, in a major speech in Bruges, Belgium, assailed the idea of a supernational European State. In an address to the European Parliament in Strasbourg, France, Jacques Delors had predicted that by the mid-1990s, the EU would develop "an embryo European government." Thatcher referred to these possible developments as "a nightmare" that would create "bureaucratic centralism" in the EU. She also warned: "We fought two world wars to make the world a safer place for democracy. Here we are preaching more democracy to the old Communist Soviet Union and ourselves practicing less democracy and more bureaucracy."

During Thatcher's Prime Ministership, she stood as a strong opponent of a federal Europe and represented the lone ranger among the other members of the European Council. In her later years she gave speeches against a European superstate. Mrs. Thatcher stated that a United States of Europe will endanger world peace. Thatcher uttered her strongest statement when she called the European Federalist project, "a nightmare." She asked: "Were it to come about does anyone suppose that such a power would not soon become a rival to America? Thatcher then affirmed: "If this new Europe were not to follow the path to separate great power status, it would be the first such power in history to renounce its independent role."[99] Margaret Thatcher saw from the beginning that the Commission held too much power in the institutional power balance. She understood that this amount of centralized power can lead to a dictatorship. While she never directly stated these words she used other lighter terms which place the Union's structure in a similar sphere.

Maurie Duverger commented in *L'Express* of Paris, reprinted in *World Press Review*, that:

> After 1992, nearly 80 percent of economic regulations will be enacted by the EU in Brussels, not in the capitals of the

Member States. That means that decisions will be taken away from parliaments elected by universal suffrage and handed over to a political system that will largely escape the grasp of such parliaments. Europe invented democracy. But the more Europe unites, the more democracy is whittled away. As national powers are gradually reduced by the growth of a supra-national power, citizens will be chagrined. [100]

Former EU European Parliamentarian David Martin, commenting on the EU's "democratic deficit" and need for institutional reform, stated: "If the EC was a state and applied to join the Community, it would be turned down on the grounds that it was not a democracy."[101] Tony Benn, one of the most prominent figures in postwar British politics, and a longtime Labour Party member, affirmed: "The European Community is entirely undemocratic. It is run largely by commissioners who are not elected and cannot be removed. The Council of Ministers is the only legislative body in what's called the 'free world' that meets in secret."[102]

Secretiveness is a common characteristic of dictatorships. Certain EU legislation is fashioned in a secretive, undemocratic fashion. The Belmont European Policy Center stated that: "Unfortunately, the EU Treaty contains certain provisions, which govern Co-decision Procedure...having the effect of making the legislative processes unnecessarily secretive and prima facie inconsistent with the principles of democratic government."[103] This report emphasized the secretiveness of Council of Ministers meetings, which echoes throughout several foreign affairs journals and articles.

The Antichrist's federation will have secret agendas. Amazingly, when the Antichrist takes his position as President of the European Union Commission, he will have the platform for his dictatorship. Of all the Institutions, the Commission holds the greatest powers, and the other EU governmental bodies do not balance its authorities. The former journal *European Affairs* stated: "At present the European institutions are upside down. The only institution with democratic legitimacy on a European scale, the European Parliament, has consultative powers only. The most dynamic body, the one that has the power to get things moving, is arbitrarily appointed and accountable to only one: the Commission of the

European Communities."[104]

The American Free Press upon Estonia's admission into the EU quoted former Estonian Prime Minister Edgar Savisaar, and others as comparing the EU with the Soviet Union. "The forced propaganda of the European Union is reminiscent of the Soviet Union's methods and brainwashing," Rolf Parve, wrote in Kesknadal, the weekly paper of the Center Party.[105] "Moscow and Brussels differ in one point," Professor Igor Grazin, one of the leading anti-EU voices in Estonia says: "The Soviet Union theoretically allowed nations to leave the union. Brussels is creating organs, however, which would kill that idea in the bud." Savissar compared the "big bureaucratic system" of the EU with that of the Soviet Union. Currently, the EU is regarded by several politicians as a superstate, and they state this derogatorily.

According to *Wikipedia*: "a superstate is an agglomeration of nations and or/states, often linguistically and ethnically diverse under a single political-administrative structure. This is distinct from the concept of superpower, although these are frequently seen together. It is also distinct from the concept of empire where one nation dominates other nations through military, political, and economic power, as in the Roman Empire, although and empire may also be a superstate, as in ancient Persia, India and China.[106]

HIS KINGDOM WILL BE DIVIDED AND WILL INVOLVE MANY MEN

Nebuchadnezzar's vision in Daniel 2:28-45 illustrates the Beast's complexity. The Bible states that the fourth kingdom is *"strong as iron,"* and *"breaks in pieces and shatters all things,"* Daniel adds that there is weakness amidst its strength. Daniel 2: 41-43 records:

> *Whereas you saw the feet and toes, partly of potter's clay and partly of iron, the kingdom shall be divided; yet the strength of the iron shall be in it, just as you saw the iron mixed with ceramic clay.*

> *And as the toes of the feet were partly of iron and partly of clay, so the kingdom shall be partly strong and partly fragile.*
> *As you saw iron mixed with ceramic clay, they will mingle with the seed of men; but they will not adhere to one another, just as iron does not mix with clay.*

The iron and clay which makes up the image's toes do not mix. The iron legs have power to break in pieces and crush all that opposes the Beast. The Bible states that clay represents the seed of men. The potter's clay signifies a divided kingdom and the complexity within this kingdom—iron is firm, clay is brittle. The kingdom divides at the legs into feet and toes mingled with clay. John F. Walvoord, in his book *Daniel: The Key to Prophetic Revelation*, discusses this passage and relates the various interpretations from well known Bible expositors. A. C. Gaebelein states that "monarchies and clay represent democratic rule." Lutheran Hebrew Old Testament scholar Johann Karl Friedrich Keil argues that "it is all the means employed by rulers to combine the different nationalities, a sort of intermarriage." Walvoord concludes that this diversity, "whether this refers to race, political idealism or sectional interests,… will prevent the final form of the kingdom from having any real unity."[107]

The vision depicts an analogy of the European Union's institutional structure as it exists today. One iron leg represents the EU Commission, while the toes symbolize the Council of Ministers. The toes mingled with clay represent the sovereign nations who still hold elections and rule their countries while handing over specific powers to the EU Commission. Clay, or the democratic electoral process, conflicts with totalitarian rule. The Scriptures stand unprecedented in their accuracy. One must pay tribute to those Bible scholars who successfully interpreted prophetic passages while there no telltale signs in world affairs manifested. Some Bible Eschatologists teach that the Beast has ten toes which represent the ten nations because the Scripture refers to the feet of the image and feet have five toes a piece thus ten toes. The Scripture does not specify the number of toes which can be many.

Dwight Pentecost sited Kelly's observation who that: "There will be, before the age closes, the most remarkable union of two apparently contradictory conditions—a universal head of empire, a separate independent kingdom besides, each of which will have its own king; but that one man will be emperor over all these kings... God has said they shall be divided....In virtue of the iron there will be a universal monarchy, while in virtue of the clay there will be separate kingdoms."[108]

Europa the EU's website elaborates by stating about the EU's institutions:

> The European Union (EU) is not a federation like the United States. Nor is it simply an organization for co-operation between governments, Like the United Nations. It is, in fact, unique. The countries that make up the EU (its 'Member States') remain independent sovereign nations but they pool their sovereignty in order to gain a strength and world influence none of them could have on their own. Pooling sovereignty means, in practice, that the Member States delegate some of their decision-making powers to shared institutions they have created, so that decisions on specific matters of joint interest can be made democratically at the European level.

While the nation's pool their sovereignty, conflict and disunity arises as each nation responds protecting its own culture, people and industries. The EU is a kingdom divided. While linked by the Treaty of Rome, each government still holds autonomy. The Member States speak their own languages and retain identity with their individual histories and cultures. EU citizens elect the leaders of the EU Parliament and Council of Ministers, and clay (i.e., the seed of men) represents this democratic practice. The EU's motto is "united in diversity," which literally can be the plaque underneath the image of toes mingled with clay.

Due to the Union's many languages, which numbers 23 official languages, EU officials must make sure that all 27 Member States understand the legislation. They provide interpretation at many hundreds of meetings held every week. Twenty-five percent of university graduates employed by the Commission directly engage in language work. In the smaller Community institutions, this figure can be as high as 70 percent of graduates. Along with each new member accepted into the European Union, this number increases.[109] The EU Parliament is the biggest employer of interpreters in the world employing 350 full time and 400 freelancers when there is higher demand.[110]

Further magnifying the Union's diversity are each nation's differing governments and politics. Although the Union refers to the nations as Member States, they are separate sovereign countries. Some of the nations hold grievances with other nations, for historical or economic reasons. This world power will never have any real unity while it is both united and divided. In examining EU citizens' views and gripes toward other Member States, this division further intensifies. Nevertheless, Scripture tells us that this world power will be dreadful and terrible and exceedingly strong (Dan. 7:7).

These facts have caused some to believe that the EU will never have any real unity or strength. What the European Union is seeking to do has never been done in the world's history. Separate sovereign nations are joining to become a single economic and political unit. The Bible spoke about this in ancient history. In our day we will see it happen.

We know from Scripture that the European Union federalists will attain economic and political union. The ideal of retaining each member state's government, language, and culture within this federation will be the weakness amid its strength.

The Vice President of the Commission

The Lisbon Treaty created the position called High Representative of the Union for Foreign Affairs and Security Policy which in actuality will serve as the European Union's Foreign Minister. The Former position of High Representative merged with the European Commissioner for External Relations to produce the new Foreign Minister position. The rejected Constitution called the position, *Union Minister for Foreign Affairs*. The Minister would also be a Vice-President in the Commission. [111]

The European Parliament

The Parliament directly represents the people of Europe and links to the toes on the image in the book of Daniel. As with all other EU institutions, the EU parliament has evolved since its inception. In 1974, the Heads of Government agreed to permit direct elections. In 1979, the EU held the first direct elections. Although the EU Parliament is the second largest democratic electorate in the world, second to India, but unlike most national parliaments, the EU parliament does not have legislative initiative. The Parliament's 736 members, elected every five years by voters in all Member States, have significant power over budgetary matters. They scrutinize, draft EU legislation, question the Commission and Council of Ministers on their conduct of EU affairs, and debate topical issues.

Acting as a check upon the Commission, Article 140 of the Treaty of Rome requires Commissioners to appear before Parliament to respond to questions. The Commission submits an annual report of its activities to the Parliament. The Commission is required to resign as a body if the Parliament adopts a motion of censure against it. Of the four attempted motions of censure, none succeeded.

A majority of Parliament must approve international treaties—save certain trade agreements. In many other areas the Parliament may amend laws, unless the European Commission and all members of the Council object. The Parliament may ask the Commission to propose laws, and may challenge acts of the Commission or Council in the Court of Justice. The Council must consult the Parliament on who heads the Commission, and must approve the choice of a new team of Commissioners. The EU Parliament compares to the US Congress with its President, which the people elect for two and a half year terms acting as its speaker. [112]

Some end time watchers reported on the European Parliament Presidency as the possible launching pad for the Antichrist, assuming this President led the Union. The Union's institutional structure comprises of five presidents: the Council's, Parliaments, Court of Justice's, Court of Auditors and the Commission. Of the five, the Commission President heads the European Union.

The Court of Justice

The Court of Justice, located in Luxembourg, is comprised of 27 judges, one from each member state plus one other, assisted by 8 advocates-general. The Council of the European Union appoints the judges and advocates-general for six-year renewable terms. The judges elect the President of the Court of Justice for a renewable term of three years. The President presides over hearings and deliberations, directing both judicial business and administration. The EU's Court parallels the US Supreme Court. It enforces EU treaties, determines the interpretation and implementation of Union legislation, and resolves conflicts between Union and national laws. Basically it makes sure that the Member States effectively apply the laws. Union law (based on the Treaties of Rome) and national law of the individual member countries now intertwine. Its decisions attracts more and more of the national courts' attention. Court decisions strengthen EU institutions and promote EU policies. Verdicts reached by simple majority are binding on all parties, and are not subject to appeal.[113]

The Court of Auditors

The Maastricht Treaty established the Court of Auditors as the fifth institution of the EU. The Court of Auditors examines the accounts of all of the Union's revenues and expenditures. One member from each EU member state and a President, make up the Court. The Court has no judicial functions. It is rather a professional external investigatory audit agency. The Court checks if officials implement the budget of the European Union correctly, and ensures that EU funds are spent legally and with sound management. A staff of approximately 800 auditors, translators and administrators supports the Court.[114]

The European Council

The European Councils held their first meeting in 1961 and formalized them after 1974. These brought together the Commission President and the leaders of the EU countries in deciding political guidelines for the Union. The Council has no formal executive or legislative powers, it deals with major issues and meets about four times a year in Brussels. The Lisbon Treaty made the European Council a full fledged European institution. It is headed by a President. Elected by the Council for two and a half years; the President prepares the Council's work, ensures its continuity and works to secure consensus among member countries. The position is a non-executive, administrative role. The highest political body of the EU, it is chaired by a member of the Council of the European Union formerly known as the Council of Ministers President. He can call meetings beyond the four that are formally required to take place. Lisbon gave the Council greater say over a variety of EU related matters. While the Commission and Council of the European Union are two separate institutions that work together, the European Council brings these two groups together as one institution. [115]

The European Central Bank

Established in 1998 and modeled on the German Bundesbank, the bank which was once independent from any European or national institution is now a governmental institution of the European Union. The Governing Council, the supreme decision making body of the ECB takes decisions on monetary policy, interest rates and reserves of the ESCB along with other matters. The Union only allows the President of the European Council, the President of the EU Commission and members to attend its meetings. Governing Council members represent the interests of the Eurozone as a whole.

Also Within The Institutional Structure

The Economic and Social Committee represents the views and interests of EU nationals.
The Committee of the Regions ensures the respect of regional and local identities and prerogatives.

In addition the EU has other bodies that play specialized roles, the European Investment bank, European Investment Fund, European Ombudsman, European Data Protection Supervisor, Office for Official Publications of the European Communities, European Personnel Selection Office and the European Administrative School.[116]

The False Prophet

Revelation 13:11 tells us that John saw another beast, but this beast comes out of the earth vs. the Antichrist's empire, which rises from the seas. He has two horns like a lamb but speaks as a dragon. The Bible describes in Revelation 12-15:

> *And he exercises all the authority of the first beast in his presence, and causes the earth and those who dwell in it to worship the first beast, whose deadly wound was healed.*
>
> *He performs great signs, so that he even makes fire come down from heaven on the earth in the sight of men.*
>
> *And he deceives those who dwell on the earth by those signs which he was granted to do in the sight of the beast, telling those who dwell on the earth to make an image to the beast who was wounded by the sword and lived.*
>
> *He was granted power to give breath to the image of the beast that the image of the beast should both speak and cause as many as would not worship the image of the beast to be killed.*

While the Beast rises out of the sea as a giant monster the False Prophet in contrast comes out of the earth like a lamb and possesses two horns. The "False Prophet" might be a spiritual leader, his designation as prophet and his comparison to a lamb signifies this. Since the Antichrist abolishes religion, he may act as a spiritual occultist. Hitler consulted occultists during his time in power. His possessing two horns might mean that he holds a leadership position in addition to his position in the Antichrist's federation.

The False Prophet can rise from the EU Commission holding the title of Vice President of the Union. This Prophet has similar powers of the most powerful Biblical prophets: Elijah and Elisha. Both raised someone from the dead and performed great miracles. The False Prophet breathes life into the Beast's image, which is either a statue or an actual human clone of the Antichrist. God made man in his image and in the same wording the Bible states that this replica is the image of the Beast. Antichrist might use the science of cloning to try to deceive the people that he can create life. God allows the False Prophet the power to breath life into the image so that it speaks and the world worships his likeness. [117] His clone fits the description of the "abomination of desolation" that stands in the holy place (Matt: 24:26, Mark: 13:14).

All who do not worship the image of the Beast, Antichrist's henchmen will kill. Nebuchadnezzar, King of Babylon foreshadows the Antichrist and is one of the titles given to him. He leads the first world empire seen in Daniel's dream image and represents the head of gold. As the Antichrist whose little horns grows to the host of heaven, (Dan. 8:10) the Scriptures depict Nebuchadnezzar as a tree whose height also reaches the heavens (Dan. 4:11, 20). For seven years God gives Nebuchadnezzar a mental illness that makes him act like an animal (Dan. 4:15-16). Similarly, the Antichrist reigns as a Beast for seven years.

Like the Antichrist, he sets up a golden image which stood 60 cubits tall and six cubits wide, i.e. 66. Babylonian officials played music and commanded those who heard the music to fall down and worship the golden image. Those who refused to worship the image soldiers cast into a fiery furnace. As with the Antichrist the King of Babylon required all nations and peoples to worship the image (Dan. 3:7.) Daniel and two of his friends refused to worship the idol. Soldiers cast them into the furnace and they survived and one like a son of God walked amongst them in the furnace, which soldiers heated seven times hotter than usual. As Daniel, the tribulation saints will experience the captivity under Babylon as the Jews did the year Jeremiah predicted the invasion. At this time the EU functions as the dictatorship described in Scripture.

In reviewing the EU's undemocratic institutional structure which places too much power in the European Commission, and the Commission Presidency which will allow the Antichrist all of the powers outlined in Scripture, one can only stand in awe at the accuracy of the Bible.

DIAGRAM of EU INSTITUTIONS

COMMISSION PRESIDENT
▲
EU COMMISSION
▲
COUNCIL OF MINISTERS
I I I I I I I I I I
1 2 3 4 5 6 7 8 9 10
▲
EU PARLIAMENT

MEMBER NATIONS 27+

I	I	I
I	I	I
Court of Auditors	European Central Bank	Court of Justice

The Economic and Social Committee
The Committee of the Regions
The European Investment Bank
European Investment Fund
European Ombudsman
European Data Protection Supervisor
Office of Official Publications of the European Communities
European Personnel Selection Office
European Administrative School

EUROPEAN UNION TREATIES
I
ASSOCIATE MEMBERS
I
Nations at varying places of membership status based on the body of laws that they adopt.
Nations within the EU's free trade area adopting reciprocal trade laws.

BIBLICAL DIAGRAM OF THE BEAST

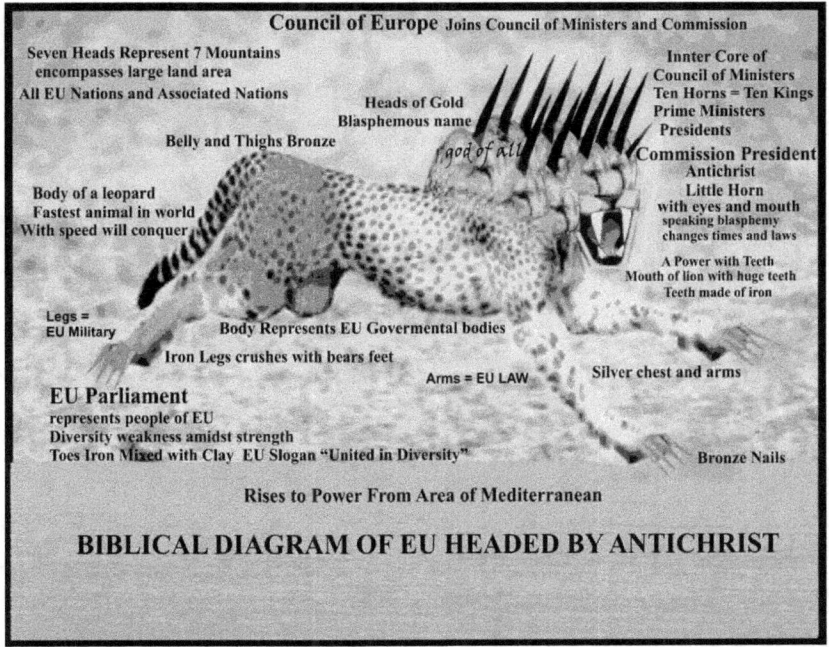

CHAPTER 7

TEN HORNS TEN NATIONS

27 European Nations?

The Bible specifically states that ten nations head the federation and align with the Antichrist. Presently 27 nations are members of the European Union. The 27 nations are Austria, Belgium, Bulgaria, Cyprus, Czech Republic, Denmark, Estonia, Finland, France, Germany, Greece, Hungary, Ireland, Italy, Latvia, Lithuania, Luxembourg, Malta, Netherlands, Poland, Portugal, Romania, Slovakia, , Spain, Sweden and the United Kingdom.

There is talk of the Union's expanding to include even more members. Some experts estimate that up to thirty-five countries could make up the Union within a generation. Some even suggest that the Soviet Union could become a member of the Union. After the revolution of 1989, the list of would-be members of the European Union grew. Even Israel joins the list.

Twenty seven members do not resemble the ten-nation federation spoken of by Daniel and John in the Revelation. Currently, discussions concerning the Union going forward with political union with an inner core of nations are underway. A few decades ago when the number of nations which opted for EU membership grew, various bureaucrats determined that the Union must deepen the process of integration before enlarging. The Union must unify politically, economically, and militarily before accepting any new members. Union delegates fiercely debated widening the EU's membership to include nearby countries. The prevailing view was that the EU should strengthen itself inwardly before it took on any new members. The Commission and the Council of the European Union formerly the Council of Ministers determined that the EU will have to achieve both political and economic union. [118]

In a larger EU, decisions become harder to reach. Solving language questions becomes extremely difficult. In a nine-language EU, any meeting of ministers requires twenty-seven interpreters. A sixteen-language EU, needs forty-two interpreters at each meeting. Some took this as evidence that a wider community required a stronger central government. With twelve members in the European Council, each representative speaks for ten minutes. This takes two hours, and rises to three hours for eighteen members, and four hours for twenty-four. Unanimous decision making becomes impossible, and a thirty-member Commission and larger European Parliament becomes too unwieldy.

The EU's founders designed the EU's institutions for six members. When membership reached twelve, these members expanded its capacity to the full. [119] According to the Federalist Journal *Crocodile*, the newsletter of "The Crocodile Club" founded in 1980 by an informal group of members of European Parliament that favored greater European integration and greater powers to the European Parliament:

> There are no clear objective criteria for determining the optimum or maximum size of the Union. No one can say how many Member States it can cope with without risking paralysis or regressing into a mere free trade area. It is therefore impossible to lay down the number of Member States admitting of no further enlargement of the Union. No one can gauge the maximum absorption capacity which the Union could not exceed without bringing about its destruction, but it is indisputable that a limit exists.
>
> The Community as presently constituted cannot encompass enlargement. Without further reform, enlargement to include 15 or more Member States would eventually spell its destruction. The choice for the Union is consequently not between deepening or widening but rather between deepening or dissolution. [120]

With enlargement, the EU sought to strengthen itself politically and suggested that a strong united core proceed ahead of the other nations. [121]

According to *European Affairs*, a publication which devoted itself to European Union issues:

> It might be possible to envision by the end of this century a Europe of concentric circles: (1) the EU at the core; ... trying to bring the two parts of Europe closer together responds to a historical urge that both sides feel. The historical basis of a whole Europe or common home after all goes back to the Empire of Charlemagne, and then the holy Roman Empire, and should at a minimum encompass the territories of those empires; both were culturally and geographically primary West European. The EU will become a community of different speeds, tiers and forms of association. [122]

As the Union prepared to enlarge its membership it went to work on internal strengthening in order to facilitate the incorporation of new members. Each country that joined the Union met strict criteria. They must be sound economically, have secure democratic institutions and adopt the body of EU law.

Former German foreign minister Joschka Fischer called for the relaunch of the process of unification through the creation of a federal core. This core will comprise of a limited number of countries, and will constitute "the centre of gravity" to which all the other states of the Union will be attracted. Another possibility is for Europe to progress at different tiers and speeds. Former French President Valéry Giscard'Estaing published what he called a *Manifesto for a Federal Europe*. In his manifesto, he calls for the formation of a core group of federalist countries within a wider European Union. Giscard calls this core the "European Power." It consists of all and only those countries which are a part of European Monetary Union (EMU).

Heads of state meeting in Nice decided to undertake an in-depth review of the future of an enlarged Union and called European citizens to take part in it. The European Policy Centre, a think-tank for EU policy, devoted its resources to this debate. In the fall of 2000, Notre Europe, a think-tank founded by former European Commission President Jacques Delors, held a debate on the structure of an enlarged Europe, which had several contributors including Joschka Fischer. Although they used different metaphors—a multi-speed Europe, a pioneer group, three spheres formed on the basis of a Eurozone, which is the politically integrated area, the avant garde; some writers have referred to this inner political core as the Union's "avant-garde" for political union —all of the speakers echoed the same message: that with the Big Bang of members about to enter the Union, institutionally the Union cannot go forward as it is currently structured without the new members' leading to its demise. [123]

Guy Verhofstadt, former Beligan Prime Minister and EU Parliamentarian authored a manifesto for Europe titled, *The United States of Europe: Manifesto for a New Europe*, in it he discusses the inner core and added his own proposals and summarized them in his article, "Only a New 'political core' can drive Europe forward again." He stated:

> Only through adopting a unified approach in all these areas will Europe really count as a world player. ...In such a scenario, Europe would comprise two concentric circles: a political core that is a "United States of Europe" based on the Eurozone, and surrounding it a confederation of countries, or a "Organization of European States".
> Naturally, this political core must never prevent or oppose any form of broader cooperation. All EU Member States wishing to join it, old or new, should be able to do so; the sole precondition should be their willingness to work unconditionally on pushing ahead with the overall political project. The notion of a "United States of Europe" is the only option for the old continent. [124]

The suggested next step after the Lisbon Treaty, which will insure that the Union continues to strengthen and not be diluted by all of its members will be to form this inner core. This solid core will become "the engine of the union." [125] Knowing that the Union will have a ten nation federation and that discussions are underway for an inner core, we see that the evolution of the Union lines up with Scripture. Europe will become a giant empire with the EU governmental power house of the Commission and ten nation Council at the center. The next step for the EU is to form this core and when we see the EU number a political core of ten we know that the Tribulation is right at the door.

The Three Horns Plucked by the Roots

Daniel, in three separate verses, tells us that the Antichrist plucks out by their roots, three of the first horns (Daniel 7:8). Daniel envisions the ten-nation federation at its pinnacle of power. He describes the appearance of a little horn, *"before whom three of the first horns were plucked out by the roots."* Disturbed by his vision, Daniel talks to an angel who discloses the truth of the fourth beast. *"And about the ten horns that were on its head, and about the other horn which came up (the little horn) before which three fell."* The angel explains: *"The ten horns are ten kings who shall arise from this kingdom: and another shall rise after them; he shall be different from the first ones, and shall subdue three kings."*

One view holds that this verse refers to three of the ten kings that the Antichrist subdues. In the Hebrew translation, to subdue means to humble, put down, or humiliate. This contradicts the precept of the ten-nation federation. The ten kings willingly give their power and strength unto the Beast, and have one mind. They receive power with the Beast (Rev. 17:12-13).

The Antichrist, unlike any of the other leaders who held his position, subdues them. These three kings follow his policies unwillingly, unlike the others, and he expels them from the federation. There exist many variables. The Scriptures can indirectly be stating that thirteen kings exist when the Antichrist subdues them. He expels three of them, leaving his final federation with ten. Or he can subdue three of the member nations of the wider group of 27 nations. When the Antichrist subdues three nations, this verifies his position as the man of sin. The Antichrist raises the EU to its zenith of power with his select ten nations (Rev. 13:1).

No article in the Treaty of Rome allows the EU to expel a member. Denmark, for example, rejected the Treaty on Political Union and opted out of specific policies, but it remains a full-fledged member of the European Union. No nation within the Union wishes to forfeit the economic benefits of membership. Each nation relies on its role to influence the EU's evolution. Previous rocky relations with Greece caused EU partners to lament the absence of an expulsion clause. A petition circulated requesting signatures for the expulsion of Greece.[126] The Constitution that voters rejected included a clause that allowed for expulsion of members. When Denmark rejected the Treaty on European Union (Maastricht Treaty), there was talk in Bonn, Paris, and Brussels that Denmark could face expulsion. According to *The Economist*: "The eleven would renounce the Treaty of Rome and start again with a new treaty that excluded Denmark. The Council of Ministers' legal service claimed that this would be legal."[127]

Which three members will the Antichrist expel? Those which probably did not fit into the Old Roman Empire's original borders? Denmark happens to be one. It presently takes an anti-Federalist stance and initially voted no to the Maastricht Treaty, which caused a stir in the whole Union. It agreed to sign, but only under its provisions. The future world ruler will not tolerate Member States half-hearted in their commitment. A ten-nation federation within the EU's present institutional structure ensures its strength. It is no coincidence that EU policy makers wish to limit the Union's membership from the inner core which various EU leaders have proposed since the early 1990's.

If EU founders originally designed the Union for six members and maxed out at twelve, ten nations will end up being a good number. Taking ten of the most ambitious leaders will help the union reach important decisions quicker and more efficiently. The number might start with fewer or more but will end up at ten.

The leaders of the participating nations will form some sort of agreement like the Schengen agreement which eliminated border controls between the member countries of the Union in the mid 1980's. Schengen added impetus to the completion of the Common Market and the Amsterdam Treaty of 1997 incorporated the agreement into EU law. An Executive Committee ran Schengen and when it became part of EU legislation, the duties of the Executive Committee transferred to the EU's institutions in the co-decision procedure; the process by which they adopt directives and regulations. The Union will most likely incorporate the political core in the same way. They will draw up an agreement with the aim of moving the Union forward politically. Based on the Bible's description, the ten nation federation and the Antichrist run the Union. The ten king federation will bring together the ten Council members and the President of the Commission.

The other option is to streamline the European Council which brings together the Commission President and the leaders of the EU Member States to contain members of the political core only. The Vice President of the Commission currently attends its meetings. Or the Council of the European Union which comprises of the Heads of the Member States will be revamped to reduce it to the ten strongest and add the Commission President, i.e. Antichrist. Either way the other Council will comprise of the leaders of the remaining Member States. The EU can also add the core as an additional Institution which would comprise of the ten prime ministers and the Commission President. However the EU makes these changes, the student of prophecy should keep an eye on its evolution.

Meanwhile the EU as a whole will continue to add more members. Despite the EU's apparent willingness to consider taking in so many new members, there are strict conditions for admission. The criteria for the inner core will be those nations that possess the greatest ambition and commitment to move forward politically to evolve the Union into a full fledged political world empire. These leaders of all the remaining Member States will be ripe for the Antichrist's leadership and vision to move the EU into becoming the most powerful and crushing world empire that has ever existed. When the Union becomes the ten-nation federation, the ten leaders will be ready to meet and assist their leader in the same way the twelve apostles assisted Jesus. When this core forms the Tribulation will practically be at the door.

MAP OF 27 NATION EU

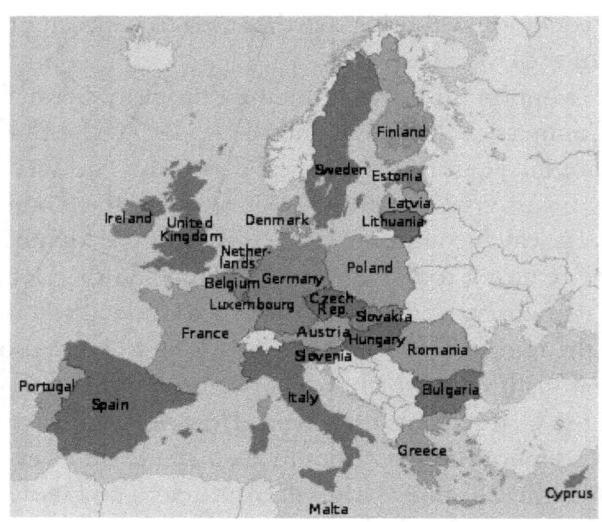

MAP OF OLD ROMAN EMPIRE

STATES ON THE CURRENT AGENDA

Recognized candidates	Applied	Potential Candidates
Croatia, Macedonia, Turkey	Albania, Iceland, Montenegro	Bosnia & Herzegovina, Kosovo, Serbia

States Not on the Current Agenda	States Outside Europe	Eastern Europe States Outside ENP & Eap
Liechtenstein, Norway, Switzerland	Cape Verde, Israel, Morocco	Kazakhastan Russia

Special Territories of Member States	Microstates Within western Europe, there are five microstates:	Eastern Partnership States
British Dependencies, Danish self-governing communities, French overseas departments and collectivities	Andorra, Monaco, San Marino and Vatican City. The fifth, Liechtenstein is a member of EFTA. Monaco, San Marino and Vatican City have all signed agreements allowing them not only to use the euro, but to mint their own coins.	Armenia, Azerbaijan, Belarus, Georgia, Moldova, Ukraine

PROGRESS

Croatia may be expected to join first, possibly around 2012, Macedonia possibly around 2016, and Albania, Bosnia and Herzegovina, Kosovo, Montenegro, Serbia, and Turkey following, either together or in smaller groups.

CHAPTER 8

THE MARK OF THE BEAST

I want to talk about a very different revolution that is taking place right now, quietly sweeping the globe without bloodshed or conflict...Its effects are peaceful, but they will fundamentally alter our world, shatter old assumptions and reshape our lives...as its emblem, one might take the tiny silicon chip—no bigger than a fingerprint. **Ronald Reagan**

God commanded Ezekiel to place a mark on the foreheads of the men he would spare from the judgment inflicted on the wicked living in Jerusalem (Ez. 9:4). Revelation's 144,000 witnesses—12,000 men from each of the 12 tribes of Israel—possess God's seal on their foreheads (Rev. 9:4, 14:12). Paul, in his letters to the Corinthians and Ephesians, tells Christians that the Holy Spirit seals them. Therefore they will escape eternal hell fires (I Cor. 1:22, Eph. 1:13-14, 4:30). In the new heaven and earth, God dwells among man, and his servants have his name on their foreheads. Revelation 3:12 tells us: *"He who overcomes I will make him a pillar in the Temple of My God, and he shall go out no more; and I will write on him the name of My God, and the name of the city of My God, the New Jerusalem, which comes down out of heaven from My God; and I will write on him My new name."*

Satan has always attempted to counterfeit God. His mark has been a characteristic of Satanism throughout the ages. According to Montague Summers, in her book *The History of Witchcraft and Demonology*, in 1661 the pupils of a cult confessed:

> The Devil gives them a mark, which marks they renew as often as those persons have any desire to quit him. The Devil reproves them and more severely, and obligeth them to new promises, making them also new marks for assurance or pledge, that those persons should continue faithful to him.

> The Devil's mark to which allusion is here made, or the Witches' mark, as it is sometimes called, was regarded as perhaps the most important point in the identification of a witch, it was the very sign and seal of Satan upon the actual flesh of his servant, and any person who bore such a mark was considered to have been convicted and proven beyond all manner of doubt of being in league with and devoted to the service of the fiend. [128]

During the Tribulation, Satan attempts to establish his kingdom here on the earth. His mark, on each of his followers, bears his name. According to Rev. 13:16-18:

> *And he causes all, both small and great, rich and poor, free and slave, to receive a mark on their right hand, or on their forehead:*
> *And that no one may buy or sell, except one who has the mark, or the name of the beast, or the number of his name*
> *Here is wisdom.*
> *Let him who has understanding calculate the number of the beast: for it is the number of a man; and his number is 666.*

The Antichrist will implement a system by which no man can buy or sell unless he wears a mark placed on his forehead or wrist. This etching in one's flesh represents the Beast or 666. Revelation refers to the mark in a spiritual context. Whosoever receives it spends eternity in hell (Rev. 14:11, 15:2, 19:20, 20:4). God punishes this abomination by sending a plague of foul and loathsome sores upon those who have the mark and worship the image (Rev. 16:2). Bible scholars theorize that the mark is part of a high-tech system that eliminates cash for the buying of goods. Thus, many evangelical theologians and students of prophecy follow the latest related technological developments, and note their possible evolution towards a cashless society. While this scenario provides one possible *raison d'être* for the mark, other applications must not be excluded, such as high-tech identification and human tracking systems. The Antichrist institutes this system midway through the Tribulation. He launches it as both a technological breakthrough and a prerequisite for life in his totalitarian regime.

The Technological Race Among Nations

After careful examination of the prophetic writings, and considering the current global population, we can see that the Antichrist will not accomplish the Scriptural forecasts without technological breakthroughs. At no other time in history have science and technology made greater strides, or become a greater priority for nations than today. The technological race replaced the Cold War as the new bandwagon of the superpowers. Today, technology is the key to national power. As Edward N. Luttwak, an American military strategist and historian theorized, we have gone "from geopolitics to geo-economics." He points out that methods of commerce have displaced military methods. Mr. Luttwak stated: "In this new era competitive technology projects are one of the weapons of commerce."[129] The stake is what former Chancellor Helmut Schmidt once called the struggle for the world product, rather than for traditional power.[130] The question occupying the nations of today is: who will win the technological race?

Studies over the past forty years have indicated that technological change is one of the most important factors that influence to a nation's rate of growth. A country's possession of knowledge has replaced its possession of natural resources as the key to economic prosperity. According to an EU Commission report on Science and Technology:

> In this era of rapid technological change, the economic health of a region will depend on its capabilities to capture knowledge in science, technology and to foster innovation and entrepreneurship. Knowledge and its utilization are replacing the possession of a natural resource base as the key to economic prosperity and leadership. Any region which chooses to remain competitive in this next phase of the industrial revolution must adapt to this new order and devise mechanisms to exploit the economic potential of developed knowledge and technology.[131]

For this reason, Japan aims to stay at least five years ahead of other countries in the development of new technologies.[132] Nations now pursue the economic growth that new technologies can spur. From computers to television, consumers want the latest features. This fact has increased growth and spending in commercial research and development programs by Europe, the US, and Japan. This means that nations are in a race to promote new technological breakthroughs, and they work hard at making and selling the latest technologies. The European Union jumped on this bandwagon.

In 1974, the Council of Ministers decided to extend European Union research to the whole of science and technology, and instructed the Commission to implement several major research programs. In 1987, the European Union entered into the Single Act an article that gives the Union formal powers in the field of research and technology. It stated: "The Communities' aim shall be to strengthen the scientific and technological basis of European industry and to encourage it to become more competitive at the international level....it shall encourage undertakings to exploit the Community's internal market to the full."[133]

Today, scientific research is the third largest area of EU spending, after agriculture and structural development. Information technology heads the list of basic areas of future research programs. The Federal Trust for Education and Research, a think-tank organization that aids in formulating EU policy, stated in a report that:

> Europe cannot afford to exclude itself from the profound technological transformation which is currently sweeping the world and which is expected to be the locomotive of economic development over the next two or three decades. Historians have noted that, periodically, the world brings forth a new technology, or group of related technologies, of such a revolutionary nature that it transforms the whole basis of economic activity...There is little disagreement that information technology is the mainstream technology of the current era.[134]

One cannot help but wonder if the EU will herald the Mark of the Beast as a technology of "a revolutionary nature, "to transform the world economy.

The Commission's RTD Network

Although the Mark of the Beast exists, the Antichrist must be in a political position that provides him direct access to technological programs and the power to implement them. We have established that the Commission presidency holds the seat of the Antichrist. The Commission presently oversees all research and technological development (RTD) programs in the European Union. It proposes, initiates, and implements RTD decisions. This gives the Commission direct and total control over technological projects. The Commission can even propose and suggest their own ideas. This will be the case with the Beast's mark.

The Commission has its own network. Various groups of specialized Commission officials manage the Union's RTD programs. These men, scientists by training, often come from university laboratories or industrial research centers. From their central position, they do much to speed up the circulation of ideas and the dissemination of knowledge.

Three of the most important committees with general responsibilities include CREST, CODEST, and IRDAK. CREST, the Committee for Scientific and Technical Research, consists of senior officials liable for scientific policy. It advises both the Commission and the Council of the European Union. CODEST, the Committee for the European Development for Science and Technology, enlists twenty-four members who are leaders from the scientific world. IRDAC, the Industrial Research and Development Advisory Committee, includes representatives from European industry. The advisory committees for each of the sectors concerned aid in the preparation and use of the individual programs.

One of the Commission's Vice President's is in charge of RTD. Other commissioners have the task of overseeing the individual research programs. One overlooks the development and use of advanced technology and the activities of IRDAC, while others are in scientific and technical cooperation with European Free Trade Association (EFTA) and non-member countries. This internal network will give the Antichrist direct access to new technologies.

The key RTD program devised by the Commission to create a technological base to compete with the US and Japan is ESPRIT: The European Strategic Programme for Research and Development in

Information Technology. The Commission launched it in 1984. The Commission must approve the selected projects. Proposed projects that have strategic and commercial importance receive money.[135] Concerning the ESPRIT program, the Commission wrote in the mid 1980's:

> In world trade, electronic equipment will overtake the automobile sector in the 1990's with worldwide R&D spending on information technologies rising from $35 billion in 1986 to some $90 billion in 1990. It will remain one of the dominant sources of technological advance until the end of the century ...information, in all its forms to become both one of the leading international commodities in itself and a vital element of economic activity in general. And it is rapidly becoming a driving force for social change....Information technology is therefore of key importance to the economy, both in renewing the competitiveness of established sectors and in the new opportunities it offers for a Europe rich in information skills. For Europe to make the most of opportunities offered by information technology requires strategic action....The blueprint for this emerging European Technology Community has been established in the 1980's with the European Strategic Programme for Research and Development in Information Technology.[136]

One of ESPRIT's projects deals with payment cards and electronic purses. Commission officials are testing the cards.[137] In the same way the future officials will test the Mark of the Beast.

The European Union also has links with many countries through bilateral agreements on scientific and technical cooperation. These include major industrial powers such as the US, Japan, and Canada. They also admit the new industrialized Third World countries (Mexico, Brazil, India). The EU also maintains permanent relations with other international organizations active in research, such as the specialized UN agencies.[138] As President of the Commission, the Antichrist will have knowledge of recent developments, and will support programs that suit his policies.

THE MARK OF THE BEAST

The Commission decides who will buy and sell with the Union. The Union will incorporate the "Mark of the Beast," i.e., this technological system, into EU financial policy. The mark will serve several purposes. Despite the economic benefits and other rhetoric, the technology will mainly act to mark his citizens and monitor them in his dictatorship.

Replacing the Cash System

The mark will not just happen one day; it will not occur overnight. The system's rise will occur as a gradual order of events. Prior to buying and selling with the mark, financial experts will campaign for a cashless society. This is already happening. An international consortium of market leaders which aims for a "no cash" economy has formed in the payments industry, to develop standards for a new way to pay by "electronic purse." Consumers use this card with a microcomputer instead of cash or checks when paying. The aim is to use it for everything from vending machines and public transportation to traditional passports and pay telephones. A pan-European consortium of consultants, academic institutions, and technology companies put together the EU-backed system. Banks can use the "smart cards" for many uses such as an alternative to traditional passports and credit cards, and as a method of payment for payphones, taxis, shops, and vending machines. Even police spot-checks in the EU will use an integrated system of identification using machine-readable ID cards.[139]

Smart cards and electronic purses will lay the groundwork for the Beast's mark. Payment cards and electronic banking will replace the cash system. Prompting this change is the enormous cost of paperwork. Prior to the wide use of the internet, the US spent $30 billion per year to process nearly 40 billion checks. In international trade, paperwork costs range between 4 and 15 percent of the value of the merchandise. Electronic data interchange reduces these costs.[140] The Internet has added its contribution to reducing these costs and also by offering online shopping, banking and payments debited directly out of one's bank account to pay credit cards, utilities, taxes and mortgages.

The EU plans to develop a "European Nervous System" that would connect government computers in the EU nations, to transfer data about everything from taxes to pollution levels. This nervous system will no doubt be in place before the mark is developed. The system has the potential to connect worldwide.¹⁴¹ The Antichrist will use such a system to keep track of all the marked individuals. There is also another Biblical parallel here. God's Holy Spirit indwells each Christian, and connects them (so to speak) to Jesus through his Spirit. Computers will act as the counterfeit to the Holy Spirit. As the Christian connects to the body of Jesus, the individual living during the Tribulation will connect to the Beast's "central nervous system," i.e., computers.

The devices that will become the Mark of the Beast already exist. Companies call them bio-implants. Bio-implants are now available for the identification of animals and the medical field uses them in humans for patient identification. A veterinarian places it beneath the animal's skin, and it contains information about the pet and his owner. The company VeriChip sold them to a Barcelona nightclub which used them for 125 patrons who used their chip as a debit card to debit drinks.

According to *Wikipedia*, Verichip received FDA approval in 2004 as implantable radio-frequency identification (RFID) microchip. Twice the length of a dime the medical technician implants it between the shoulder and elbow of an individual's right arm. Once scanned it responds with a unique 16 digit number which links to information about the user held on a database for identity verification, medical records access and other uses. A doctor or medical practitioner performs the insertion procedure under local anesthetic in a physician's office. In the beginning of 2007, Verichip Corporation created Xmark, its corporate identity for healthcare products. Xmark incorporates Hugs and the Halo system of infant protection: the RoamAlert system of wandering protection; the MyCall emergency response system; and the Assetrac asset tracking system.¹⁴²

An implant in the wrist or forehead of a human individual will become the future use of this technology. It will be able to carry all kinds of data about an individual. With child abductions a concern, and with heightened security since September 11, 2001, and the advent of the war on terror; implants will offer a great appeal. The new technology will also create jobs and contribute to economic growth. The Antichrist will use the mark to monitor those in his police state and even more so by taking the mark the individual will pledge their allegiance to his authority and ideology.

The Marriage of Man to Computers

EU Scientists call it "Adaptive Brain Interface (ABI), and the EU's ESPRIT program funds and sponsors its development. An individual hooked up to a computer can give the computer commands by his mind alone. Although the immediate application for ABI is to help the physically impaired, as this technology further develops, its potential within a police state is almost unimaginable. In March 2000, in Brussels, a paraplegic named Gabriele Taonconi demonstrated before EU officials his ability to walk thanks to a computer chip implanted near his spine and wired to his legs. They postponed his demonstration because of a computer glitch that prevented commands from communicating to the computer chip. Professor Pierre Rabi Schong of Montpellier University of France, a project coordinator, said the implanted chip allows the user to create artificial muscle movement. "We are trying to reproduce what happens in the brain...with electrodes to nerves and muscles."[143] Eventually a computer chip will not only track one's movements, but control individuals, reducing men to robots performing acts against their will.

The Mark of the Beast

Never before in history have new technologies moved to the forefront of national policies. The European Union is able to research, develop, and, through the Commission, implement whatever system it chooses. The Antichrist will enter his position in a world market where the development of new technologies governs economic growth. Initially, the system will offer all kinds of economic and social benefits. With a secured identification system for buying and selling, all kinds of crimes will diminish. Those who receive the mark will suffer the wrath of God. The Bible predicts the horrific side effect of grievous sores that breaks out on the bodies of the implanted. The Antichrist will not just implement the system for economic and social benefits; this is his mark, his label on those he rules. It will act as his tie to them, and it counterfeits God's seal of redemption. The born-again Christian must accept the good news of the Gospel before he receives the Holy Spirit and God's seal of redemption. In the same way, before one receives the mark, one will have to accept the

Antichrist's gospel concerning his deity.

The Number of His Name

The Book of Revelation provides the one riddle found in Scripture and it concerns the identity of the Beast. Revelation 13:17-18 states: *"and that no one may buy or sell except one who has the mark or the name of the beast or the number of his name. Here is wisdom. Let him who has understanding calculate the number of the beast, for it is the number of a man: His number is 666."* The Mark is also the name of the Beast who is a man. Scripture names no other man with a number except Antichrist who God assigns the number 666. The two other times the number 666 is used in Scripture is mentioned in 1 Kings 10:14 and 2 Chr. 9:13. The Bible tells us that after the Queen of Sheba's visit, Solomon yearly took in 666 talents of gold from the surrounding nations. Deuteronomy 17:15-17 warns that a king of Israel shall not multiply wives, silver or gold which Solomon did in addition to going after the gods of his foreign wives and building high places for them. 1 Kings Chapter 11 describes Solomon's descent into idolatry. [144]

In addition, Nebuchadnezzar's idolatrous golden image was 60 cubits high by 6 cubits wide, thus 66. Throughout history, ancient and modern nations use gold for currency. Only after World War II did the world stop using gold as a reserve for currencies. Gold, i.e. money is synonymous with idolatry. The number calculates to his name and relates to the currency system under the Antichrist, which he ties into his dictatorship and his blasphemous identity. He will cause the world to worship him and commit mass idolatry. The riddle which will be solved during the Tribulation further identifies him as the son of Satan and his mark as the means by which one gives one's soul to the Devil and ends any hope of redemption.

The start of the Tribulation ends the age of grace and ushers in a final dispensation. The Beast's government while rich and powerful becomes a monotheistic dictatorship with the worship and adoration to the State and its leader. The wheat and the tares divide into two categories of persons; those who take the Mark of the Beast and those who say no. Those who do not take the Mark of the Beast will refuse because of their belief in the true God and His Son Jesus Christ.

CHAPTER 9

THE US-EU PARTNERSHIP

Of the "latter day" nations mentioned in the Scriptures, America receives no direct citation, except possibly in two passages. For those who live during America's present era of prosperity and strength, this fact is puzzling. Some experts solve this puzzle by teaching that America is Babylon, and Jeremiah foretells its destruction. Babylon represents the European Union. Given that the Union becomes the most powerful world empire to ever exist, the United States must lose its sole superpower status in the interim. Since the entire world worships the Beast, it is safe to conclude that the US will remain in a strong alliance with the EU.

America is the daughter country of its mother Europe. Without America, the EU would never have united. The unified Europe of 1992 evolved, perhaps inevitably, from the Marshall Plan. American leaders of the postwar period believed that a strong, independent Europe stood in the best long-term interest of the United States. The US supplied Europe with the funds to rebuild itself, and even provided for its defense against Communist forces in postwar Europe.

Since the 1950s, the United States has consistently supported the Union's development. A stronger and more united Europe can share the burden of global responsibilities. Conservative President Ronald Reagan stated to the European Parliament in 1985: "We continue to see a strong and unified Europe not as a rival, but as an ever stronger partner." The Bush Sr. Administration gave greater priority to improving ties with the Union than any previous American administration. Former President Bush

Sr. stated that "a stronger Europe, a more united Europe, is good for my country, and it is a development to be welcomed, a natural evolution with an alliance, the product of true partnership, 40 years in the making."

Bush viewed Europe as "a partner in world leadership." He stated that he believed that a strong, united Europe meant a strong America. George Bush's administration upgraded the diplomatic status of the EU Commission in Washington. President Bush strongly supported the Common Market. He urged the EU to continue with intense efforts towards European Unity.[145]

After the fall of the Berlin Wall, the European Union became the "cornerstone" for the new European architecture. These changes strengthened the EU's desire to speed unification and assume its newfound role as a political leader. The US encouraged such a role as a major step toward the kind of global "burden sharing" it has long urged upon its European allies. Former US Secretary of State James Baker proposed "that the United States and the European Union work together to achieve, whether in treaty or some other form, a significantly strengthened set of institutional and consultative links." Baker believed that since the US and EU shared common ideals and values, and both faced the same challenges in economics, foreign policy, and a host of other fields, it was a matter of common course for both governments to work together.

The EU is America's most important trading partner. Their combined GDP is around 60% of the world total while they constitute only around 10% of the world's population. Together they account for 40% all world trade. They form the largest trading partnership in the world. The political, economic, and corporate links between the two are broad and deep. Even more important is their cumulative mutual investment stake in each other's economy.

Europe's investment in the US represents 75% of all European investment abroad and roughly 60% for all foreign direct investment in the United States. By 2001, the US investment stake in Europe grew to roughly half of all US investment abroad, and in 2001, this investment yielded half of all foreign earnings for US companies. Each has a significant stake in the prosperity of the other.[146] For this reason former EU Commission President Jacques Delors called for a new and profound partnership between the EU and the United States.[147]

An EU Economic Affairs Commissioner in the 1990's made it clear that a stronger and larger EU would be in the best interest of the US. According to the Commissioner, by the end of the 1990s, Europe would be a political and economic entity with a crucial role, as a major engine of the world economy and as a stabilizing factor in world affairs. He believed that it was in America's best interest that this evolution continues with as little friction as possible. He assumed the US would lend this process its full moral and political force. The EU's new role will present the US with a challenge. Experts believe that the American ability to influence the policies of the European Union will decline.[148]

Former President Clinton noted that he felt more favorably than his predecessors about "European Unity and...the European defense capacity to greater strength and unity within Europe." He labeled Germany as the leader of Europe, and as the privileged partner of the US. Clinton viewed the Union as "America's most valued partner in trade and investment." He believed that a "strong and more unified Europe makes for a more effective economic and political partner."[149]

The Trans-Atlantic Declaration

In 1990, the US and EU agreed to strengthen their relations, when both sides signed the "Trans-Atlantic Declaration." The US President and the Presidents of the European Council and EU Commission agreed to meet twice a year, and the US-EU relationship continues to evolve. At each summit, the EU and US set further goals for cooperation and joint action.

In 1995, the US and EU agreed to work together in promoting peace and democracy worldwide. Issues on their agenda are international crime, drug trafficking, terrorism, refuge problems, environmental damage, and the spread of infectious diseases. They also pledged to support the Middle East peace process, and to commit to developing a full and equal partnership. Initially, leaders met to create the world's largest free trade zone. Instead, defense and social issues came to the forefront.

In 1997, the EU and US intensified their cooperation on key foreign policy issues, and made progress in issues of world trade and other global concerns. They signed the "Science and Technology and Cooperation Agreement," which promotes closer cooperation between EU and US scientists and scientific institutions.

In 1998, the EU and US turned their attention to the new trans-Atlantic marketplace, after recognizing that they shared the world's largest and most complex economic relationship (each accounting for half of the other's foreign investment abroad), and that the prosperity of their populations intertwined. They decided that it was their task to work together to maintain open markets, and sustain the momentum of liberalization. They agreed to pursue their objectives together through the World Trade Organization, and renewed their commitment to political and economic support of the Middle East peace process. The EU and the US launched the Transatlantic Economic Partnership (TEP) at the London summit in May 1998.

In 1999, the EU and US added small arms and light weapons control to their agenda, and agreed that the destabilizing accumulation and spread of such weapons demanded the urgent attention of the international community. In the Bonn Declaration adopted at the 1999 EU-US summit in Bonn, both sides committed themselves to a "full and equal partnership" in economic, political and security affairs.

The next year, the EU and US agreed to work on accelerated action to combat AIDS in Africa, and continued to discuss the development of their joint role as peacekeepers. They committed to the construction of a new European Security Architecture in which NATO, the EU, the Western European Union (WEU), the Organization for Security and Cooperation in Europe (OSCE), and the Council of Europe would have complementary and mutually reinforcing roles to play.

At their 2001 summit, the EU and US discussed how they might use their partnership to solve trade disputes, and to promote peace and stability throughout the world. The US welcomed the efforts of the EU to acquire a civilian and military crisis management capability, which would reinforce the Union's ability to contribute to international peace. They also agreed to strengthen and revitalize the UN. In May of 2002, the EU and US held a Quartet meeting that also included the UN and Russian Federation, to work jointly in support of a secure and lasting peace in the Middle East.

At the 2007 EU-US summit, leaders formed the Transatlantic Economic Integration Framework, creating the Transatlantic Economic Council (TEC). In the economic area the EU and the US mostly work together within the framework of the Transatlantic Economic Partnership and under the multilateral umbrella of the WTO. They conducted a number of dialogues. The transatlantic business dialogue, a transatlantic labor dialogue, a consumer dialogue, an environmental dialogue and also the European Parliament/US Congress and Senate legislative dialogue. Other important projects such as the EU Centers in the US are also included under this chapter.

The European Union and the United States are the two largest economies in the world. They account together for about half the entire world economy. The EU and the US have also the biggest bilateral trading and investment relationship. Transatlantic flows of trade and investment amount to around $1 billion a day, and, jointly, their global trade accounts for almost 40% of world trade. With so much invested in each other's economies the ties between both continents so deep their partnership will only continue to deepen. [150]

The EU-US partnership does not imply that all leaders and political experts view the EU as an entity of light. Conservative spokespersons such as Pat Buchanan, and magazines of conservative thought and opinion such as *National Review*, speak out against a federal united Europe. Their views reflect Thatcher's position against bureaucratic centralism or a superstate that will rule all of Europe.

The Decline Of The US

With the rise of the EU to world empire status one cannot help but ask of the US's position and standing alongside this final power. As the EU rises to superpower status, the role of the US will decline. Some say this decline has already begun. Jacques Attali, the former president of the Bank for Reconstruction and Development, referred to Bush's victory in the Gulf War as the "last hurrah of a weakening global power."[151] The US's influence is declining and America is eroding from within. Drugs and crime, are rampant. Its families are falling apart, and its educational system produces test scores at an all-time low. According to a writer for the Academy of Political Science: "It has become cliché to say that unsatisfactory economic performance is undermining the United States' global leadership position. The budget deficit, trade deficit, and the need to finance these deficits with a large inflow of foreign capital into the United States have seriously weakened the American claim to global economic leadership—and possibly to political leadership as well."[152] This deficit exploded with the onset of the Great Recession.

The dollar is no longer the world's most stable currency. It has become a source of uncertainty and instability in the world economy. The US debt burden is so great that at the time of the fall of the Berlin Wall, aid to Eastern Europe on the scale of the Marshall Plan had become impossible. EU countries led by Germany made the main contributions.

America's economic position will decline further as Asia and Europe continue to grow more rapidly than the US. Zbigniew Brzezinski commented in the last decade: "Unless America pays more attention to its domestic weaknesses, a new global pecking order could emerge early in the next century, in the event that a unifying Europe and an economically dynamic Japan were to assume large political and military responsibilities."[153] In the Gulf War, the US had to rely on the political and financial support of other countries. A *New York Times* editorial stated: "Superpowers can afford to pay for their own wars; we cannot."[154] Some experts argue that the United States needs a new vision of its role in the world, and that it will have less and less influence in world affairs.

Walter Russell Mead, senior fellow for international economics of the World Policy Institute, cited events that prove America's decline and the erosion of its influence. He stated:

> The East European countries decided to link their new trading regime to the European monetary system, rather than to the dollar. Sweden... took the dollar out of the basket of currencies against which the Kroner would float and based its value directly to EC currencies. Poland, too, downgraded the dollar.
> The formerly Communist countries...It was to Bonn first and to Brussels second that they would turn for assistance, guidance, and models of economic and political behavior. ...For the first time, prominent European financial and political leaders could be heard to say that Washington was a nonentity. ... Jacques Atali, head of the European Bank for Reconstruction and development, spoke dismissively of the United States as a

failed nation; he argued that the great struggle of the future would be the battle between Europe and Japan for the global leadership that Washington had already and irretrievably lost.[155]

The Europeans are creating a new Europe centered on the EU. They do not see the US as a partner in this process. In the early 1990's commentators such as Lionel Barber, the editor of the *Financial Times* who then served as the Washington correspondent for the newspaper, commented: "Plenty of signs indicate that the United States will find it difficult to adjust to the 'New World Order' in which Washington's leadership is open to challenge."[156] It was speculated that "the US will be a major player in the world economy but not a dominant one, and that it will achieve its goals only as part of a consensus with other countries."[157]

At the same time, Dominique Moisi, who was acting as the Associate Director of the Institute Français Des Relations Internationales, predicted: "The American Century is coming to an end. The United States will undoubtedly remain the strongest power in the community of North Atlantic democracies, but its days as a hegemonic and sole protective power for Europe are counted." Mr. Moisi believes that "it is unlikely even that the twenty-first century will be dubbed, like the twentieth, the American Century." Mr. Moisi stated: "The US has neither the desire nor the means to recapture that privileged moment it experienced after the Second World War. We are witnessing a transitional stage in the international system....The role of the US will remain crucial, but it will stand alongside the other powers, and will no longer be alone in its category."[158]

The US's position further deteriorated the first decade of the millennium. Since the millennium, the United States has fought two wars and funded the disasters left behind from the devastating hurricanes which included hurricane Katrina, which nearly sunk New Orleans. In addition the US funded the bailout for the Great Recession. The US deficit is now in the trillions. In 2009 the US deficit reached 12.3 % of the nation's GDP. [159] The Financial Crisis which started with the US subprime mortgage market caused a domino effect around the globe and the loss of confidence of global powers in the US Financial system. From the BBC to the Financial Times, leading news services quoted experts who said that the US's role as the leading superpower changed and would not be the same after the financial crisis. That the world was now multipolar with the emergence of better capitalized centers in Asia and Europe.

Former Belgian Prime Minister and EU Parliamentarian Guy Verhofstadt, summed up perfectly in his essay, "The Financial Crisis – Three Ways Out for Europe:"

> The economic downturn in the West, and particularly the United States, will undoubtedly also cast a shadow over the former's political dominance in the world. Not that this dominance will suddenly collapse: the power of the US, in particular, is too great and too multifaceted for that. Put another way, America's absolute power will remain huge into the near future, but its relative power will crumble, thereby shifting the balance of power. For whereas the weight of other nations and blocks (China, India, Russia, Brazil, etc.) is increasing that of the United States has quite clearly reached its peak. [160]

The dollar's decline is causing alarm for many countries that peg their currencies to the dollar and for countries that hold sizeable positions of US assets. Financial experts are questioning the dollar's status as a global reserve currency. In addition no one knows the long term results of President Obama's bailout plan, or the possible consequences of the US printing more money to fund the bail out. Quantative easing i.e. the printing of money, if not done properly can destroy an economy by causing inflation and devaluing its currency. The policy destroyed the nation of Zimbabwe. [161]

The aftermath of the Great Recession will change the global pecking order and the US will lose its position as the leading nation in the world. The BBC reported in 2008, that "the US Superpower Status is Shaken." They quoted political philosopher John Gray and former professor at the London School of Economics as writing in the London paper, *The Observer*:

> Here is a historic geopolitical shift, in which the balance of power in the world is being altered irrevocably...The era of American global leadership, reaching back to the Second World War, is over...The American free-market creed has self-

destructed while countries that retained overall control of markets have been vindicated...In a change as far-reaching in its implications as the fall of the Soviet Union, an entire model of government and the economy has collapsed...How symbolic that Chinese astronauts take a spacewalk while the US Treasury Secretary is on his knees."[162]

Even the *Financial Times*, the world's leading financial newspaper reported that "the US will lose its role as a global financial "superpower" in the wake of the financial crisis. The article quoted German finance minister Peer Steinbruck as blaming Washington for failing to take the regulatory steps that might have prevented the crisis. He stated: "The US will lose its status as the superpower of the world financial system. This world will become multipolar with the emergence of stronger, better capitalized centers in Asia and Europe, the world will never be the same again...if we look back 10 years from now, we will see 2008 as a fundamental rupture."[163]

Director of National Intelligence, Dennis Blair, told Congress that instability in countries around the world caused by the global economic crisis and its geopolitical implications, rather than terrorism, is the primary near-term security threat to the United States.[164]

Paul Craig Roberts who was Assistant Secretary of the Treasury in the Reagan administration and Assistant Editor of the *Wall Street Journal* summarized the US economy in his article, "The Dollar's Reserve Currency Role is Drawing to an End," and commented that the US's economic profile is that of a third world economy. According to Mr. Roberts: "If the US government cannot balance its budget by cutting its spending or by raising taxes, the day when it can no longer borrow will see the government paying its bills by printing money like a third world banana republic. Inflation and more exchange rate depreciation will be the order of the day."[165]

If all of this is not bleak enough, Fred Bergstein, the Director of the economic think-tank The Peterson Institute, wrote in *Foreign Affairs*:

> The Peterson Institute for International Economics projects that the international economic position of the United

States is likely to deteriorate enormously as a result, with the current account deficit rising from a previous record of six percent of GDP to over 15 percent (more than $5 trillion annually) by 2030 and net debt climbing from $3.5 trillion today to $50 trillion (the equivalent of 140 percent of GDP and more than 700 percent of exports) by 2030. The United States would then be transferring a full seven percent ($2.5 trillion) of its entire economic output to foreigners every year in order to service its external debt.[166]

The Rise of the Almighty Euro and The Fall of the Dollar

The Great Recession prompted by the financial crisis and America's enormous deficit is affecting America's greatest asset: the US Dollar. The US dollar has been the most widely held currency in the world and it stood as symbol of US strength and prosperity. It is the world's reserve or anchor currency, this means that many governments and institutions used the dollar as part of their foreign exchange reserves. This number totaled about two thirds of the allocated reserves. The dollar became the international pricing currency for products traded on the global market such as oil and gold. This allowed the US to purchase the commodities at a marginally lower rate than other nations and to borrow at a better rate because there existed such a large market for the dollar. This allowed the US to run its high trade deficits and greatly postponed the economic impact. The dollar has been losing its role as the reserve currency and as Mr. Roberts noted above, "The Dollar's Reserve Currency Role is Drawing to an End." The dollar's loss of its reserve status will have terrible effects on the US economy.

If the dollar looses it status of reserve currency, the US as we know it will be no more. According to financial guru Michael Murphy:

> The US government will have less economic leeway to deal with the current financial mess, because excess Federal debt creation will lead immediately to a lower dollar and higher imported inflation. Longer term, the government will have to find another way to pay its debts than just selling

THE US-EU PARTNERSHIP

Treasuries to the Fed. Most likely, they will have no choice. The price of gold and silver will go up as they are used more as a currency asset, competitive with the world and regional currencies. The price of oil and all other internationally traded commodities will go up in most currencies, and go up a lot in US dollars. American lifestyles and financial habits will be forced to change radically in a world where we have to pay as we go. Longer term, economic power and wealth will shift from the West to the East and, to a lesser extent, the Middle East. The US government will have no choice but to tax US citizens and businesses more heavily.[167]

While the US dollar erodes, the euro since its launch in 1999 has risen to become the second largest currency holding of foreign reserves. As early as 2007 Alan Greenspan was quoted in a weekly German magazine *Stern* saying it was "absolutely conceivable that the euro will replace the dollar as the dominate foreign reserve currency, or will be traded as an equally important reserve currency." According to Vanessa Cross a business writer, who wrote "Can the Euro Replace Dollar as Dominate Foreign Reserve Currency," in supporting her view she quoted econometric analysis by Jeffrey Frankel and Menzie Chinn who indicated that the euro could replace the US dollar as the major reserve currency by 2020 if the dollar continued to depreciate and if the UK adopted the euro by 2020. She also noted the so-called BRIC nations – Brazil, Russia, India, and China – demanding the establishment of an international currency and for the dollar's replacement as the world's benchmark currency. China suggested that a new currency reserve system controlled by the International Monetary Fund (IMF) would be more stable.[168]

In September of 2009, the UN followed China and Russia and called for a new global currency to replace the dollar. The US dollar is not Russia's basic reserve currency anymore. The euro-based share of reserve assets of Russia's Central Bank increased to the level of 47.5 percent as of January 1, 2009 and exceeded the investments in dollar assets, which made up 41.5 percent. Also in September of 2009, *The New York Times* reported that Robert Zoelick president of the World Bank came out and said that America's days as an unchallenged economic superpower might be numbered and that the dollar was likely to lose its favored position as the euro and the Chinese renminbi assumed bigger roles. He added that the euro provided a "respectable alternative" for financing international transactions and that there was "every reason to believe that the euro's acceptability could grow." [169]

According to former Federal Reserve Chairman Alan Greenspan the dollar no longer had much of a lead over the euro, he said, adding that the European Central Bank had "developed into a global economic force to be taken seriously."[170]

Ambassador Guenter Burghardt, Head of the Delegation of the European Commission to the United States, noted in a speech to the Federal Reserve Bank in Atlanta Georgia, in as early as 2003, that "the euro has established itself as the second-most important currency after the US dollar on the world's financial markets." He noted that in 2003 the outstanding amount of bonds and notes in euros increased to 41% compared to the US's 43%, and the euro's money market instruments rose to almost 46%. Also by 2003 over 50 countries operated and managed exchange-rate arrangements that include the euro as a reference.

Meanwhile banks around the world such as the Central Bank of Russia, the Bank of Canada, central banks in Asia, Taiwan, Singapore and China have increased their euro holdings. He added that "the European Central Bank itself contributes to the prevailing role of the US currency as the official reserve currency." Mr. Burghardt also pointed out in that speech that:

> This enhanced profile in the monetary sphere has not yet translated into an appropriate external representation of the euro area. Despite the fact that the euro area today is the largest trading partner, main aid donor and second largest GDP producer in the world, its influence in the shaping of global economic decisions does not yet correspond to those capabilities. To borrow and American analogy, we are punching far below our weight. [171]

We know from Scripture and in reviewing the climate within the EU that the day is coming when the EU will assert itself on the world stage. The Secretary General of the Union of European Federalists, Joan-Marc

Simon reiterated and summarized what European think-tanks and leaders have been stating when she wrote:

> The 20th century has seen the rise and consolidation of the US as the world superpower which has been interlinked with the establishment of the dollar as the world currency. The current economic crisis, with the US decline and the emergence of new world powers, is leading towards a multipolar world and this will result in a new world monetary order which will reshape economics, internal policies and international relations for years to come. During the last decades the US has been exploiting the condition of the dollar as a reserve currency to run colossal deficits in its trade and current-accounts with which it has financed its economy and has managed to keep its status of the world superpower. This time it looks like the dollar domination is over and during next years most probably we will assist to the birth of a new monetary world order.[172]

There are other variables that will also come into play such as the European Central Bank greatly reducing its dollar holdings, and other nations that will join the euro increasing its strength. When the dollar ceases to be the world reserve currency, this will officially mark the end of the US as the leading superpower. The economic impact will once again effect the global marketplace.

Spain's former Secretary of State of Economy and Secretary General of Commerce, Guillermo de la Dehesa wrote an article questioning if the euro will ever replace the dollar as the reserve currency. He pointed out that if the UK joined the euro, given London's position as one of the world's two leading financial markets both in Euros and US Dollars, and because it has the EU's second largest GDP after Germany, this would provide a major boost to the euro. He stated that the EU's present union is a handicap because the EU is not an actual federal state but a union of independent nations.[173] We know from Scripture this will change especially when the Union moves forward with its political core of members.

The Next Superpower

Ironically, in the early 1990's, the US became concerned that Japan would become a dominant power that would undermine the economic security of the US and Europe by the middle of the next century. A CIA report stated: "Japan is a fundamentally amoral society that will dominate the world through its economic power."[174] At the time, *The Economist* stated that "while Americans fret over whether Japan will overtake them as an economic power, Uncle Sam is more likely to be knocked off his pedestal by the European Community."[175] The article pointed out that the EU's population is a third larger than America's, and that the EU, taken as a whole, is the world's biggest exporter. Where America will take its biggest knock is at the IMF and the World Bank. Under institutional rules, the headquarters of these institutions are located in the territory of the member nation with the biggest quota. The headquarters will one day move from Washington to Brussels and The EU will have the dominant role in world economic management under the Antichrist.

European leaders have spoken out against Pax Americana, the American determination to enforce a worldwide peace. They observe that the UN and Europe could counterbalance what they view as the imperial outreach of the US.[176] Europe will go beyond counterbalancing the US; it will be aiding the US's economy through its policies. America views the Common Market as a bolster to the US economy. America, who once shouldered the world's problems, views a burden-sharing Europe as a benefit. The European Union will grow above and beyond the expectation of any American administration. It will rise to superpower status and evolve into the most powerful dictatorship that ever existed.

America's Last Stand

When the dollar officially collapses and we know this crash will happen, and when its effects ripple around the globe, the crisis will provide the Antichrist with the perfect platform to enact solutions that will bring the EU prosperity along with the nations of the world. As US President Obama shaped and instituted policy to help remedy the Great Recession, the Antichrist will do the same, only Scripture tells us that his policies succeed. During America's broken condition, the EU will have opportunity to rise to its forecasted position of the greatest political power to ever have existed.

The Antichrist will bring the world back on financial tract and global economies will experience prosperity in the same way that Adolph Hitler brought wealth to Germany in his first few years of power. A writer stated that if Adolph Hitler died three years after gaining the chancellorship in Germany, history would have recorded him as Germany's greatest chancellor. It will be exactly the same with the Antichrist.

Once the Antichrist signs the peace treaty with Israel, about three and a half years afterwards, he places the abomination of desolation in the Jewish Temple. At this time, his evil, diabolical side surfaces and the nations react. The destruction of the EU (Babylon) occurs just before the Battle of Armageddon. Rumors from the east and north trouble the Antichrist. He then sets out to conquer many nations, and he establishes himself in Jerusalem.

A people from the north and a great nation will come to destroy the land of Babylon (Jeremiah 4:6-7, Daniel 11:40, 45). This great nation may be the US, which unites with the Soviet Union to destroy the European Union. Jeremiah reiterates this, and tells us that the great nation is from the farthest parts of the earth (Jer. 6:22). After destroying Babylon (Europe), they come to take Jerusalem, which the Antichrist controls. China follows. Jeremiah 5:15-16 states: *"Behold, I will bring a nation against you from afar, O house of Israel, says the Lord: it is a mighty nation, it is an ancient nation, a nation whose language you do not know, nor can you understand what they say. Their quiver is like an open tomb, they are all mighty men."*

The US position in the world will continue to decline as the EU rises to superpower status. When the EU becomes the final world empire, the US will remain a strong nation, though not a lone superpower. After the dollar's fall, America's prosperity will result from the Antichrist's solutions. The US will endorse EU policy and support the Antichrist until near the end of the Tribulation. When the US discovers the Antichrist's true colors and takes action, the nation will aid in carrying out Biblical prophecy. Fulfilling Babylon's judgment, the US will launch an attack on Europe. From there, the US will join the world's armies at the Battle of Armageddon. The US is a very trusting nation, and places great faith in its allies, especially in Europe. Their ties reach far and go deep. This reliance and the US's weakened position will prevent the US from taking action until it is too late.

A View to the Past

It was American armed forces who claimed the victory at the end of World War II and undertook the task of rebuilding Europe. The Soviet Union, which lay on Western Europe's borders, threatened to spread Communism to the ends of the earth. The Cold War between communism and Western democracy began, and global stability depended heavily on the United States. No country possessed America's combination of military power, wealth, and political authority. The US supplied Europe with the funds to rebuild itself, and even provided for its defense against Communist forces in postwar Europe.

The US will never view the EU as a future military threat, or as the potential cause of war and conflict. America will follow the Antichrist blindly, just as the nation has endorsed other dictators throughout its history. In part, its blindness will be a symptom of its own internal problems. A lack of effective US leadership will also be responsible.

Many skeptics view the EU as an economic grouping with too many differences to ever amount to anything politically. Others blinded by the Antichrist himself, will believe in his solutions for the world's ills. The rest will not care about world events while absorbed in their own personal lives, and will have no inkling that God's judgments are about to be unleashed upon the world. By the time America realizes the depravity of the Antichrist and takes action, the armies of the world will be on the road to Armageddon.

CHAPTER 10

THE PEACE TREATY

The Tribulation begins when the Antichrist negotiates a peace treaty with Israel, guaranteeing its security. Three and a half years after these negotiations, he stands in the Jewish Temple and declares himself a god. The Antichrist then lays siege to Jerusalem, and seeks to exterminate the Jews. Zechariah 13:8 tells us that two-thirds of the Jewish population dies due to his exploits. The verse affirms: *"And it shall come to pass, in all the land, says the Lord, that two-thirds in it shall be cut off and die; but one-third shall be left in it."* The remaining third, God refines. They call upon His name and He hears them. There are 13.3 million Jews worldwide. This would amount to the deaths of over eight million Jewish people in a three-and-a-half-year time period!

Nearly all Bible prophecy centers on Israel, including the prophecies dealing with the Tribulation. Today the Middle East is a primary focus in international affairs. The Center for Contemporary Arab Studies at Georgetown University concluded: "This very quick trip through history shows that, for several millennia, the Middle East was at the very center of the world stage. In the few hundred years between the sixteenth and the twentieth century's, it drifted to the wings. Now it has once again been recalled, by a mysterious providence, to the center."[177]

Jews Return to Their Own Land

Bible scholars view the reestablishment of the Israeli nation as the most important sign of the end times, because so much of Bible prophecy

The Seat of the Antichrist

centers on Israel. Many commentators regard Ezekiel 37:1-22, which prophecies about God's bringing the Jews back to their land from the valley of dry bones, as a reference to the restoration that took place in 1948. Ezekiel 37 predicted Israel's rebirth as a nation, and in 1948 this prophecy saw fulfillment. The skeletons in the valley are a picture of the way many Jews appeared after the Holocaust. The bones cry, "*our hope is lost.*" At the moment of their great despair, God brings about this miracle, which is exactly what occurred. The passage discusses God's bringing the Israelites from all of the nations where they lived, to their own land. During the Cold War, Communist nations did not allow Jews who desired to go to Israel to leave their countries. With the fall of the Berlin Wall in 1989, another prophecy saw fulfillment. Ezekiel 36:24 states: "*For I will take you from among the nations, and gather you out of all countries, and bring you into your own land.*"

With the fall of communism, Jews who lived under the oppression of totalitarian regimes returned home. Restrictions on Jewish emigration lifted in the Soviet Union, and twenty thousand immigrants per month poured into Israel.[178] The US, which had always provided open doors to immigrating Jews, decided to limit the number of Soviet Jews entering the country. Israel and some American Zionist organizations pressured the US not to admit them unless strong family links to current residents existed. Some 90 percent of refugees preferred the US to Israel as a destination, but this restriction forced them to go to Israel. Many remained there because of an Israeli requirement for a refund of fares and related costs should such refugees attempt to move to another country.[179] Politics did not force Jews to return to Israel, but God's divine hand brought them into their land.

Although Israel became a nation, it does not possess all the land God promised to Abraham. Under King Solomon, Israel came to possess most of it. The land promised was Palestine, stretching from the Sinai Desert north and east to the Euphrates River. This includes present day Israel, Lebanon, and the West Bank of Jordan, plus substantial portions of Syria, Iraq, and Saudi Arabia.[180]

Israel's History of Conflict

- In 1948, Israel became a nation.

THE PEACE TREATY

- Five Arab countries—Egypt, Jordan, Iraq, Syria, and Lebanon—declared war and attacked the new nation.
- In 1949, Israel signed a series of truces with the Arab countries.
- In 1956, Egyptian President Gamal Abdel Nasser barred Israeli ships from using the Suez Canal. He launched guerrilla attacks against Israel. Israel attacked Egypt and occupied the Sinai Peninsula and the Gaza strip.
- In 1957, Israel withdrew from these territories under strong pressure from the UN, US, and Soviet Union.
- In 1964, in Cairo, at an Arab League meeting, activists formed the Palestinian Liberation Organization.
- In 1967, after a marked rise in activities against Israel by the Arab countries, Israel launched a preemptive strike. The Israelis destroyed the Egyptian Air Force on the ground. Israeli troops swept to the banks of the Suez Canal, and fought the Syrians in the Golan Heights. Jordan entered the war. When the armies declared a cease-fire, the Israeli army occupied the Sinai Peninsula and Gaza strip, East Jerusalem, the West Bank, and the Golan Heights.

Theologian and author John Walvoord commented concerning Israel's victories in this war:

> As a result of the war, Israel increased her territory from eight thousand to thirty-four thousand square miles and doubled her population. Most important from the prophetic point of view, Jerusalem was back in the hands of Israel. The prospect of another war averted for the time being. Israel had suffered less than a thousand battle fatalities in contrast to thirty thousand Arab dead. Israel had tremendously increased her stature as a nation among nations and left the military might of her enemies in shambles. The world had begun to notice the prophets' predictions that the Jews will "*never again...be uprooted from the land I have given them* (Amos 9:15). [181]

- Israel absorbed East Jerusalem in 1967.
- The UN Security Council adopted resolution 242, which calls for Israeli withdrawal from "territories occupied" in the June War. It also calls for Arab recognition of Israel's "right to live in peace within secure and

recognized boundaries." The United Nations invited the PLO to take part in a General Assembly discussion of the Palestine question. It approved a resolution recognizing the right of the Palestinian people to independence and sovereignty, and gave the PLO observer status at its sessions. The Arab League endorsed the PLO as the "sole legitimate representative of the Palestinian people."

• In 1970, PLO guerrillas from Jordan made raids on Jerusalem. President Nasser died, and Anwar el-Sadat succeeded him.
• In 1973, Egyptian and Syrian forces attacked Israel on Yom Kippur. A Soviet- and American-sponsored cease-fire resolution ended the fighting and led to an international peace conference at Geneva.
• In 1974, Israel and Egypt signed a disengagement agreement, and Israel signed a similar one for the withdrawal of its forces from Syria and from part of the Golan Heights.
• In 1975, Israel signed a second disengagement treaty with Egypt. In that year the General Assembly adopted a resolution denouncing Zionism "as a form of racism and racial discrimination." The move outraged Israel and its supporters.

Menachem Begin became Prime Minister of Israel. President Sadat of Egypt went to Jerusalem. This marked the first visit by an Arab head of state to Israel.

• In 1978, the top leaders of Israel, Egypt, and the US met at Camp David for twelve days and agreed on two bases for Middle East peace. In 1979, these leaders signed the Camp David Peace Treaty.
• In 1982, Israeli forces invaded southern Lebanon with the goal of ousting the PLO. They besieged Beirut for ten weeks, and sent in American troops. The next year, Ronald Reagan sent Secretary of State George Shultz to the Middle East to conclude an accord on the withdrawal of all foreign troops from Lebanon. Israel and Lebanon signed the agreement.

King Hussein of Jordan and Yasir Arafat of the PLO agreed on an initiative that called for an international peace conference under United

THE PEACE TREATY

Nations auspices. The initiative foundered because the two sides could not agree on how to include the Palestinians, and because Mr. Arafat refused to accept United States participation.

The Peace Process

In 1991, after the Gulf War, former President Bush sent Secretary of State James Baker on a series of trips to the region to explore compromises that would begin the Arab/Israeli peace process.

Israel and Lebanon would discuss the future of Israel's declared "security zone" in southern Lebanon, which Israel had held since 1982. Syria would promise peace in exchange for the Golan Heights, captured by Israel in the 1967 Middle East War. Israel and Jordan would find a solution to the twenty-four-year Israeli occupation of the West Bank of the Jordan River, territory that Israel seized from Jordan in the 1967 war. Former King Hussein formally renounced his claim to the territory in 1988, clearing the way for a Palestinian state there. Sixty percent of Jordan's population is Palestinian.

The major dispute is between Israel and the Palestinians. Palestinians in the West Bank and Gaza Strip seek autonomy over their affairs, in the form of Arab elections in the occupied territories, independent Palestinian municipal governments, and Palestinian administration of police forces, schools, and health care centers. Palestinians say the Arab eastern half of the city should be their capital. Israelis adamantly oppose negotiations over Jerusalem.[182]

The Oslo Accords

In 1993, Israeli and Palestinian delegations secretly negotiated in Oslo, Norway. They signed the Oslo accords at a Washington ceremony on September 13, 1993, during which former Palestinian leader Yasser Arafat and Israeli Prime Minister Yitzahak Rabin shook hands, ending decades as sworn enemies. The Israelis and Palestinians recognized each other's mutual political rights, and agreed to strive to live in peaceful coexistence. They set up a time table in which Israeli troops would withdraw from Gaza and Jericho, and for Palestinians would set up their own government. They looked to 1999 for the finalization of a permanent settlement.

Despite Israel's special thirty-year relationship with the US, Israel met secretly in Oslo, Norway, for this historic conference with Palestine. They notified the US barely a few days before its finalization. US Secretary of State Warren Christopher first viewed the "Declaration of Principles" in an Israeli newspaper. Israeli Political commentator Daniel Ben-Simon stated that "the Oslo agreement put Israel's patron to shame."[183]

On September 28, 1995, at a White House ceremony, Israelis and Palestinians signed another deal known as the "Interim Agreement," or "Oslo 2." The four-hundred-page pact allowed for a second stage of autonomy for the Palestinians, giving them self-rule in various Arab cities and villages while allowing guarded settlements to remain. The Oslo Accords have not gone according to plan. The continual conflicts that have arisen between the Israelis and Palestinians have caused the peace process to reach many impasses. Former President Clinton sent former Secretary of State Warren Christopher to the region for talks. Madeline Albright followed in his footsteps. The European Union has sent several delegations to the area. Still the peace process has barely moved along.

On September 28, 2000, Israeli opposition leader Ariel Sharon led a delegation on a visit to the Temple Mount for a message of peace. After his visit, crowds of Palestinians in Gaza and the West Bank attacked Israeli security forces with guns and rocks. Palestinians blamed Sharon's visit to the Muslim holy site for sparking the conflict, which continued into 2001 with each side blaming the other.

In July of 2000, Bill Clinton, Ehud Barak, and Yasser Arafat met at Camp David to work out the final arrangements for a Palestinian state. Barak made concessions above and beyond the framework of Oslo. He offered the Palestinians control over a large portion of Jerusalem, but Arafat walked away without making any counter-proposals. Both sides did not demonstrate flexibility during the summit to negotiate a settlement. When it became clear to the Palestinian authority that Israel could not fulfill every demand of the necessary reciprocal compromises, the Palestinian Authority chose to break off negotiations without offering any of its own proposals. Clinton placed the blame for the failure of the talks squarely at Arafat's feet.

THE PEACE TREATY

Israel transferred virtually every Arab City and town in the territories to Arafat's control, supplied the Arab militia with weapons, began paying Arafat a multi-million-dollar monthly allowance, and lobbied for additional financial support to permit the Palestinian authority to build an airport, operate radio and television networks, and deal with other countries as a sovereign power. But the terror and violence accelerated. The Israeli death toll soared, and captured documents proved that Arafat and his Palestinian authority schemed with terrorist states such as Iran and Syria to acquire armaments and fund terrorism. Their aim remains the same—the destruction of Israel. Again, at the Taba Talks in January 2001, Israel once again showed its willingness to make far-reaching political and strategic compromises in order to achieve peace.[184]

In February 2001, Sharon defeated Ehud Barak for the position of Prime Minister. In December 2002, Sharon made a speech at the Herzliya Conference Institute of Policy and Strategy, and stated that the next phase cannot continue until there is a calm from terrorism and until the Palestinian government reforms, that peace cannot occur with Arafat as president of the Palestinian Authority, nor without the dismantling of all existing security bodies, the majority of which are involved in terror.[185] In 2004 Yassr Arafat died.

The EU and Israel

For the Tribulation to begin, the European Union must sign a treaty with Israel, guaranteeing Israel's peace. The US sponsors the current peace initiative. Henry Kissinger suggested in late November of 1990 that US leadership in the Middle East might be ending. "We are in a transitional period," he said. "I would think that over a period of ten years, many of the security responsibilities that the United States is now shouldering in the Gulf ought to be carried by the Europeans who receive a larger share of the oil from the region."[186]

For many years, the EU has followed developments in the Middle East closely, particularly the Arab-Israeli dispute. Only since the late 1970s has the EU taken a common West European stand on the Arab-Israeli conflict. They support a peaceful solution based on the 1980 Venice declaration. It affirms the right of all states in the region, including Israel, to exist within

155

secure frontiers, and the right of the Palestinian people to self-determination. The Union believes an international peace conference on the Middle East would provide the most suitable framework for negotiations and provides aid and economic assistance to the territories.[187] It is now an EU plan to become a leading player in the Middle East. Garret Fitzgerald stated in his report to the Trilateral Commission on the Israeli-Palestinian issue:

> In some European capitals, where there has for a long time been a feeling that Europe's interest in the Middle East is greater than that of the United States but where the United States' much greater influence in the region is recognized albeit with some sense of frustration, this American approach has been criticized as too limited and narrow, and also as being too optimistic....If, however, the policy fails, many in Europe would wish to see their governments in the European Union taking up the torch, without, perhaps, having a very clear idea as to how they could succeed where the United States had failed.[188]

In a statement by the EU Presidency to a joint meeting of members of the European Parliament and the Knesset on January 17, 1990, EU diplomats made it clear that if the Baker initiative failed: "The Twelve will be active in seeking an alternative to the Israeli-Palestinian dialogue as a means of advancing the kind of settlement advocated by the EU."[189] The EU feels qualified to play an important role in the advancement of peace, security and development in the Middle East, both by reason of its geographic proximity and its long-standing ties with the region. The Union regards itself as the most important economic group in the world today, with corresponding political influence. It also provides two of the permanent members of the UN Security Council.

The Mediterranean area is the Union's third main market for Community products, and the source from which the Union obtains some of its basic needs. On the EU's current agenda of foreign policy aims is "to play a very active part in efforts to achieve a lasting peace and stability in the Middle East."[190]

On the day the fighting ended in the Gulf, Luxembourg Foreign Minister Jacques Poos declared that the EU must help to establish peace and security in the Middle East. EU foreign ministers discussed the challenge of promoting stability in the Middle East after the war, hoping to play an influential role in rebuilding the region. Poos said in an interview that "the Middle East needs a Marshall Plan—a Europe and, if possible, worldwide plan." The foreign ministers have underlined their willingness to do everything possible to ensure lasting peace in the region.

At a meeting in Luxembourg, EU members pleaded with then US Secretary of State James Baker for a role in the peace process. The European request evoked a lukewarm response. He suggested that the EU have observer status. During an emergency meeting the EU expressed fears that Washington will sideline the Union.[191] They issued a statement to the *New York Times* in 1992, in which they stated that they "hoped for a full role as cosponsor of any Middle East peace conference. Israel stated that it wants the EU to have only observer status at any peace talks. It has long been concerned over the EU's contacts with the Palestine Liberation Organization. One EU aide, however, noted that [the EU] would have to live with the peace, and wants to be part of the creation of it." He added that it firmly believed that "the more international the conference, the better its chances."[192] Israel fears that the EU, which has proclaimed the need for Palestinian self-determination, has a strong pro-Palestinian and pro-Arab bias.

EU Middle East experts say the Union can make a "positive contribution" to the peace talks through its close historical, political, and economic links with the Arab world. The EU used political and economic pressure to persuade Israel to invite the Union to the negotiating table. Several EU ministers insisted that Union aid for Israel—and the Arab countries—depended on a heightened EU role in the Middle East. EU diplomats admitted that in Israel's case, the trade and economic argument was probably more effective. The EU is Israel's leading trading partner; the EU is Israel's largest market for exports and its second largest source of imports after the US. EU ministers promised Israel a closer economic relationship with the EU. They offered it on the condition that Israel recognize the Union's hopes of playing a "special role" in the Middle East. Of all the EU states, the Netherlands is an especially keen defender of

Israel's political and economic interests.[193] According to former Italian Prime Minister Gianni de Michelis:

> We insisted on being among the countries promoting the conference, on equal footing with the United States and the Soviet Union. We would find it difficult, if not unfathomable, to accept a lesser role, considering the contribution the Twelve can make to the peace process and to subsequent developments. We wish to be present not because we are seeking prestige, but because of the clear advantages our presence would bring to everyone. We have explained this several times to our Israeli friends who up until now have been those most reluctant to accept the Europeans, whom they consider as favoring the Arabs and thus wanting to transform the future conference into a court against Israel... However, vital its tie to the United States may be, the one to Europe is perhaps even more so in the long term. Israel is the daughter of Europe's history, and not only of the holocaust that was a tragedy not only for the Jews, but also for Europe....Anchoring Israel to Europe means eliminating one of Israel's motives for insecurity, that of having to rely on an ally that is geographically distant, not only in terms of military assistance but also in terms of development.[194]

The EU believes it can play an important role in the peace process by providing Israelis and Arabs with economic incentives to reach a diplomatic solution. They have begun work on a regional Arab-Israeli economic cooperation program. The EU will aim at the creation of new and binding trade, industrial, and environmental links between Israel, the Palestinians, and all Arab countries in the region. The EU's Middle East experts underline that "a precise program for cooperation, the economic advantages clearly spelt out, would be an added incentive to finding a solution to all political problems."

Former Italian Prime Minister Gianni de Michelis and Former French Foreign Minister Roland Dumas met in Sicily along with the Middle East ambassadors. They called for "a renewed, dynamic role" for Europe, including a seat at the negotiating table. At a press conference, Dumas said Europe must take on the role the Soviet Union could no longer play. It was no good asking Europe to make a major economic contribution while virtually excluding it from the key questions of disarmament and regional security.[195]

The Conference on Security and Cooperation in the Middle East

The EU bases its Middle East proposals on the Conference on Security and Cooperation in the Middle East. This proposal, issued in 1990 by the foreign ministries of Italy and Spain, is a regional arrangement for the Middle East. It takes in the Arab world, Israel, and Iran. The CSCE's global approach promotes peace in the Middle East. It acts as a multilateral forum covering the entire region. Agreed on will be guidelines on several issues: security, economic development, water and other natural resources, environmental issues, and human rights.

The Conference on Security and Cooperation in the Mediterranean and the Middle East reserves a special role for the UN. Participants include the US, Soviet Union, the EU and some of its member countries, and other states from Morocco to Iran. The euro-Mediterranean conference met for the first time in Barcelona in 1995. It marked the first time foreign ministers from Syria and Israel attended the same conference.

The EU took a lead role by pledging more aid to Gaza and the West Bank than the US. It is at work creating a free trade zone with Israel. The conference launched the euro-Mediterranean Partnership and established the euro-Mediterranean Free Trade Area.[196]

The EU Demands a Leading Role in the Middle East

The European Union took a leading role in the first Palestinian elections. They coordinated an international observation operation to ensure their success. The Union voiced anger at Washington shutting it out of an emergency summit held in Washington in 1996. The French foreign minister's spokesman stated that "the European Union has its place in the peace process. It is bound to be part of a peace settlement because it finances 75 percent of aid to the Palestinian territories." To establish its role, the Union invited Arafat to meet its foreign ministries before he went to Washington. Italy's foreign minister stated: "Tonight's meeting of the European troika with President (Yasser) Arafat in Luxembourg underlines the role of Europe in the Middle East peace process, especially since it is being held before the Washington Summit." The European Union on several occasions voiced its anger over being a money box for the Middle East without having any say in the region. They desired a role alongside the United States. Shireen Hunter, visiting research fellow at the Brussels-based Centre for European Policy Studies, stated: "If Europe is going to have any reality whatsoever, Europe has to act in one of the most important strategic areas otherwise Europe can't be taken seriously as a global actor." Europe continues to press for a greater role in the region, voicing its desire to have a political role as strong as its economic one.[197]

The Palestinians and Arab countries have been pushing for a greater European role to counter what they see as Washington's pro-Israeli stance. The Union is convinced that peace in the Middle East depends on the full implementation of the existing agreement between Israel and the Palestinians. They also believe in a final solution based on international law as set by the United Nations and the principle of land-for-peace. The Union calls for "total withdrawal for total security."

The European Parliament stated that the Union "cannot nor should not, accept East Jerusalem to be considered part of the territory and sovereignty of Israel." The Union urges the option of a Palestinian state and they refer to east Jerusalem as a Palestinian city. The Union wrote former President Clinton to propose a joint American-European initiative to revive the Middle East peace negotiations. The United States politely brushed off the European proposal. Although the US welcomed European efforts and said they had a productive role to play, the US reaffirmed its position as having the central role in the Middle East peace negotiations.[198]

Europe essentially put its foot in the door of Middle East diplomacy. At a meeting of European and Mediterranean foreign ministers, the Dutch foreign minister brought together Yasser Arafat and Israel's foreign minister on the sidelines of the conference. The EU president exclaimed, "it's indispensable, the political role of Europe here." He was speaking of the euro-Mediterranean forum. In the Amsterdam Treaty negotiated in the Summer of 1997, the Union called for and committed itself to peace in the

Middle East. European diplomats hoped to get the two men together again at the next Euro-Med meeting, to win a greater role in the Mideast Peace Process. [199]

In early 1998, the EU Commission urged the European Union to review its aid program to the Middle East peace process, demanding concessions from Israel and a bigger say in the US led negotiations. In the policy paper, the Commission said that the EU should insist that Israel stop sealing off Palestinian territories from the outside world. It noted that living conditions deteriorated despite the mounds of money the EU dumped into the region. The paper said the EU should insist on participating alongside the United States in all talks between Israel and the Palestinians, and should take the lead in coordinating international economic aid. The Commissioner responsible for Middle East policy stated: "We think it is perfectly logical, as may happen in a private company if you are the main shareholder. It wouldn't be normal for you not to be included on the board."[200]

Since 1998, the EU's aggressive determination to be part of the peace process helped to evolve its role as a "key player in the political and economic process." The EU's recent stated position on the Middle East peace process is that of a "promoter of a comprehensive, just and lasting peace and of prosperity for the region."

The EU also acts as a "facilitator in the peace process." It holds regular meetings with the main actors involved. The EU Troika (present and incoming Presidency, the High Representative for CFSP, and the Commission) make routine visits to the Near East. The activities of the EU Special Envoy for the Peace Process, the political talks with all parties, aimed at promoting the EU's positions, contribute to strengthen the role of the Union in the negotiations for the final settlement of the Israeli-Arab conflict.[201]

The EU presidency issues frequent statements concerning the various stalemates that have occurred in the peace process. They also have partaken in monitoring the early Palestinian elections of 1996 and the training of Palestinian policeman. The EU has also teamed up with the US, as agreed in the Trans-Atlantic Declaration, to work together in the peace process.

At the US-EU summit in Washington on December 18, 1998, the EU stated in their Declaration on the Middle East Peace Process:

> We will work together, including through our respective envoys, in the political and economic area, to build on this achievement and to help the parties move the peace process forward to a successful conclusion. We will use our partnership to support the implementation of seek ways to help the parties in the Lebanese and Syrian tracks to restart negotiations with the aim of reaching a comprehensive settlement.

The EU lends a good deal of economic support to the Middle East region. They are the largest donor of non-military aid to the peace process. The EU is the first donor of financial and technical assistance to the Palestinian authority. They are the first trading partner and a major economic, scientific and research partner of Israel, and are also a major partner of Lebanon, Syria, Jordan, and Egypt. In 2000, they signed the EU-Israel Association Agreement and committed themselves to establishing a partnership which provides for close political and mutually beneficial trade and investment relations together with economic, social, financial, civil scientific, technological and cultural cooperation.[202]

In the Laeken Declaration, which resulted from the European Council's meeting in Laeken on December 14 and 15, 2001, EU leaders issued a "Declaration on the Situation in the Middle East," stating that "it is imperative to put an end to violence." The EU reaffirms Israel's right to live in peace and security, and supports the establishment of a Palestinian State. The EU appeals to the Palestinian authority to end terrorism, and demands that they dismantle the Hamas' and Islamic Jilhad's terrorist networks, "including the arrest and prosecution of all suspects: a public appeal in Arabic for an end to the armed intifada." The EU demands that the Israeli government withdraw all military forces, and lift all closures and restrictions—including freezes on settlements and operations—directed against Palestinian infrastructures.

A key statement of interest to students of prophecy reads: "The European Union remains convinced that setting up a third party monitoring mechanism would serve the interests of both parties. It is prepared to play an active role in such a mechanism." Could this lead to the guarantee of peace in the region and the Covenant of Death?[203]

In May of 2002, when President George Bush, Jr. met with

Commission President Prodi during a summit, he affirmed the EU's importance in the Middle East Peace process by stating:

> The United States and the EU share a common vision of two states, Palestine and Israel, living side by side in peace and security. This vision offers the Palestinian people a new opportunity to choose how they live. We should take this opportunity to help build institutions that will serve the Palestinian people, a Palestinian state and its neighbors, as well....The EU, as well and the United States has an important role to play. When the EU and the United States work together we multiply our effectiveness.[204]

In the July 2002 issue of *The Federalist*, Guido Montani, the Secretary General of the UEF in Italy, stated:

> Presently the European Union does not have the means necessary for intervening adequately in the Middle East. The Federalists therefore are calling on the Union's governments to convene urgently a meeting of the European Council and to declare a State of Emergency, granting the European Commission all the military and budgetary powers for solving the crisis in the Middle East.

He adds that the European Commission will act as a "provincial European government," which should call for an international conference. He refers to "The European Peace Plan," which must call for "the immediate creation of a Palestinian State." Mr. Montani also adds that "the European Union, unlike the USA and Russia, has an interest in proposing to all of the Middle East countries (and not just to Palestine) a Marshall plan for development and peace."[205]

In August 2002, the Danish presidency of the European Union announced that it was working on a three-stage Middle East peace plan, which envisioned the creation of an independent Palestinian state in 2005. The Danish plan hoped to signal to the Arab world that Europe is still a major player in the Middle East region. Former Danish president Per Stig

Moeller stated: "We must make progress on security, political and economic issues to strengthen the belief among Palestinians in a state that will be theirs and that is within reach, and reassure Israelis that they will at last have security within their own borders."[206] Thus the groundwork for the treaty spoken of in Scriptures exists and only awaits the arrival of the Antichrist to formalize and sign it, yet the events still continue to evolve.

In December 2002, the EU, US, UN, and Russia held a Quartet meeting to discuss Middle East peace, and put forth a road map that envisions two states, Israel and Palestine, living side by side in peace and security.[207]

On Apr. 30, 2003, the Roadmap for Peace took place based upon a speech by President Bush and the principles of the Oslo Accords, this plan is supervised by the Quartet: the United States, the European Union, the Russian Federation and the United Nations. It called for serious alterations in the Palestinian government and resulted in the appointment of Palestinian Authority Prime Minister Mahmoud Abbas. Afterward a summit took place with Sharon and Abbas reaffirming their commitment to the Roadmap. Sharon promised withdrawal of Israeli troops from Palestinian areas, and Abbas pledged an end to the Intifada and the Palestinian culture of hate against Israel. Despite the agreement, Palestinian terrorists carried out a suicide bombing in Jerusalem and the Israeli Cabinet waged war against Hamas and other terrorist groups, and halted the diplomatic process.

Later that year at the Fourth Herzliya Conference, Prime Minister Sharon presented a plan for Israel's unilateral disengagement from the Gaza Strip and northern Samaria in exchange for peace. The disengagement plan, called for evacuating nearly 9,000 Israeli residents living in Gaza and the West Bank.

In 2005, at the Sharm el-Sheikh Summit I, Sharon met with PA President Abbas, Egyptian President Hosni Mubarak and King Abdullah of Jordan to announce the implementation of Israel's disengagement from the Gaza Strip and parts of the West Bank. Abbas and Sharon agreed upon a Ceasefire. Later in August Israel pulled all of its citizens out of the Gaza Strip and the Northern West Bank.

In 2007, Israeli Prime Minister Ehud Olmert's accepted the revised Arab Peace Initiative. In response to the March 28, 2007 Arab League

THE PEACE TREATY

Summit at Riyadh, Olmert invited the Arab heads of state to a meeting in Israel to further discuss the initiative and collaborate on improving it. Olmert met with Abbas, Mubarak and Jordan's King Abdullah II. They discussed containment of Hamas in the Gaza Strip and to strengthen Abbas' Fatah party in the West Bank. Later that year, Israeli Prime Minister Ehud Olmert and Palestinian Authority President Mahmoud Abbas signed a joint statement in Annapolis, Md. to lay the groundwork for peace talks.

In 2008, President Bush embarked on a tour of a number of Middle East countries, starting with Israel. The purpose of the visit was to advance peace negotiations initiated at the Annapolis conference in Nov. 2007. Bush urged the Palestinian side to dismantle the terrorist infrastructure and also called on Israel to halt settlement construction and remove unauthorized settler outposts.

The Peace Valley plan is an effort personally supported by Israeli President Shimon Peres, which seeks to promote a new approach based on economic cooperation, and promotion of joint economic and business projects. In May 2008, Tony Blair, the special envoy for the Quartet announced a new plan for peace and for Palestinian rights, based heavily on the ideas of the Peace Valley plan.

In December 2008, the EU expressed the hope that Lebanon – Israel peace talks would be possible. The EU has praised the Arab Peace Initiative, as a major step forward for the Middle East Peace Process, since it offers a basis for peaceful and normalized relations between Israel and all 22 members of the Arab League.

The Resolution of the Arab-Israeli conflict is now a strategic priority for Europe. They believe that without this peace, there will be little chance of dealing with other problems in the Middle East. The EU's objective is a two-state solution with an independent, democratic, viable Palestinian state living side-by-side with Israel and its other neighbors.

The Bible tells us that the Antichrist confirms the covenant with Israel, and guarantees Israel's peace. In 1993, the Federalist Trust, a European think-tank organization that aids in formulating EU policy, and is ahead of its time usually suggesting policy that the EU adopts a few decades later, published a report on the Middle East. They wrote up a proposed treaty that guarantees Israel's peace. The proposal offers the security that the US initiative fails to offer. The report proposes the establishment of a "regional security community" as the basis for the Arab-Israeli peace settlement. The proposed treaty states that the guarantor states would protect the community against external attacks. The Union would secure Israel's peace with its army. The Scriptures state that the Antichrist confirms the covenant with many. The proposed treaty includes the world's great powers and reads:

> Moreover, the incorporation of the great powers into the security package as both the guarantors and supervisors of this arrangement raises the costs of violation dramatically. Should a certain state decide to defy the superpowers (and the other co-signatories to the agreement) and to embark on a belligerent/irredentist course, it will clearly identify itself as an aggressor and will run the risk of losing the political goodwill as well as the economic and military support of the international community, thereby dooming such a move. Hence, a security community consisting of a militarily constrained Palestinian state and a demilitarized Golan, guaranteed and strictly supervised by the great powers may satisfy Israel's security concerns and ally its apprehensions of the adverse implications of loosening of the US-Israeli strategic relationship, caused by such a proposed arrangement.[208]

It is likely that this proposed treaty is "the covenant of death" spoken of in Scripture. According to Amos Perlmutter: "People who live in a constant state of war naturally yearn for peace; for a nation, security is the equivalent of sanity for an individual. The Israelis search for security is an obsession, a quest for an almost metaphysical security, even if they know that such protection is beyond their political and military capabilities."[209]

When the Antichrist signs the peace treaty with Israel, this covenant assures Israel total peace. The Israelis will feel safe from the threats of their neighbors. The CSCM is the skeletal form of the proposals yet to come. The EU will guarantee Israel's peace in the region and will act as her protector. The world will view it as one more event in history, no cause for concern. This covenant marks the beginning of the Tribulation and ends the dispensation of grace. With events occurring at unprecedented speed, anything is possible and leaders can sign a treaty almost overnight. According to *The European Journal of Internal Affairs*:

> Disarmament creates a fourth paradox. Never before has history seen such an acceleration. There was a time when governments determined their security priorities on a long-term basis and when diplomats negotiated for many years the finer details of acts, verification, ceilings and the like. Those items seem well and truly passed. Today, diplomats are called upon to establish treaties within six months or a year (as was said by President Bush at the Brussels summit last May), whereas the negotiating process, though working at maximum speed, will nevertheless still be unable to keep pace with the political changes which are speedily occurring both East as in the West.[210]

In Israel's ancient past the nation became part of the empire that took it over. Thus, Israel was Assyria, Babylon, Persia and Rome. Israel will also be part of the EU. Coincidentally Israel voiced a desire to join the European Union and the Union considers Israel a possible candidate country. If the country joined it will have the security of the EU and its territory will belong to the empire. According to Michael Sctender-Auerbach from the think-tank the Century Foundation:

> For Israel, EU membership would not only provide a strong security guarantee, but would afford them all of the economic advantages of the vast EU market. For the security establishment, it could possibly mean even opening the door to membership in NATO. The EU and Israel already have a formal Cooperation Agreement—ratified five years ago by the Knesset, Israel's parliament—and this relationship has influenced economic, political and cultural exchanged.

Auerbach pointed out that Israel joined the Euro-Mediterranean zone, which will boost Israel's financial gains in the textile industry. For Israel to gain entry into the EU it will need to negotiate a peace settlement with the

Palestinians consistent with Security Council resolution 242 and to settle its border disputes with Syria and the Golen.

He also added that "as an EU member at peace with its neighbors, Israel would bolster Europe's status as a world leader and international power broker. This will also provide Israel with the security and membership in a community of nations that accept and protect them." He added that "the EU can currently guarantee peace without Israel becoming a member of the EU, but Israel as a member will no doubt solidify any peace agreed by providing the same protection as it would for the rest of the Member States."[211] For the first time in history, geopolitical speak now matches what the Scriptures predicted.

Israel's Covenant of Death

Because the EU holds strong relations with the Arab world, the Antichrist will also use these relations to guarantee Israeli peace. He will campaign for peace in Israel and the region as a whole. Israel will trust him and feel secured by his promises. With him they will sign what the Bible calls their covenant with death. Concerning Israel's signing this agreement, in several places in Scripture the Bible elaborates on the deceit behind this promise. In the book of Isaiah, God reveals the truth of this covenant. Isaiah 28:15, 18 reads:

> *Because you have said, We have made a covenant with death, and with Sheol we are in agreement: when the overflowing scourge passes through, it will not come to us; for we have made lies our refuge, and under falsehood we have hidden ourselves.*
>
> *Your covenant with death will be annulled, and your agreement with Sheol will not stand; when the overflowing scourge passes through, then you will be trampled down by it.*

God is telling the Jewish nation that *"with hell they are in agreement"* because the man they are dealing with is none other than the Devil in a man's body. The phrase *"we have made lies our refuge"* exposes that the guarantees of the treaty are false, for this leader who promises to guard

Israel will seek to destroy it. He tells them that *"when the overflowing scourge passes through, you will be trampled down by it."* Another words, when this man wages war against Israel, the nation will be destroyed by it. God elaborates on the Antichrist's deception and intention as he signed this agreement. In Psalm 55: 20-21 it says:

He has put forth his hands against those who were at peace with him:
He has broken his covenant.
The words of his mouth were smoother than butter,
But war was in his heart;
His words were softer than oil,
Yet they were drawn swords.

Scripture provides a view to the emotional and physical picture of Israel once the Antichrist breaks the treaty and lays siege to the nation. Isaiah 33:7-9 states:

Surely their valiant ones shall cry outside: the ambassadors of peace shall week bitterly.
The highways lie waste, the wayfaring man ceases.
He has broken the covenant, he has despised the cities, he regards no man. The earth mourns and languishes; Lebanon is ashamed and shriveled: Sharon is like a wilderness: and Bashan and Carmel shake off their fruits.

Daniel 11:37 emphasizes the Antichrist's regard for no man. It states: *"He shall regard neither the God of his fathers, nor the desire of women, nor regard any god: for he shall magnify himself above them all."* Genesis 3:16 teaches that Eve represented all of womanhood. Her *"desire shall be for your husband."* The desire of women is man. Thus, the Antichrist will regard no man.

The Antichrist?

The most shocking event took place in February 1998, when former Commission President Jacques Santer went on a weeklong tour of the

Middle East to promote Europe's political role in the region. Santer actually spoke of guaranteeing Israel's peace. According to Reuters: "European Commission President Jacques Santer said on Saturday that the Middle East peace process could best move forward if Israel's security was guaranteed and the Palestinians were able to develop their economy."

Santer stated: "It is very important that the people of Israel live in security. The best condition is also to give the Palestinians the right to economic development." Santer asserted that "Europe has to play a stronger role in the peace process." The whole purpose of his visit was to ensure Europe's political involvement. Santer affirmed: "We want political involvement and that's why I'm here." It does not get any closer than this, as one of the future commission president's identity will be the Antichrist and he will mirror Santer's words.

We know that the Antichrist must be pro-Israel in his policies. Despite some of the Union's pro-Palestinian positions, Santer stated: "We are as pro-Palestinian as we are pro-Israel." As if already holding a preeminent place in the peace conference, Santer added: "We have to see how we can have a real balance to make a breakthrough in the involvement and that's why I'm here." [212]

Santer's visit was the first by a European Union president to the region. Despite having a Commissioner who is responsible for the Middle East region, Santer took it upon himself to act alone. During Santer's visit he met with the Israeli leader.

Only since this last decade has the European Union made such inroads into the peace process. The Union evolved from desiring a role to achieving one. It is haunting that in 1993 the Federalist Trust drew up a treaty proposal and the Union is now in the place to initiate it. There is coming the day when the Union will broker the peace. It is possible that European leaders are negotiating this treaty this very moment.

CHAPTER 11

IT WILL SURELY COME

When the disciples asked Jesus, "What will be the sign of your coming?" As was pointed out in an earlier chapter, Jesus provided a series of predictions that all point to a world in utter turmoil and chaos. Many of the signs specifically relate to the Tribulation period, but several predict the times leading up to the start of the Tribulation. Jesus first forecasts that *"many will come in My name saying, 'I am the Christ' and will deceive many"* (Matthew 24:5).

While society has already experienced a rise in self-proclaimed prophets, during the Tribulation, due to the perilous times, they will proliferate. Jesus next added: *"And you will hear of wars and rumors of wars. See that you are not troubled for all these things must come to pass, but the end is not yet"* (Matthew 24:6). In 1993, the *New York Times* listed forty-eight trouble spots around the globe.[213] The Middle East conflict continues to escalate. With the attack on the US on September 11, 2001, the discord came within America's borders with a serious attack. Thus, the US is currently engaged in a war on terrorism, waged war against Iraq, is keeping a watch on Iran and North Korea which threatened a preemptive strike against the US. The American government has issued a high alert against terrorist attacks from Al Qaeda, and is experiencing first-hand the anxiety that comes from Jesus's statement about upcoming "wars and rumors of wars." Along with the US, terrorism, wars and various conflicts threatens nations around the globe.

Jesus continues with "And there will be famines, pestilences and earthquakes in various places" (Matthew 24:7). In 1996, *Newsweek* commented in response to the floods, hurricanes, droughts, and earthquakes that struck in so many localities around the globe in that year that "the only plague missing was frogs."[214] Since then these events have only increased. Other natural events such as polar ice caps, glaciers and mountain top ice melting which will effect habitat and water levels some attribute to global warming. [215] Jesus concluded that "these are the beginning of sorrows" (Matthew 24:8).

Nearly all of the Scriptures' criteria are in place for the Tribulation to begin. Daily, the EU is gaining more stature in our world. In the early 1990s, many skeptics doubted that the EU would succeed in uniting economically, and regarded the 1992 program as a project doomed to failure. Not only did 1992 succeed as planned, the EU went onto reach its goals for monetary union, another area that critics regarded as a potential disaster for the Union. Today the euro is worth more than the American dollar. The US media has provided very little coverage of the political evolution of the EU, which is currently evolving into the final world power described in the Scriptures.

The Middle East peace process evolves daily. The European Union's role over the last two decades increased considerably in the region and the Union can guarantee the peace, especially since it made Middle East peace a foremost priority. As events unfold in the peace process, we can expect to see the Union gain an even stronger footing in preparation for the Antichrist's treaty.

Even if one disregards the Biblical writings, the Union should raise serious concerns by virtue of its undemocratic institutional structure and its political ambitions. The Union is at a crucial stage in its evolution. As it evolves into a political empire, society will continue to grow wicked, resembling more and more the days of Noah and Lot.

We know that the Antichrist is going to be one of the leaders appointed to the EU Commission Presidency. This man will be responsible for raising the EU to its pinnacle of power. He will virtually be unknown when he takes power and will become strong with a small people. Former Italian Health Minster Tina Anselmi urged people "not to undervalue the possibility of a new and dramatic fascism." She stated that Mussolini "only had 2,000 votes in Milan at the start of 1922 and yet by the end of the year, he was in charge of the country."[216] We know that history repeats itself, and despite our knowledge of the process by which dictators come to power, they continue to rise and fall.

The world will not be battling an evil man like Hitler, whom some consider to have been demon possessed, but will be up against Satan himself in a man's body who will make Hitler look mild. Antichrist launches his fury and rage against the world because he knows that the second coming of Jesus Christ dawns on the horizon. God gives him this time because the Antichrist acts as an instrument of God's judgment upon the earth. What the conquests of the Antichrist do not destroy, the plagues, earthquakes, and other disasters will. Those who do will have to contend with the Antichrist and his henchmen, and some will end up martyred.

The Mark of the Beast will distinguish the Antichrist's followers from those of God. By not taking the Mark, one will not be able to buy or sell. Children and relatives will turn over their family members to the Antichrist's SS. Jesus tells us in Mark 13:12: *"Now brother will betray brother to death, and a father his child; and children will rise up against parents and cause them to be put to death."* Fathers turn against their own children and have them put to death which epitomizes the belief in the police state that will exist at that time. Jesus tells us regarding this betrayal that "because lawlessness will abound, the love of many will grow cold" (Matthew 24:12). We see some of this today in various faiths and have heard horror stories of children turning against their parents and even killing them.

The Headlines to Watch For

The signs and events leading to the Tribulation are so in place that we can speculate on the next main developments to watch for, which are:

•The continued rise of the EU and the demise of the US.
•The building of the third Temple and the Temple Mount area to change for the building of the Temple.
• The forming of the ten or thirteen member political core, which can also start with fewer members and increase upwards to ten or thirteen.
• The Antichrist eliminating three members from either the 27, or 13.

- The increased globalization of this world which will come about via the European Union once it takes the lead as the world's leading superpower.
- The fall of the US dollar as the world's reserve currency.
- The further strengthening of the euro.
- A possible global currency, but the euro will suffice.
- Increased earthquakes and natural disasters.
- More wars and conflicts.
- Further elimination of cash in society.
- More use of bio implants.
- Evolution of bio implants, i.e. further technological advances.
- Evolution of computers and their use potentially for a police state.

The God of the Bible and the Tribulation

Despite God's warnings and the evidence that supports the Tribulation, many believe that it will not happen. Somehow, they think, man will turn his fate around. For others, the prospect of the European Union's creating a world dictator seems impossible. Others do not believe in God or the Bible as the Word of God. Some cannot fathom that a loving God would allow such destruction and suffering. Why does God allow so much human suffering especially as will happen during the Tribulation. Why would he create man and annihilate him.

The God of the Bible is not an entity that a finite limited mind can understand. Why would God allow the injustices in this world and human suffering. One cannot fathom that God will allow such suffering to happen to the beings he created. When God's judgments come and the people living are experiencing them they will become angry at God rather than turn to him.

We think of God as all loving and that our lives should be heaven on earth because a loving God will only give us good things. The God of the Bible is a peculiar God. One who has emotions like us, who created us in his image, yet remains incomprehensible to us. God's ways are not our ways, as anyone who reads through the Bible discovers. He is just in all of his dealings with men. We are finite and God is infinite; thus we cannot completely understand Him. Man fashions the character of God around his sympathies, and rejects Him. We tell God that if He is not who we think He should be, we want no part of Him. To know God is to realize that we do not fully know, nor can we in this life understand Him. He tells us that His ways are not our ways, or His thoughts ours. The wisdom of God seems like foolishness to men; such as the preaching of the cross. Yet it is the power of God to those who believe.

God tells us that we must have the faith of a child to believe in Him. In examining the God of the Holy Bible objectively, we see that this God is much more complex, peculiar, and esoteric than one's conception of Him. The more one learns of Him, the less one really understands Him. This is a God who created all things, is everywhere at once and who knows every language and thought of the roughly six billion people who are on the planet. He formed the world in six days and rested on the seventh, and produced a fantastic garden with trees and fruit capable of giving man knowledge and eternal life.

God created the angels and afterwards his next highest form of life: man. Man has never seen his face and if he did he would die. He appeared as a pillar of cloud and a flaming bush. He elects a particular people, the Jews, whose bloodline His Son would come into this world and to whom He reveals Himself. He promises these people a fruitful land; Israel, and leads them to it. He fights wars for them and drives out their land's inhabitants. In fighting those battles God orders the Israelites to kill every man, woman and child of the nations and tribes that come up against them.

This same God expects his chosen people to love him and if they go after other gods and pagan practices he eventually becomes angry with them and brings on them pain, suffering and calamity in an effort to get them to turn to him.

He set up a system of worship the included the Ark of the Covenant, and a Temple that He designed and He specifies every detail and it is here He comes and meets with His people. He provided Moses with over 600 laws He expected the people to follow. Some pertain to social behavior and others are dietary and others which only make sense to the Creator and He requests animal sacrifice.

One can only question at this point why the God of all ages would request animal sacrifice and such a peculiar set of laws to abide by. Animal sacrifice atoned for the people's sin. All of this foreshadowed the ultimate sacrifice—His Son who was born of a woman, in a manger, alongside the beds of animals. The men of His day reject and sentence Him to a brutal and cruel death for the most serious of offenders for no greater crime than stating that He was the Son of God. He was born in the most humble of places, lives as a man, and dies unjustly at the hands of His own creation, revealing the meek nature of this mysterious God. But, He rises from His death conquering it. All who put their trust in Him for their salvation and believe that He paid the penalty for their sin which is death will have eternal life and follow Him in the afterlife. He calls this the Gospel. God Himself calls this a foolish Gospel but refers to it as the power of God.

This God also chose to speak through eccentric prophets, some of whom took vows not to cut their hair and to eat only certain foods. While they forecasted His prophecies, these prophets spoke through seemingly bazaar symbolic actions that God commanded them to do.

We know from the prophet Isaiah that he witnessed the Lord sitting on a throne, and the train of His robe filled the Temple. Above the throne stood seraphim—six-winged angels, with two wings to cover their faces, two to cover their feet, and two for flying (Isaiah 6:2). He lives in the heavens, in a throne room with jeweled walls and giant winged creatures, and four faced beings surrounded by lighted wheels. His throne burns with fire and He shines brighter than the sun. He created beings called angels and one of those He created wanted to be like God and He cast him and all of his affiliates from heaven. This event caused the battle between good and evil, God and Satan which will culminate in the battle of Armageddon.

The Lion of the Tribe of Judah (Jesus) will defeat the roaring lion which walks to and fro from the earth seeking who he may devour. In this not fully understood battle lies the reason for all that is evil in this world.

This God who can part seas, bring fire down from heaven, raise the dead back to life, and perform all kinds of miracles, chooses to work through the natural order of events and requires faith as the prerequisite for pleasing Him as if knowing the difficulty of this for men and women. As Hebrews 11:6 states: *"Without faith it is impossible to please Him for he who comes to God must believe that He is and that He is a rewarder of those who diligently seek him."*

IT WILL SURELY COME

The figurative language of the prophets seems to belong to another world, and its way of looking at life is alien to our own, yet it is through this language that we have the end time prophecies.

Many scholars have tried to speculate on the future, based on both present and past events. During the Gulf War, some stated that terrorism would greatly increase, there would be thousands of US casualties, and the war would drag on like the one we fought in Vietnam. None of these predictions occurred. Others forecasted that the EU's economic union would fail. Concerning Islamic fundamentalism, there are a myriad of opinions. Some believe they will be responsible for the next world war. Others state that this is not even a remote possibility due to the various sects within the movement. The US Pentagon issued a report stating that the threat to America's future might come from Japan. One fact is sure, and that is that the major events that occurred in the past several years remained unforeseen. It seems that in the secular world the events one least expects are more likely to occur than what one anticipates.

The people to whom the prophets directed the predictions disregarded them in their time. The prophetic writings sometimes act at times as a general guide and in some passages a precise road map. When Jeremiah foretold the Babylonian invasion, the Israelites could not fathom its taking place, and did not listen to Jeremiah. False prophets predicted peace. Nevertheless the captivity of the Israelites occurred. Most men would not give a second thought to the idea that the threat to world peace will come from the EU. Not Europe, our allies! It is a mere economic grouping. Many individuals warn about the coming Tribulation. Unfortunately, as in the days of Jeremiah or Noah, most will not believe until the day that the EU, under the leadership of the Antichrist, unleashes its fury. Only then, no historians will comment on how the events that shook the world all came about; for along with these events come the culmination of the age and the second coming of Jesus Christ. It is a remote and distant reality that will never occur in their lifetime. Thus for all of these arguments, I will conclude with the Words of the Lord, out of Habakkuk 2:3: *"For the vision is yet for an appointed time, but at the end it will speak, and it will not lie: though it tarries, wait for it; because it will surely come it will not tarry."*

THE BIBLE'S MESSAGE OF HOPE

Bible prophecy presents frightening truths to the reader, but its message is not entirely one of doom and gloom. Believers in Jesus Christ will not go through the Tribulation. God will take them out of the world in the Rapture just before it begins. God provides a way out. His way offers refuge and eternal life.

God's gift of eternal life with Christ is simple to obtain, but few will take it. All men are sinners. Sin is anything that we say or do that does not bring glory to God. God is righteous, and the slightest sin within us makes us unrighteous in His sight. There is nothing in and of ourselves that we can do to obtain the favor of God. Isaiah 64:6 states: "*And all our righteousness are like filthy rags.*" God will not even accept one into heaven for his good works. Salvation is by faith alone. Ephesians 2:8-9 tells us: "*For by grace you have been saved through faith; and that not of yourselves: it is the gift of God: not of works lest anyone should boast.*"

But Romans 10:13 promises, "*For whoever calls upon the name of the Lord shall be saved.*" God promises eternal life to anyone who accepts Jesus Christ as his personal savior. John 5:24 states: "*Most assuredly, I say to you, He who hears My word, and believes in him who sent me, has everlasting life, and shall not come into judgment; but has passed from death into life.*" If you want to be sure that you are saved and that heaven will be your home, pray this simple sinner's prayer and mean it with all of your heart: "Oh God, be merciful to me as a sinner, I believe that Jesus died for my sins, and trust Jesus as my Lord and Savior. Thank you Lord Jesus for saving me."

He that believes in the Son has everlasting life: and he who does not believe the Son shall not see life; but the wrath of God abides on him.
(John 3:36)

ENDNOTES

CHAPTER 1

1. "The Deadliest Tsunami in History?, "*National Geographic News*, January 7, 2005, http://news.nationalgeographic.com /news/, Dan Fletcher, "Top Ten Deadliest Earthquakes," Time in partnership with CNN, January 13, 2010,http://www.time.com /time/specials/packages/article/0,28804,1953425_1953424,00.html,
2. Wikipedia contributors, "Timeline of the United States History (1990-present), *Wikipedia, The Free Encyclopedia*, http://en.wikipedia.org/w/index.php?title=Timeline_of_United_States_history_(1990-present)&oldid=326271835 (accessed November 12, 2009)
3. Avi Zenilman, "Eight Days That Shook The World," *The New Yorker*, September 14, 2009 http://www.newyorker.com/online/blogs/newsdesk/2009/09/eight-days-that-shook-the-world.html, see also Andrew Leonard, "The Day the Economy Almost Stopped," *How The World Works*, February 10, 2009, http://search.salon.com/salonsearch.php?breadth=salon&search=the+day++the+world+economy+almost+stopped
4. Seth Mydans, "Bullets and Crayons: Children Learn Lessons for 90s," *New York Times*, 16 June 1991.
5. American Survey, "Guns and Children in Schools Protection Racket," *Economist*, 30 November 1991.
6. William F. Buckley, "Guns and Children," *National Review*, 21 October 1991.
7. This figure was based on the numbers recorded in the following articles: Kerstin Witt, "Abortion in the Soviet Union," *World Press*, August 1989. See also Susan Greenhalgh, "Socialism and Fertility in China," *The Annals: World Population Approaching the Year 2000*, July 1990.
8. Donald E. Wilmon, *The Case Against Pornography*, Wheaton: Victor Books, 1986, p. 13.
9. Sara Rimer, "Crime Visits New York's Children and Dread Haunts Many Parents," *New York Times*, 19 January 1992.
10. Thomas W. Wedge, *Satan Hunter*, Canton: Daring Books, 1988, p. 196.]]
11. Wikipedia contributors, "Jim Jones," *Wikipedia, The Free Encyclopedia*, http://en.wikipedia.org/w/index.php?title=Jim_Jones&oldid=335808313 accessed December 5, 2009, Wikipedia Contributors, "Heaven's Gate (religious group)," *Wikipedia, The Free Encyclopedia*, http://en.wikipedia.org/w/index.php?title=Heaven%27s_Gate_(religious_group)&oldid=336632291(accessed December 5, 2009, Wikipedia contributors, "Aum Shinrikyo," *Wikipedia, The Free Encyclopedia*, http://en.wikipedia.org/w/index.php?title=Aum_Shinrikyo&oldid=333113722(accessed December 10, 2009
12. Ibid. pp. 13, 24-5, 63.

13. New World Encyclopedia Contributors, "Falun Gong," *New World Encyclopedia*, http://www.newworldencyclopedia.org/entry/Falun_Gong (accessed December 14, 2009), Wikipedia contributors, "Falun Gong," Wikipedia, The Free Encyclopedia, http://en.wikipedia.org/w/index.php?title=Falun_Gong&oldid=338626170(accessed December 15, 2009)
14. Joseph S. Nye, "What New World Order," *Foreign Affairs*, vol. 71, no. 2, Spring 1992.

CHAPTER 2

15. A good portion of this list is found in Dwight J. Pentecost, *Things to Come: A Study in Bible Eschatology*, Grand Rapids: Zondervan, 1971, p. 334.
16. Ibid. Dwight J. Pentecost, pp. 317, 319-323. See also Lehman Strauss, *Commentaries-Revelation*, New Jersey: Neptune, 1964, Loizeaux Brothers, 1985, p. 248.
17. William Smith L.L.D., *Smith's Bible Dictionary*, Thomas Nelson Publishers, 1979, pp. 715-718.
18. Will and Ariel Durant, *Our Oriental Heritage: The Story of Civilization 1*, New York: Simon and Schuster, 1963, pp. 227-229.
19. Stanley Hoffman, "The European Community and 1992," *Foreign Affairs*, Fall 1989, p. 33. See also Donald S. Zagoria, "The China Challenge: American Politics in East Asia," The Academy of Political Science, vol. 38, no. 2 (New York, 1991), p. 4.
20. Wikipedia contributors, "Dome of the Rock," *Wikipedia, The Free Encyclopedia*, http://wikipedia.org/w/index.php?title=Dome_of_the_Rock&oldid=331219660 (accessed January 2, 2010)
21. William L. Shirer, *The Rise and Fall of the Third Reich*, New York: Simon and Schuster, 1960, p. 43.
22. John F. Walvoord, *Daniel: The Key to Prophetic Revelation*, Chicago: Moody Press, 1971, p. 283.

CHAPTER 3

23. Op. Cit. Pentecost, p. 368.
24. Will Durant, *The Story of Civilization: I Our Oriental Heritage*, New York: Simon and Schuster, 1963, pp. 234-236, 244, 256, 258.
25. Op. Cit. Pentecost, pp. 365-367.
26. Op. Cit. Will and Ariel Durant, p. 240.
27. Elisa Carrillo, *Alcide de Gasperi: The Long Apprenticeship*, Notre Dame: University of Notre Dame Press, 1965, pp. 49, 149.
28. Merry and Serge Bromverger, *Jean Monnet and the United States of Europe*, New York: Coward McCann, 1969, pp. 84-89, 92. See also, Jean Monnet, "A Grand Design for Europe," European Documentation, Periodical 5/1988, Luxembourg: Office of Official Publications.
29. "A New Holy Roman Empire," *Economist*, 4 September 1993.
30. Op. Cit. Stanley Hoffman, p. 32.
31. "Churches Preparing for Major Role in New European Union," *United Methodist News Service*, June 1998.
32. The "See Change" Broadside #1, 27 March 2001, http://www.seechange.org/media/Broadside%20(March%20%27%202001).htm
33. State of the World, According to John Paul II, Address to the Diplomatic Corps Accredited to the Vatican, 13 January 2003, Zenit News Agency, http://www.zenit.org/english/visualizza.phtml?sid=29883,

34. United Press International, "Pope Seeks EU Recognition of Christian Roots," *Washington Times*, 24 January 2003, http://www.washingtontimes.com/world/20030124-41210892.htm,
35. Ian Paisley, M.P., M.E.P., "The Vacant Seat Number 666 in the European Parliament," 22 July 1999, http://www.ianpaisley.org/article.asp?ArtKey=666
36. The EU Must Keep Sunday, Says Catholic Church, the Trumpet.com November 18.2008 http://www.thetrumpet.com, "Pope says Europe needs Christian values to prosper, help others," Cindy Wooden, Catholic News Service, October 19, 2009, http://www.catholicnews.com
37. Wikipedia contributors, "European Union-Holy See relations," *Wikipedia, The Free Encyclopedia*,http://en.wikipedia.org/w/index.php?title=Europen_Unioin_%E2%80%93_Holy_See-relations&oldid=292976117(accessed November 12, 2009, see also http://en.wikipedia.org/wiki/Category:The_European_Union_and_the_Catholic_Church
38. Europe is in love with symbols but the reality is much more dull, Damian Chalmers" The Independent November 19, 2009 http://www.independent.co.uk/environment/, Israel & The Nations-Europe, The Madonna, The Anthem, The Tower of Babel, The Woman Riding A Beast, www.godspromisedland.com, Wikipedia contributors, "Symbols of Europe," *Wikipedia, The Free Encyclopedia,* http://en.wikipedia.org/w/index.php?title=Symbols_of_Europe&oldid=324684669 (accessed December 30, 2009), Wikipedia contributors, "Ode to Joy," *Wikipedia, The Free Encyclopedia,* http://en.wikipedia.org/w/index.php?title=Ode-to_Joy&oldid=326051031, (accessed December 30, 2009)
39. Op. Cit. Will and Ariel Durant, p.222.
40. Ian Harding, "France's Lost Souls Take the Mystic Path," *European*, 22-24 February, 1991.
41. "Divining Executive Talents," *Europe: Magazine of the European Communities*, October 1990, pp. 36-37.

CHAPTER 4

42. Richard Mayne and John Pinder, *Federal Union: The Pioneers: A History of Federal Union*, London: Federal Trust for Education and Research, 1990, pp. 3-4, 8-13, 23, 49, 51, 57, 62-63, 73, 76, 86, 109, 112-113, 119, 124. See also Benjamin B. Ferenez and Ken Keye, Jr., *Planethood: The Key to Your Future*, Coos Bay: Love Line Books, 1991, pp. 23, 35.
43. Wikipedia contributors, "World Federalist Movement," *Wikipedia, The Free Encyclopedia*, http://en.wikipedia.org/w/index.php?title=World_Federalist_Movement&oldid=331194908 (accessed January 19, 2010).
44. "Jean Monnet: A Grand Design for Europe," European Documentation, Periodical 5/1988, Luxembourg: Office of Official Publications of the European Communities, p. 7. See also Merry and Serge Bromverger, pp. 9-11, 224-225.
45. Op. Cit. Richard Mayne and John Pinder, pp. 112-113, 119, 124.
46. Op. Cit. "Jean Monnet: A Grand Design for Europe," pp. 5, 7.
47. Op. Cit. Richard Mayne and John Pinder, pp. 143-145, 210-212.
48. "Quotes," *EUROCOM Bulletin*, February 1991, p. 3.
49. "From Luxembourg to Maastricht, 100 Critical Days to Maastricht," Brussels: European Belmont Policy Centre, August 1991, p. 6.
50. Frans H.J.J. Andriessen, "The Integration of Europe: It's Now or Never" *European Affairs*, No. 6, December 1991, p. 7.
51. Publius II, "Introduction to World Federalism," Brussels: *New Federalist*, No. 2, 1992, p. 18.

52. Jim MacNeill, Pieter Winsemius, and Taizo Yakushiji, *Beyond Interdependence: The Meshing of the World's Economy and the Earth's Ecology*, New York: Oxford University Press, 1991, p. 4.
53. "GATT towards a New Round," European Community Economic and Social Committee, Brussels, Luxembourg: Office for Official Publications of the European Communities, 1986, pp. 14, 33.
54. "New Ways to Run the World," *Economist*, 9 November 1991.
55. Dennis Healy, "Pax Americana Is a Dangerous Illusion," *European Affairs*, August/September 1991, p. 44.
56. Lucio Levi, "Globalization and a World Parliament," *Federalist Debate*, Year XIV Number 2, Torino, Italy, July 2001.
57. Francesco Rossolillo, "European Federation and World Federation," *Federalist*, Year XLI, Number 2, Pavia, Italy, 1999.
58. Pat Buchanan, "The US of Europe Versus the US of A.," *New York Post*, 20 July 1991.

CHAPTER 5

59. "Quotes," *EUROCOM Bulletin*, four issues: June 1989, July/August 1989, July 1990, December 1990.
60. Jean-Claude Casanova, "Dealing with Europe: The Dream of the Wisemen," *European Journal of International Affairs*, 1991.
61. Edward Heath, "Britain and the European Community," *Mediterranean Quarterly*, vol. 1, no. 1, Winter 1990, p. 23.
62. Axel Krause, "1992's Impact on American Business Accelerates," *Europe Magazine*, June 1989.
63. Lester C. Thurow, "Europe Will Write the Rules of Trade," *European Affairs*, April/May 1991.
64. Leigh Bruce, "Europe's Locomotive," *Foreign Policy*, Spring 1990, pp. 69-70.
65. "Delors Delivers 'State of Community' Address," *EUROCOM Bulletin*, vol. 2, no. 2, February 1990.
66. "Quotes," *EUROCOM Bulletin*, October 1990.
67. Robert J. Guttman, "Interview: Valéry Giscard D'Estaing," *Europe Magazine*, May 1997.
68. Stephen Kinzer, "Kohl Calls the Path to European Unity Irreversible," *New York Times*, 14 December, 1991.
69. "Quotes," *EUROCOM Bulletin*, January 1992.
70. "EMU in Motion: 1878 vs. 1992," *Economist*, 22 April, 1989.
71. "Luxembourg: Use the ECU," *Europe Magazine*, November 1989.
72. Santer Sees Expansion to East Near Turn of Century," Reuters, 12 December, 1994. "Santer Says Single EU Currency by 1999 Is Essential," Reuters, 16 December, 1994. "Santer Says No Reason to Worry about French on EMU," Reuters Financial Report, 20 June, 1997. "Focus Davos US Officials See Solid Stable Euro," Reuters World Report, 31 January, 1998. "EU Sees euro Bolstering Global Political Clout," Reuters World Report, 30 January, 1998.
73. Klaus Engelen, "Why US Is Beginning to Worry about the Euro," *European*, January 9-15, 1997.
74. "Euro: An International Currency," *Federalist Debate*, Torino, Italy, Year XV, Number 1, March 2002.
75. "Dublin Summit," *Europe*, May 1990.
76. Bruce Barnard, "Making Sense of Maastricht," *Europe*, January/February 1992.
77. Feld, "European Political Cooperation," *Mediterranean Quarterly*, p. 79. See also European Political Cooperation (EPC), Luxembourg: 1988, p. 5.
78. "Europe: The Deal Is Done," *Economist*, 14 December, 1991, p. 51.

79. Alan Sked, "The Case Against the Treaty: Maastricht Made Simple," *European*, 1992, p. 27.
80. Margaret Thatcher, "It's Time to Walk Away from Europe," *Financial Times*, March 18, 2002.
81. For more on treaties see The European Constitution Website, which contains information on the various treaties, http://www.unizar.es/euroconstitucion/Home.htm, "Background Briefing: How the Treaty of Lisbon will make the EU more Democratic," *Federal Union*, December, 2007, "EU Constitution," *United Press International*, November 3, 2009, http://www.upi.com/Daily-Briefing/2009/11/03/EU-Constitution/UPI-62631257257635/ Article 1, The Treaty At A Glance, "On 13 December 2007, EU leaders signed the Treaty of Lisbon, thus bringing to an end several years of negotiation about institutional issues." http://europa.eu/abc/treaties/index_en.htm,Wikipedia contributors, "European Central Bank," *Wikipedia, The Free Encyclopedia*, http://en.wikipedia.org/w/index.php?title=European_Central_Bank&oldid=324222667 John Rummo, "Final signature acquired on the Lisbon Treaty,"November 4, 2009 http://www.worldmarketmedia.com/801/section.aspx/489/post/final-signature-acquired-on-the-lisbon-treaty, Rudolf Stohr, "The Growth and Evolution of the European Union," January 2008, Times of Malta.com, "Highlights of the Lisbon Treaty," October 20, 2007 http://www.timesofmalta.com/articles/view/20071020/local/highlights-of-the-lisbon-treaty,Wikipedia contributors, "Treaty establishing a Constitution for Europe," *Wikipedia, The Free Encyclopedia*, http://en.wikipedia.org/w/index.php?title=Treaty_establishing_a_Consitution_for_Europe&oldid=324178952
82. Robert Haslach, "The Western European Union: A Defense Organization in Search of a New Role," *Europe*, Jan/Feb 1991. See also Ian Davidson, "Building New Security Structures, View from Europe," *Europe*, Jan/Feb 1991. See also Seamus O'Clireac, "Long Term Implications of the Unified European Market: Birth of an Economic Superpower?" *Mediterranean Quarterly*, Fall 1990.
83. Assembly of the Western European Union, The Interim European Security and Defence Assembly, "Revising the European Security Concept—Responding to New Risks," Colloquy Berlin, 2-3 May 2001, Official Record, Office of the Clerk to the Assembly.
84. Bruno Waterfield, "Blueprint for EU army to be agreed," *Telegraph.co.uk*, February 18.2009, http://www.telegraph.co.uk/news/, EDA Background Information 2005-2009, *European Defense Agency*, http://www.eda.europa.eu/genericitem.aspx?area=Background&id=121 Stephan Nicola, "EU Dreams of Common Army," UPI Germany Correspondent, Berlin, March,27,2007,http://www.spacewar.com/reports/EU_Dreams_Of_Common_Army_999.html,Craig S. Smith, "Europeans Plan Own Military command Post" *The New York Times*, September 3, 2003,http://www.nytimes.com/2003/09/03/world/europeans-plan-own-military-command-post.html
"Italy's Foreign Minister says Post-Lisbon EU Needs a European Army, *The Timesonline.co.uk,* November 17, 2009, http://www.timesonline.co.uk/tol/news/world/europe/article6917652.ece Wikipedia contributors, "Military of the European Union," *Wikipedia, The Free Encyclopedia*, http://en.wikipedia.org/w/index.php?title=Military_of_the_European_Union&oldid=324939563,James Slack, Mathew Hickley, "Now all of our Armed Forces are on offer as part of an EU catalog" April 3, 2009 http://www.dailymail.co.uk/news/article-1167247/Now-Armed-Forces-offer-EU-catalogue.html, Wikipedia contributors, "Synchronized Armed Forces Europe," Wikipedia, The Free Encyclopedia, http://en.wikipedia.org/w/index.php?title=Synochronized_Armed_Forces_Europe&oldid=323985108 and also Wiki:Synchronized Armed Forces, *Wapedia,*

Bruno Waterfield, "Blueprint for EU Army to Be Agreed, Telegraph.co.uk, Brussels, February 18, 2009,
http://www.telegraph.co.uk/news/worldnews/europe/eu/4689736/Blueprint-for-EU-army-to-be-agreed.html
85. "Quotes," *EUROCOM Bulletin*, May 1991.see also Wikipedia contributors, "European Economic Area," *Wikipedia, The Free Encyclopedia*,
http://en.wikipedia.org/w/index.php?title=European_Economic_Area&oldid=324160492
86. "EU eyes Mediterranean free trade area by 2010" Eurativ.com, November 2005, http://www.euractiv.com/en/east-mediterranean/eu-eyes-mediterranean-free-trade-area-2010/article-149382
87. Guy Verhofstadt, "The Financial Crisis Three Ways Out for Europe," Gütersloh, November 2008
88. Barrosso: European Union is 'Empire' short version, EUXTV, July 10, 2007
Jose Manuel Barroso, Lisbon Treaty: What they Said: Jose Manual Barroso, *BBC.co.uk*, September 30, 2009
89. Leigh Bruce, "Europe's Locomotive," *Foreign Policy*, Spring 1990, p. 88.
90. EU-Forgotten Flag, AP, 24 March 1997.

CHAPTER 6

91. Op. Cit. European Union Treaty, p. 82.
92. "Europe: Rings-Doves and Openness," *Economist*, 22 August 1992.
93. Andrew Willis, "Eastern States Counter EU's Secretive Nomination Process, "*EU Observer*, November 13, 2009, http://euobserver.com/9/28985
94. Wikipedia Contributors, "European Commission," *Wikipedia, The Free Encyclopedia*,
http://en.wikipedia.org/w/index.php?title=European_Commission&oldid=325819644 (accessed December 6, 2009)
95. John F. Walvoord, "Prophecy Knowledge Handbook," Wheaton: Victor Books, 1990, pp. 268-270.
96. "Unknown Duo chosen as New Face of Europe," *Euranet: European Radio Network*, November 20, 2009
http://www.euranet.eu/eng/Archive/News/English/2009/November/Unknown-duo-chosen-as-new-faces-of-Europe
"Europe Unity Tested by Talk of President," Associated Press, November 15, 2009
Stephen Castle, Steven Erlanger, "Belgian Prime Minister Picked as European President" *International Herald Tribune*, November 19, 2009
97. Peter Ludlow, "Maastricht and the Future of Europe," *Washington Quarterly*, Autumn 1992, pp. 120, 124, 126.
98. "Treaty of Lisbon: Taking Europe Into the 21st Century: A More Democratic and Transparent Europe: , *Europa.eu*,
http://europa.eu/lisbon_treaty/glance/democracy/index_en.htm
Christopher Bollyn, "Estonians Wary of European Union," *American Free Press*, November 19. 2003, http://www.thetruthseeker.co.uk/article.asp?ID=1065
99. "World Affairs: Western Europe," *Encyclopedia Britannica*, p. 444. Stephen Prokesch, "Thatcher Will Leave the House of Commons but Plans to Keep Speaking Out," *New York Times*, 29 June, 1991. "Quotes," *EUROCOM Bulletin*, June 1996.
100. Maurice Duverger, "The Evolving European Parliament," *World Press Review*, September 1989, p. 32.
101. "Quotes," *EUROCOM Bulletin*, "August/September 1990.
102. Tony Benn Interview by Kent Worcester, "Europe's Democratic Defecit," *World Policy Journal*, Fall 1991, p. 741. See also George Ross, "After Maastricht," *World Policy Journal*, p. 507. See also Stephen Woddard, "The Lessons of the Vote in Denmark," *New Federalist*, March 1992, p. 3.

103. "From Luxembourg to Maastricht, 100 Critical Days to Maastricht," p. 46.
104. Alaine Lamassoore, "Three Houses, One Home," *European Affairs* October/November 1992, no. 5, p. 21.,
105. Wikipedia contributors, "President of the European Commission," *Wikipedia, The Free Encyclopedia,* http://en.wikipedia.org/w/index.php?title=President_of_the_European_Co mmission&oldid=325347588 (accessed December 15, 2009)
106. Wikipedia contributors, "Superstate, *"Wikipedia, The Free Encyclopedia,"* http:en.wikipedia.org/w/index.php?title=Superstate&oldid=325729983 (accessed January 5, 2010)
107. Op. Cit. Walvoord, pp. 70-71.
108. Op. Cit. Dwight Pentecost, pp. 319-320.
109. Richard Hay, "The European Commission and the Administration of the Community," European Documentation periodical 3/1989, Luxembourg: Official Publication of the European Communities, May 1989, pp. 21-22.
110. For more information see Wikipedia contributors "European Parliament," *Wikipedia, The FreeEncyclopedia,* http://en.wikipedia.org/w/index.php?title=European_Parliament&oldid =324812904(accessed December 9, 2009)
111. Wikipedia contributors, "High Representative for Common Foreign and Security Policy," *Wikipedia, The Free Encyclopedia,* http://en.wikipedia.org/w/index.php?title=High_Representative_for_Comm on_Foreign_and_Security_Policy&oldid=325763093(accessed December 6, 2009)
112. "European Parliament: The Appointment of the Commission President and the Rest of the Commission," *Europa.eu* http://www.europarl.europa.eu/parliament/public/staticDisplay.do;jsessionid=27BC70E7 D1F26252ED0CE49E68F1235F.node1?id=146&language=en
113. For additional commentary on EU institutions see Seth Elliot, "The European Parliament," *Europe*, June 1990, p. 8. See also "Talking Shop Become Hyper-Market," *Economist*, 1 February 1992, p. 50. See also *Europe*, November 1989, p. 40, and Emile Noel, *Working Together: The Institutions of the European Community*, Luxembourg, 1988, p. 38.For more on Court of Justice see Wikipedia contributors, "European Court of Justice," *Wikipedia, The Free Encyclopedia,* http://en.wikipedia.org/w/index.php?title=European_Court_of_Justice&old id=325957550(accessed December 10, 2009)
114. For more on see Wikipedia contributors, "Court of Auditors," *Wikipedia, The Free Encyclopedia,* http://en.wikipedia.org/w/index.php?title=European_Court_of_Auditors&o ldid=326156770 (accessed December 7, 2009)
115. For more on see Wikipedia contributors, "European Council," *Wikipedia, The Free Encyclopedia,* http:en.wikipedia.org/w/index.php?title=European_Council&oldid=324262 075(accessed December 6, 2009"What is the Difference Between the "Council" and the "European Council," *Folketinget.dk,* http://www.folkentinget.dk"Q&A What are the EU President and Foreign Policy Jobs," *Reuters* November 19, 2009, Valentina Pop, "New Treaty Will Not Create 'One Phone Number' for Europe," *EU Observer*, November 18, 2009 http://euobserver.com/9/29010
116. "European Union Institutions and other bodies," *Europa.eu,* http://europa.eu/institutions/index_en.htmWikipedia contributors, "Institutions of the European Union," *Wikipedia, The Free Encyclopedia,* http://en.wikipedia.org/w/index.php?title=Institutions_of_the_European_U nion&oldid=325971759 (accessed December 15, 2009)
117. Susan Anderson, "The Cloning of Human Beings" University of CT: August 10-15, 1998 Boston, http://www.bu.edu/wcp/MainBioe.htm

CHAPTER 7

118. "European Community from Atlantic to Where?" *Economist*, 30 August 1991. See also "From Luxembourg to Maastricht," p. 4. See also Wikipedia contributors, "Enlargement of the European Union, "*Wikipedia, The Free Encyclopedia*, http://en.wikipedia.org/w/index.php?title=Enlargement_of_the_European_Union&oldid+324890035(accessed November 30, 2009)
119. "Survival of the Fattest," *Economist*, 11 April 1992, p. 54. Bernard Cassen, "How Large Is Europe?" *European Affairs*, August/September 1991, no. 4, pp. 19-20. See also "Leading to a Community," *Eurocom*, September 1991, and *Economist*, 12 March, 1993.
120. "The European Daisy," *Crocodile: Letter to the Parliament of Europe*, Brussels, October 1992, Wikipedia contributors, "Crocodile Club," *Wikipedia, The Free Encyclopedia*, http://en.wikipedia.org/w/index.php?title=Crocodile_Club&oldid=317606870 (accessed February 5, 2010)
121. Report La Commission reporte l'ecamen de cu point a sa 1112eme reunion du z juillet 1992. "Europe and The Challenge of Enlargement," EC Commission, June 1992. "A New Partnership" #34-38.
122. Robert D. Hormats, "Redefining Europe and the Atlantic Link," *Foreign Affairs*," Fall 1989, pp. 80, 84. See also Gregory F. Treverton, "The New Europe," *Foreign Affairs*. America and the World, 1991-1992, p. 97.
123. "The Debate on the Structure of an Enlarged Europe," *Notre Europe*, 10 October 2000. See also Robert J. Gutman, Valéry D'Estaing, *Europe*, May 1997.
124. Guy Verhofstadt and 'The United States of Europe': The Eurozone as a new core Europe: Manifesto for a New Europe, *The Federal Trust for Education and Research*, London, January 2006,Guy Verhofstadt, "Crisis-busting I: "Only a new 'political core'can drive Europe forward again" *Europe's World*, Spring 2006 http://www.europesworld.org/NewEnglish/Home_old/Article/tabid/191/ArticleType/ArticleView/ArticleID/21046/CrisisbustingIOnlyanewpoliticalcorecandriveEuropeforwardagain.aspx
125. Olivier Vedrine, "Analyze: A "solid core" to build a political European Union"www.multipol.org, April 30, 2009
126. "Europe: The Sick Man of Europe," *Economist*, 9 May 1992.
127. "Europe Ways Round That Little Danish Inconvenience," *Economist*, 13 June, 1992. See also "How to Leave the Stage Gracefully," *European*, 13-19 June, 1996.

CHAPTER 8

128. Montague Summers, *The History of Witchcraft*, New Hyde Park, New York: University Books, 1956, p. 70.
129. Edward N. Luttwak, "From Geopolitics to Geo-Economics: Logic of Conflict, Grammar of Commerce," *National Interest*, Summer 1990, no. 20, pp. 17, 20-21.
130. Op. Cit. Stanley Hoffman, p. 33.
131. "STRIDE Science and Technology for Regional Innovation and Development in Europe," Commission of the European Communities, Luxembourg: The European Communities, November 1988, p. 11.
132. James C. Carlson, "Japan's America Bashers," *ORBIS* vol. 34, no. 1, Winter 1990, p. 92.
133. "Research and Technological Development Policy," European Documentation Periodical 1/1988, Luxembourg: The European Communities, pp. 18-19.
134. "Europe's Future Four Scenarios," Federalist Trust for Education and Research, London, 1991, pp. 15-16.
135. Wissee Dekker, "Redefining ESPRIT," *European Affairs*, Spring 1990, vol. 69, no. 2, p. 129. "EU Proposes Increased Research Funds," *Europe*, October 1989.

136. "ESPRIT: European Strategic Programme for Research and Development in Information Technology," Commission of the European Communities, Brussels, p. 3.
137. Paola Buonadonna, "Smart Cards Lighten Brussels' Pockets," *European*, 3-9 March, 1995. See also Barry Fox, "New Credit Cards Pass the Smart Test," 24-30 August, 1995, p. 10. George Cole, "Smart Ways to an Easy Life," *European*, 13-19 March, 1997. Sandra Smith, "Smart Card Offers a Passport to the Future," *European*, 17-23 March, 1995.
138. Op. Cit. Research Technological Development Policy, pp. 58-59.
139. "Visa Checks Out Cashless Idea," *European*, 8-14 April 1994. Tom Forester, *High-Tech Society: The Story of the Information Technology Revolution*, Cambridge: MIT Press, 1987, pp. 230-231. Richard Clutterbuck, "Eurocops and Euroterror," *European Affairs*, February/March 1991, pp. 16-17.
140. Tom Forester, p. 218. See also Herbert Unger, Nicholas Costello, "Telecommunications in Europe: European Perspective," Commission of the European Community, Luxembourg: The European Communities, 1988, p. 58.
141. "Europe's Electronic Rescue Plan," *New York Times*, 4 September 1992.
142. Penn Bullock, VeriChip's Merger With Credit Monitoring Firm Worries Privacy Activists, December 9,2009, http://www.wired.com/threatlevel/2009/12/positive_id/ Wikipedia contributors, "Verichip." *Wikipedia, The Free Encyclopedia*, http://en.wikipedia.org/w/index.php?title=Solomon&oldid=3334219083 accessed, November 25, 2009
143. Science Net: "Adaptive Brain Interfaces (ABI) - Reading Your Mind," http://www.sciencenet.org.uk/slup/CuttingEdge/Nov00/abi.html. Shield Healthcare: "Computer Chip offers hope to the paralyzed as European scientists unveil implant that can enable walking," http://www.shieldhealth.com/news-chip.html. "Adaptive Brain Interfaces (ABI) 28193," http://sta.jrc.it/sba/esprit/abi-esprit.htm. Quotes taken from Warren Brooks, "Computer Revolution Made Berlin Wall Ineffective Obsolete," *American Freedom Journal*, vol. 4, no. 1, December 1989/January 1990, p. 7.
144. Wikipedia contributors, "Solomon," *Wikipedia, The Free Encyclopedia*, http://en.wikipedia.org/w/index.php?title=Solomon&oldid=334219083(accessed November 20, 2009)

CHAPTER 9

145. *The European Community Pamphlet*, EC Information Service, Washington, D.C. Robert S. Guttman, "Letter from the Editor," *Europe*, April 1990, p. 8. Robert D. Hormats, "Redefining Europe and the Atlantic Link," *Foreign Affairs*, Fall 1989, p. 75. Axel Krause, "What Ever Happened to Bush's Europhoria?" *European Affairs*, June/July 1991, p. 45.
146. Reginald Dale, "December a Month of Diplomatic Activity," *Europe*, January/February 1990, pp. 35-37. "European Union a Call for US Support" and "Quotes," *Eurocom*, May 1991.see also Bertrand Benoit, "US 'will loose financial superpower status,' *Reuters*, September 25, 2008, http://uk.reuters.com/article/idUKLNE48O02G20080925
147. Horst Krenzler, "Toward Healthy and Open World Markets," *Europe*, December 1989, p. 16. Keith M. Rockwell, "On the Way Up," *Europe*, p. 68. "A New Europe, A New Atlanticism: Architecture for a New Era," Address by Secretary of State James Baker, III, to the Berlin Press Club, Stegenberger Hotel, Berlin, Tuesday, 12 December, 1989.
148. Carola Kaps, "Delors Proposes New Partnership with US" *Europe*, July/August 1989, p. 14.
149. "EU-Clinton," Associated Press, 3 December 1995. See also "US Sign Covenant for Tranatlantic Relations," Reuters, 3 December 1995. "Clinton Meets with EU Leaders in

Brussels," *Eurocom Bulletin*, January 1994, p. 1. The European Press Survey, vol. 1, issue 13, 27 July-August 1994.
150. The Council of the European Union, Brussels, "2009 EU-US Summit Declaration" November 4, 2009
151. Leon T. Hadar, "United States, Europe, and Middle East Hegemony," *World Policy Journal,* Summer 1991, p. 447.
152. Stephen Cooney, "The Impact of 1992: The New Europe: Revolution in East-West Relations," New York: Academy of Political Science, vol. 38, no. 1, 1991, p. 185.
153. C. Fred Bergsten, "The World Economy after the Cold War," *Foreign Affairs*, vol. 69, no. 3, Summer 1990, pp. 96-97. Zbigniew Brzezinski, "Selective Global Commitment," *Foreign Affairs*, vol. 70, no. 3, Fal 1991, pp. 18-19.
154. James Chase, "The Pentagon's Superpower Fantasy," *New York Times*, 16 March, 1992.
155. Walter Russell Mead, "Saul Amongst the Prophets: The Bush Administration and the New World Order," *World Policy Journal*, Summer 1991, pp. 407-409.
156. Lionel Barber, "The View From America," *Europe*, December 1990, p. 20.
157. Robert D. Hormats, *Europe Magazine,* November 1991, p. 27.
158. Dominique Moisi, "The US: An Anchor for Wary Europeans," *European Affairs*, December 1991. See also Dominique Moisi, "Europe is Coming of Age," *European*.
159. Edward Hugh, "US Fiscal Deficit Projected at 12.3% of GDP in 2009," "*FistfulofEuros,'*February 26, 2009, http://fistfulofeuros.net/afoe/economics-and-demography/us-fiscal-deficit-projected-at-123-of-gdp-in-2009/ Wikipedia contributors, "List of countries by current account balance," *Wikipedia, The Free Encyclopedia,* http://en.wikipedia.org/w/index.php?title=List_of_countries_by_current_account_balance&oldid=320301145 (accessed November 20, 2009)
160. Op. Cit. The Financial Crisis: Three Ways Out for Europe Guy Verhofstadt Wikipedia contributors, "Potential superpowers," *Wikipedia, The Free Encyclopedia,* http://en.wikipedia.org/w/index.php?title=Potential_superpowers&olddid=327137992 (accessed December 5,2009),Jeff Unger, "US No Longer Superpower, Now a Besieged Global Power, Scholars Say," May 8, 2008, http://news.illinois.edu/NEWS/08/0508superpower.html
161. Brad Bishop, "Quantative Easing and the US Dollar: Friends or Foes? Cayman Financial Review, October 5, 2009,http://www.compasscayman.com/cfr/cfr.aspx?id=6885
162. Paul Reynolds, "US Superpower Status is Shaken," BBC News, October 1, 2008, http://news.bbc.co.uk/2/hi/business/7645743.stm
163. Op. Cit. Bertrand Benoit, "US 'will loose financial superpower status, *Financial Times,* September 25, 2008 http://www.ft.com/cms/s/0/1d6a4f3a-8aee-11dd-b634-0000779fd18c.html?nclick_check=1 Wikipedia contributors, "Potential superpowers," *Wikipedia, The Free Encyclopedia,* http://en.wikipedia.org/w/index.php?title=Potential_superpowers&olddid=327137992 (accessed December 5,2009),Jeff Unger, "US No Longer Superpower, Now a Besieged Global Power, Scholars Say," May 8, 2008, http://news.illinois.edu/NEWS/08/0508superpower.html
164. Dick K. Nanto, "The Global Financial Crisis, Analysis and Policy Implications," Congressional Research Service, /CRS Report for Congress, www.crs.gov, July 10, 2009
165. Paul Craig Roberts, "The Dollar's Reserve Currency Role is Drawing to an end," *GlobalResearch.ca*, February 6, 2008, http://www.globalresearch.ca/index.php?context=va&aid=8021
166. c. Fred Bergstein, "The Dollar and The Deficits," Foreign Affairs, November/December 2009 http://www.foreignaffairs.com/articles/65446/c-fred-bergsten/the-dollar-and-the-deficits
167. Michael Murphy, "Heads Up on the Dollar Today: The World's Reserve Currency is Changing," March 25, 2009, http://seekingalpha.com/article/127730-heads-up-on-the-dollar-today-the-world-s-reserve-currency-is-changing, Wikipedia contributors, "Reserve

currency," Wikipedia, The Free Encyclopedia, http://en.wikipedia.org/w/index.php?title=Reserve_currency&oldid=337299725 (accessed December 21, 2009)

168. Vanessa Cross, "The Dollar vs. Euro: Can the Euro Replace Dollar as Dominate Foreign Reserve Currency," November 27, 2009, http://business-market-analysis.suite101.com/article.cfm/the_dollar_vs_euro, "euro could replace dollar as top currency-Greenspan," *Reuters*, September 17, 2009 see also "Dollar Days as Reserve Currency Are Numbered, "Gulf News: United Arab Emirates, September 1, 2009, http://www.highbeam.com/doc/1G1-206967328.html, Interview With LeMonde, "Jean-Claude Trichet, President of the ECB
conducted by Pierre-Antoine Delhommais and Arnaud Leparmentier
17 November 2009, http://www.ecb.int/press/key/date/2009/html/sp091117.en.html, Menzie Chinn, Jeffrey Frankel, "Will the Euro Eventually Surpass the Dollar as the Leading International Reserve Currency? NBER Working Paper No. 11510* Issued in August 2005, NBER Program(s) IFM, *The National Bureau of Economic Research,* http://www.nber.org/papers/w11510, "US dollar no longer a one-way bet," Reuters, Friday November 20, 2009
http://www.reuters.com/article/idUSTRE5AJ2ZT20091120Eric deCarbonnel, "Ten Major Threats Facing The Dollar in 2009" *IStockAnalyst*, January 2, 2009, http://www.istockanalyst.com/article/viewarticle/articleid/2919378,Peter Coy, "What Happens if Dollar Collapsed," *Business Week,* October 14, 2009, http://www.businessweek.com/magazine/content/09_43/b4152000801269.htm,Pan Pylas, Worries Rise About Dollar Slide-What do do? *Associated Press*, October 22, 2009,"Are We Headed for a New Global Currency," NRH117
http://www.youtube.com/watch?v=TPentlEhbAA, September 27, 2009,The Dollar vs. The Euro, *ForaTV,* February 11, 2009, *http://www.youtube.com/watch?v=l50qElHmcfk* "Who Saw the Crash Coming," The Federal Union Blog, August 20,2009, http://www.federalunion.org.uk/blog/2009/08/who-saw-crash-coming.html
169. Russia Dumps Dollar as Reserve Currency-Adopts Euro, Wednesday, May 20, 2009 *Washington's Blog http://georgewashington2.blogspot.com/2009/05/russia-dumps-dollar-as-reserve-currency.html* Edmund Andrews, "World Bank Sees Dollar Role Diminishing, *"New York Times*, September 28, 2009, http://www.nytimes.com/2009/09/29/business/economy/29dollar.html,Edmund Conway, "UN Wants New Global Currency to Replace Dollar," Telegraph.co.uk September 7, 2009, http://www.telegraph.co.uk/finance/currency/6152204/UN-wants-new-global-currency-to-replace-dollar.html
170. Op. Cit. "Euro could replace Dollar as top Currency-Greenspan,"
171. Dr. Guenter Burghardt, "EU-US Economic Relations in the Age of the Euro: An Indispensable Partnership" Delegation of the European Commission to the United States, November 20, 2003,See also European Central Bank home page http://www.ecb.int/home/html/index.en.html
172. Jon-Marc Simon, "The New World Monetary Order and the Need for an EU Foreign Monetary Policy, September 23, 2009, *"European Federalists" http://federalists.cafebabel.com/en/post/2009/10/07/The-new-world-monetary-order-and-the-need-for-an-EU-foreign-monetary-policy*
173. Guillermo de la Dehas, "Will the Euro Overtake The Dollar as Dominant Currency? http://www.europarl.europa.eu/document/activities/cont/200806/20080618ATT32194/20 080618ATT32194EN.pdf, June 18, 2008
174. Ferry Hoogendijk, "Japan: Friend or Foe," *European Affairs*, August/September 1991, no. 4, pp. 4-5. Peter Montagnon, "EC Spies Its Big Potential in the World Economy," *Financial Times*, January 1991.
175. "The Future League of Nations," *Economist*, 24 August, 1991, p. 56.

176. Eric Cox, "Inside the Beltway," *World Federalist*, Washington, vol. 16, no. 4, Autumn 1991, p. 5.

CHAPTER 10

177. Charles Isawi, "The Middle East in the World Economy: A Long Range Historical View," The Center for Comtemporary Arab Studies, Georgetown University, 1985, p. 13.
178. Shuomo Avineri, "The Impact of Changes in the Soviet Union and Eastern Europe," *Mediterranean Quarterly*, Winter 1991.
179. Garret Fitzgerald, "The Israeli-Palestinian Issue," A Report to the Trilateral Commission, New York, May 1990, pp. 36-37. See also Robert Shawn, "A Change of Dutch Heart," *Middle East International*, December 1991, p. 14.
180. Monica Borkowski, "Israelis and Arabs: The 44 Years of Rage and Hate," *New York Times*, October 1991.
181. Op. Cit. John v. Walvoord, pp. 37-38.
182. For chronological history see Monica Borkowski, "Israelis and Arabs: The 44 Years of Rage and Hate," *New York Times*, October 1991.
183. Israel Shahak, "Israel and Iraq: Establishing a Relationship," *Middle East International*, December 1993. See also Muhammad Hallaj, "The Americans Try to Catch Up," *Middle East International*, September 1993. "The Oslo Accord Text of the Declaration of Principles," *Middle East International*, September 1993.
184. Mark R. Levin, "Not So Fast," Mark R. Levin on Bush & Mideast, on National Review Online, 25 June 2002, http://www.nationalreview.com/levin/levin062502.asp. See also Jeff Jacoby, "The Road to War in the Mideast Since the Oslo Agreements," 2 April, 2002, http://www.science.co.il/Arab-Israeli-conflict/Articles/Jacoby-2002-04-04.asp.
185. Speech by Prime Minister Ariel Sharon at the Herzliya Conference Institute of Policy and Strategy, 4 December 2002, http://www.herzliyaconference.org.
186. Leon T. Hador, "The United States, Europe, and the Middle East," *World Policy Journal*, Summer 1991, vol. VIII, no. 3, p. 21.
187. Op. Cit. European Political Cooperation, pp. 10-11.
188. Op. Cit. Garrett Fitzgerald, pp. 5, 140.
189. Op. Cit. Stanley Hoffman, p. 39.
190. A.G. Shawky, "A Secure Middle East," *European Affairs*, August/September 1991, p. 48. See also "100 Critical Days," p. 77.
191. Leon T. Hador, p. 444. See also "The War Is Over," Reuters: Europe Magazine, March 1991, p. 32.
192. Thomas L. Friedman, "US Sees New Mideast Peace Momentum," *New York Times*, 12 May, 1991.
193. "Europe and Israel: Biting the Carrot," *Middle East International*, 14 June, 1991, p. 6.
194. Gianni de Michelis, "The Mediterranean after the Gulf War," *Mediterranean Quarterly*, Summer 1991, vol. 2, no. 3, pp. 3-5.
195. Shada Islam, "Europe: Pressure from Baker," *Middle East International*, 11 October, 1991, pp. 5-6.
196. Shada Islam, "Aid for Palestinians," *Middle East International*, 6 December, 1991, p. 7. See also "100 Critical Days," p. 74. De Michelis, p. 7. Yezid Savigh, "Security and Cooperation in the Middle East: A Proposal," *Middle East International*, 10 July 1992, p. 16. Martin Kohler, "The Italian Search for Mediterranean Security," *Mediterranean Quarterly*, Fall 1991, p. 51.
197. Shada Islam, "The Shape of the Aid Plan," *Middle East International*, 8 October 1993, p. 7. See also "CFSP Statement on the Palestinian Elections," Reuters, 23 January, 1996. Paul Taylor, "EU Shut Out of Washington Summit, Invites Arafat," Reuters, 30 September, 1996. Jeremy Gaunt, "EU Wants to Be More Than Bankroller in Middle East," 7 October 1996. Miral Fahmyu, "France Says Time Ripe for Europe Role in

Mideast," Reuters, 13 December 1996. Paul Taylor, "Chirac Says EU Must Co-Sponsor Mideast Talks," Reuters, 19 October 1996. Jonathan Wright, "EU Refused to Be Mere Paymaster in Mideast-Italy," 21 October 1996. David Fox, "EU Increases Pressure for More Say in Middle East," 21 October 1996. Nashwa Hanna, "Egypt's Mubarak Meets European Team," 11 November 1996.
198. "EU draws Applause with Mideast Land-for-Peace Plea," Reuters 12 November 1996. Alister Doyle, "US, Israel Said Amenable to EU Middle East Role," Reuters 9 January 1997. "France Ready to Send Troops for Mideast Peace," 13 February 1997. Nicholas Doughty, "Hebron Deal Shows US Role Despite EU Ambition," Reuters, 15 January 1997. "Peace Talks Must Be Based on Land-For-Peace," Reuters, 17 January 1997. "EU Envoy Wants to Alter Mideast Peace Formula," Reuters 6 March 1997. Gillian Handyside, "EU Parliament Slams Israel over New Settlements," Reuters, 13 March 1997. "EU Urges Palestinian State Option," Reuters World Report, 17 June 1997. Khaled Abu Aker, "EU Asserts Palestinian Rights," Reuters, 12 November 1997. Issam Hamza, "EU Team Offers Syria Ideas to Activate Peace Talks," Reuters, 13 November 1997. "EU Proposes Joint Mideast Peace Bid with US", Reuters, 8 April 1997. "US Stresses Its Central Role in Mideast Peace," Reuters, 9 April 1997.
199. Jonathan Wright, "Europe Puts Foot in Door of Mideast Diplomacy," Reuters, 17 April 1997. Draft Treaty Amsterdam, Presidency Conclusions, Annex III European Call For Peace in the Middle East. David Fox, "EU Hopes to Bring Arafat and Levy Face to Face," Reuters, 22 July 1997.
200. "EU Urged to Review Aid to Mideast Peace Process," Reuters World Report, 16 January 1998. "Europe Wants Greater Mideast Role," United Press International, 17 January 1998.
201. "The EU and the Middle East Peace Process—The Union's Position and Role," http://europa.eu.int/comm/external_relations/mepp/index.htm.,Slobodan Lekic "EU: Jerusalem should Be Joint Capital," *Associated Press* December 8, 2009
Leon Hadar, "EU Expansion to Israel and Palestine,"*Atlantic-Community.Org,* February 25, 2008, http://atlantic-community.org/index/articles/view/EU_Expansion_to_Israel_and_Palestine
European Commission: Trade: Israel, http://ec.europa.eu/trade/creating-opportunities/bilateral-relations/countries/israel/
202. "The EU's Mediterranean & Middle East Policy-Overview," http://europa.eu.int/comm/external_relations/med_mideast/intro/index.htm.
"The European Union & Policy," *Delegation of the European Commission to the State of Israel* www.delist.ec.europa.com (accessed January 15, 2010)
203. Laeken Declaration, "Declaration of the Situation in the Middle East," p. 30. Gerald M. Steinberg, "The European Union and the Middle East Peace Process."Jerusalem Center for Public Affairs, November 15, 1999, http://www.jcpa.org/jl/vp418.htm
204. "President Bush Meets with European Leaders," 2 May 2002.
205. Guido Montani, "A European Initiative for Peace in the Middle East," *Federalist Debate*, Torino, Italy, July 2002, Year XV, no. 2, pp. 14-15.
206. "Denmark to Unveil New Mideast Peace Plan," 28 August, 2002.
207. "US, UN, Russia, EU Discuss Road Map to Mideast Peace," 20 December, 2002.
208. T*he Middle East and Europe: The Search for Stability and Integration*, ed. Gerd Nonneman, London: Federalist Trust for Education and Research, 1993.
209. Amos Perlmutter, "Israel's Dilemma," *Foreign Affairs*, Winder 1989/90, p. 121.
210. Pierre Lellouche, *European Journal of International Affairs*, Winter 1990, p. 125
211. Michael Shtender, "Israel and the EU: A Path to Peace," Century Foundation, November 3, 2005,http://www.tcf.org/list.asp?type=NC&pubid=1129
Robbie Sabel, "Israel Should Become a Member of the Council of Europe," Jerusalem Center for Public Affairs,

http://www.jcpa.org/JCPA/Templates/ShowPage.asp?DRIT=6&DBID=1&LNGID=1&TMID=111&FID=253&PID=0&IID=1824&TTL=Israel_Should_Become_a_Member_of_the_Council_of_Europe

212. "Santer Says Europe Seeks Greater Role in Middle East," *Reuters*, 7 February 1998.

CHAPTER 11

213. Benjamin R. Barber, "Global Multiculturalism and the American Experiment," *World Policy Journal*, Spring 1993, p. 49
214. "Going to Extremes," *Newsweek*, 26 January 1996.
215. Richard Black, "Earth-Melting in the heat? BBC News, May 18, 2007, http://news.bbc.co.uk/2/hi/science/nature/4315968.stm
216. "Quotes," *European*, 2 July-1 August 1993.

INDEX

A

Ancient Biblical Persons, Places & History
    Alexander the Great · 55
    Babylon · 23, 28, 31- 35, 37, 45-47, 49, 55- 57, 108-109, 133, 147, 167
    Babylonian · 9, 15, 26, 32, 35, 46-47, 55, 109, 177, See Babylonia
    Cyrus · 16, 35
    Darius · 35
    Eden · 30
    Edomites · 29
    Herod · 36, 37
    Medes and Persians · 26, 28, 32
    Medina · 37
    Nebuchadnezzar · 28-29, 32, 35, 37, 57, 101, 108, 131
    Persia · 101, 167
    Phoenicians · 29
    Queen of Sheba · 131
    Roman Empire · 11, 28- 29, 32, 34, 57, 76-77, 88-90, 101, 115, 118, 120
    Sodom and Gomorrah · 16, 18, 43
    Tyre · 24, 29- 31
    Tyrian purple · 29
    Tyrus · 29, 31-34
    Will and Ariel Durant · 47
    Will Durant · 46
Antichrist/Satan · 9, 11, 13, 19, 21, 23- 26, 28- 32, 34- 35, 37- 42, 45, 47- 49, 57-58, 67, 70, 72, 82, 87, 89-100, 105, 107-109, 113, 117- 119, 123- 124, 126- 131, 146-149, 163, 165-169, 172-173, 177
    Anton Szandor LaVey · 19
    Baal · 47
    Beast · 24, 27, 36, 41- 42, 47-49, 53-54, 59, 91, 96, 101, 108, 117, 123, 126, 127- 131, 133, 173
    Cross of Nero · 19
    Devil · 10, 23-24, 91, 123, 131, 168
    Dragon · 24, 90, 107
    False Prophet · 24, 30, 42, 107, 108
    King of Babylon · 31, 46
    Lucifer · 24, 31-32
    Molech · 15
    Montague Summers · 121
    Occultists · 19, 108
    Satan · 19, 24- 25, 29-31, 42, 90, 92, 121-123, 131, 173, 176
    Satanism · 19, 39, 121
    Satanists · 19-20, 24
    Six hundred and sixty six-666 · 24-25, 53, 123, 131
    The Satanic Bible · 19
    Unholy trinity · 24, 35

B

Biblical Prophets · 43
    2 Timothy · 20
    Amos · 166
    Daniel · 11- 12, 15-16, 24-26, 28, 31, 34- 41, 49, 57, 89, 91- 92, 94-95, 97-98, 101-102, 104, 108-109, 113, 117, 147, 154, 169
    Ezekiel · 29, 32, 34, 37, 39, 46, 121, 150
    Habakkuk · 17
    Hosea · 36, 45
    Isaiah · 31, 34, 39-40, 48, 168, 176, 178
    Jeremiah · 9, 15, 29, 31, 36, 40, 47, 57, 109, 133, 147, 177
    Joel · 18, 29-30, 38, 40
    John · 12, 24- 25, 29, 41, 43, 52, 91, 102, 107, 113, 140, 151, 178
    Mark · 16, 36, 38, 40- 41, 93, 108, 123, 126-131, 173
    Matthew · 17, 19, 38- 39, 171- 173
    Revelation · 12, 25, 27, 29, 32, 39-- 42, 45- 49, 53, 55-57, 90- 93, 96, 98, 102, 107, 113, 121-123, 131
    Zechariah · 35, 38, 149
    Zephaniah · 40

C

Commentators
   Alan Sked · 79
   Andrew Crockett · 77
   Ben-Simon · 154
   Charles H. Keathing, Jr · 18
   Cornelius van der Klugt · 73
   David Barton · 63
   Dominique Moisi · 139
   Donald E. Wildmon · 18
   Edgar Savisaar · 100
   Edward N. Luttwak · 125
   Fred Bergsten · 77· 142
   Garret Fitzgerald · 156
   George Mitchell · 90
   John Gray · 140
   Joseph S. Nye, Jr · 21
   Lester C. Thurow · 74
   Maurie Duverger · 99
   Michael Murphy · 142
   Michael Sctender-Auerbach · 167
   Paul Craig Roberts · 141
   Pat Buchanan · 72, 137
   Peter Linton · 74
   Peter Ludlow · 96
   Professor de Wijk · 84
   Professor Igor Grazin · 101
   Rolf Parve · 101
   Samuel Huntington · 73
   Savissar · 101
   Shireen Hunter · 160
   Stanley Hoffman · 51, 87
   Tina Anselmi · 172
   Vanessa Cross · 143
   Walter Russell Mead · 138
   William F. Buckley · 18
   Zbigniew Brzezinski · 138
Comspiracy Theories · 9-10, 59
   Bildeburgers · 9, 59
   Illuminati · 9, 59
   Rothschild's · 9
   Trilateral Commission · 9, 59, 156
Cults
   Aleph · 19
   Charles Manson · 19
   Comet Hale-Bopp · 19
   False prophets · 16
   Falun Gong · 20
   Heaven's Gate · 19
   Jim Jones · 19
   Li Hongzhi · 20

E

EU Institutions and Bodies
   Council of Defense Ministers · 85
   Council of Europe · 55, 70, 73, 82, 92, 136
   Council of Ministers · 53,65, 78, 92-93, 95- 97, 100, 102-104, 106, 114, 118, 125
   Court of Justice · 51, 92, 97, 99, 105, 110
   EU Commission · 51-52, 62, 64, 66, 69, 75, 79-80, 87-89, 92, 94-95, 100, 102-109, 113, 115-116, 118-119, 125-127,130, 134-135, 144,160-161, 163, 169, 172
   EU High Representative · 95
   European Council · 63, 81, 85, 99, 106, 107, 114, 119, 135, 162, 163
   European Data Protection Supervisor · 107, 110
   European Investment Fund · 107, 110
   European Ombudsman · 107, 110
   European Personnel Selection · 107, 110
   High Representative for Common Foreign and Security Policy · 80, 82
   High Representative of the Union for Foreign Affairs · 104
   Office and the European Administrative School · 107
   Office for Official Publications of the European Communities · 107
   Parliament · 51, 53, 55, 75, 80- 81, 85, 89, 91-92, 95- 97, 99, 100, 103- 104, 105, 114, 133, 137, 156, 160
   Superstate · 80, 88, 99, 101, 137
   The Charter of Fundamental Rights · 82
   The Council of the European Union · 85, 94, 97, 106, 113, 119, 127
   The Court of Auditors · 106
   The Economic and Social Committee · 107, 110
   The European Central Bank · 92, 144, 145
   The European Investment bank · 107

EU US Bodies
  The Washington Delegation of the
    European Communities · 12
EU Military
  European Defense Community (EDC) · 83
  Petersberg tasks · 85
  Political and Security Committee · 84
  Synchronized Armed Forces Europe
    (SAFE) · 85
  Western European Armaments Group
    (WEAG). · 85
  Western European Armaments
    Organization (WEAO) · 85
  Western European Union · 83, 136
  WEU · 83, 85, 136
EU Nations & Cities
  Austria · 65, 83, 86-87, 113
  Belgium · 51, 61, 89, 99, 113
  Bonn · 118, 136, 138
  Breda · 84
  Britain · 59, 64, 70, 82-83, 89, 95
  Brussels · 12, 53, 66, 74, 83, 85, 87, 89,
    93-94, 96, 99, 101, 106, 118, 130,
    138, 146, 160, 166
  Bulgari · 65
  Bulgaria · 113
  Capitoline Hill · 51, 62
  Cologne · 83
  Copenhagen · 76
  Cyprus · 65, 113
  Czech Republic · 65, 83, 113
  Denmark · 64, 113, 117-118
  Dublin · 78
  EFTA · 86-87, 121, 127
  Estonia · 65, 100- 101, 113
  Finland · 65, 83, 86- 87, 113
  France · 50-51, 56, 61, 76, 78, 89, 99,
    113, 130
  Germany · 50, 51, 56, 61, 71, 75, 78, 83,
    113, 135, 138, 145, 147
  Greece · 26, 47, 64, 83, 95, 113, 117-118
  Hungary · 65, 83, 113
  Ireland · 64, 113
  Italy · 47, 50-51, 61, 71, 86, 113, 159,
    163
  Laeken · 81-82, 162
  Latvia · 65, 113
  Lithuania · 65, 113
  London · 12, 61, 83, 136, 140, 145

  Lorraine · 51
  Luxembourg · 51, 61, 83, 86, 89, 105,
    113, 156- 157, 159
  Maastricht · *See* EU Treaties
  Madrid · 76
  Malta · 65, 113
  Marseille · 85
  Member States · 11, 33, 51, 64- 65, 69,
    77, 79, 81-82, 84, 93, 95, 97, 99, 103-
    105, 114, 116, 118-119, 121, 167
  Messina, Sicily · 62
  Netherlands · 51, 61, 78, 113, 157
  Poland · 65, 82-83, 113, 138
  Portugal · 64, 113
  Prague · 87
  Romania · 65, 113
  Rome · 51, 62, 76, 78, 89, 92, 94, 103,
    105, 117-118, 167
  Slovakia · 65, 113
  Slovenia · 65
  Spain · 64, 113, 145, 159
  Sweden · 65, 83, 86-87, 113, 138
  The Hague · 76
  United Kingdom/UK · 113, 143, 145
EU Leaders & Bureaucrats
  Alcide de Gasperi · 50- 51
  Catherine Ashton · 95
  Charles Haughey · 78
  David Martin · 100
  Dennis Healy · 70
  Edward Heath · 74
  Emilio Columbo · 80
  Fernard Braun · 62
  Franco Frattini · 86·
  François Mitterrand · 73, 76, 79, 83
  Franz Anderiessen · 66
  Jean Monnet · 60-63
  G. Amato · 81
  Gianni de Michelis · 157-158
  Guenter Burghardt · 144
  Guillermo de la Dehesa · 145
  Guy Verhofstadt · 88, 94, 116, 140
  Helmut Kohl · 73, 76
  Helmut Schmidt · 33, 125
  Herman van Rompuy · 95
  Jacques Atali · 139
  Jacques Delors · 51, 69, 75, 79, 99, 115,
    134
  Jacques Poos · 83, 156

Jacques Santer · 77, 169
Jean-Luc Dehaene · 81
Joschka Fischer · 115
Jose Manuel Barroso · 88
Konrad Adenauer · 50
Margaret Thatcher · 82, 99, 137
Paul-Henri Spaak · 55, 61· 91
Peer Steinbruck · 141
Per Stig Moeller · 163
Romano Prodi · 162
Robert Schuman · 50- 51
Roland Dumas · 158
Jacques Santer · 77, 169, 170
Tony Benn · 100
Vaira Vike-Freiberga · 93
Valéry Giscard d'Estaing · 64, 76, 81,115
EU Symbols
   EU Flag · 54, 89
   Europa · 55, 102
   Motto · 89, 103
   National anthem · 33, 89
   Shuman Day · 89
EU Trade & Finance
   Bank for International Settlements (BIS) · 77
   Completing the Internal Market · 64
   Common Market · 11, 33, 34, 51, 62, 74, 76-77, 118, 134, 146
   Euro · 11, 53, 55, 77- 78, 81-82, 86- 87, 115, 142- 145, 159-160, 167, 172, 174
   European Central Bank · *See* EU Institutions
   European Currency Unit (ECU) · 77
   European monetary system (EMS) · 76-77, 138
   Exchange rate mechanism (ERM) · 76-77
   German Bundesbank · 77, 107
   Monetary union · 11, 65, 76- 78, 172
   Schengen · 86, 118
   Xiang Huaicheng · 78
EU Treaties
   Amsterdam Treaty · 80, 82, 85, 118, 160
   Committee of the Regions · 80, 107, 110
   Common Foreign and Security Policy · 84- 85, 93
   Constitutional Treaty of the European Union · 53
   Council at Nice · 84
   European European Steel and Coal Community · 11
   EU Constitution · 53
   EURATOM · 51, 62
   European Coal and Steel Treaty · 61
   European Constitution · 82
   Lisbon Treaty · 65, 82, 85- 86, 88, 92, 97, 104, 106, 116
   Maastricht Treaty · 78- 80, 93, 106 118
   Rome Treaties · 62
   Schengen accords · 86
   Schuman Declaration · 50, 66
   The Laeken Declaration · 81
   The Nice Treaty · 81, 85
European Publications · 12
   BBC · 140
   Crocodile · 114
   Europe: Magazine · 12
   European Affairs · 12, 100, 115
   Financial Times · 139-141
   L'Express · 99
   New Federalist · *See* Political Ideology:Federalism
   Stern · 143
   The European · 12, 79
   The European Journal of Internaitional Affairs· 166

F

Financial Markets/Global
   Financial crash · 17
   Financial crisis · 13, 139-142
   Financial markets · 17, 68, 144-145
   Global reserve currency · 78, 140
   Great Recession · 68, 138-140, 142, 147
   Quantative easing · 140

H

Historical Events
   Al Qaeda · 171
   Berlin · 17, 21, 61, 74- 75, 84, 87, 134, 138, 150

Berlin Wall · 17, 21, 74-75, 87, 134, 138, 150
Bretton Woods · 70
Charles de Gaulle · 74
Cold War · 17, 33, 69, 73-75, 83, 125, 148, 150
Constantine · 47, 55
Emperor Charles V · 77
Empire of Charlemagne · 115
French Revolution · 49
G7 summits · 76
Gulf Crisis · 75, 83
Gulf War · 11, 137,-139, 153, 177
Hiroshima · 16, 61
Hitler · 39, 57, 63, 108, 147, 173
Holocaust · 150
Marshall Plan · 133, 138, 157, 163
Mussolini · 63, 173
Nagasaki · 61
Second World War · 139, 141
September 11, 2001 · 129, 171
Suez Canal · 151
Warsaw pact · 83
World War II · 11, 50, 57, 68, 70, 74, 131, 148

I

Israel · 9, 15, -16, 24, 30, 35,-40, 42, 45, 47, 55, 57, 83, 87, 89, 95, 113, 121- 121, 131, 147, 149-155, 157---160, 162-163, 164--169, 175
Abraham · 150
Ark of the Covenant · 38, 175
Ezra · 37
Hanukkah · 37
Jericho · 15
Jerusalem · 11, 16, 28, 36- 42, 57-58, 89, 121, 147, 149, 151-154, 160, 164
Jewish Temple · 9, 36, 147, 149
Judea · 37, 39
Knesset · 156, 167
Law of Moses · 38
Levitical priests · 38
Maccabees · 37
Second Temple · 11, 37
Solomon · 15, 29, 36- 38, 131, 150
Zionism · 152

Zionist · 150
Middle East /Israeli Peace
Middle East · 17, 25, 57, 75, 81, 83, 89-90, 135-136, 143, 149, 152- 153, 155-163, 164-165, 169-172
Abdel Nasser · 151
Anwar el-Sadat · 152
Arab/Israeli peace process · 153
Arab-Israeli conflict · 155, 165
Arab League Summit · 164
Arafat · 153-155, 159-160
Ariel Sharon· 154-155, 164, 169
Beirut· 152
Conference Security Cooperation MiddleEast/CSCM · 166
Declaration of Principles· 154
Dome of The Rock· 36-37
Ehud Barak · 154-155
Ehud Olmert· 164
Eretz Yisrael· 36,
EU Special Envoy for the Peace Process · 161
EU Troika · 161
EU-Israel Association Agreement· 162
Fourth Herzliya Conference · 164
Gaza · 151, 153- 154, 159, 164
Gaza Strip · 151, 153, 164
Golan Heights · 151-153
Hamas · 162, 164
Hosni Mubarak · 164
Islamic Jilhad · 162
Israeli-Arab Peace Conference · 75
King Hussein · 152- 153
King Abdullah · 164
Mahmoud Abbas · 164
Mediterranean Free Trade Area · 87, 159
Oslo 2 · 154
Oslo Accords · 153-154, 164
Peace process · 135-136, 153-154, 157-162, 160-161, 165, 169-170
Palestine · 150, 152, 154, 157, 162-163
Palestinian · 87, 151- 157, 159- 166, 169
Palestinian Liberation Organization/PLO · 151, 152
Palestinians · 153-154, 158, 160- 161, 163, 167, 169

President Nasser · 152
Quartet · 136, 163-165
Roadmap for Peace ·164
The Peace Valley plan · 165
Russian Federation · 164
Samaria · 164
Sharm el-Sheikh Summit · 164
Shimon Peres · 165
Sinai Desert · 150
Sinai Peninsula · 151
Taba Talks · 155
Temple · 36- 38, 55, 154, 173, 175
Temple Mount Faithful · 36
West Bank · 150-151, 153- 154, 159, 164
Yasir Arafat · 152
Yitzahak Rabin · 153
Yom Kippur · 152

N

Nations, Continents & Cities
    Afghanistan · 81
    Africa · 136
    Asia · 26, 138, 140- 141, 144
    Brazil · 127, 140, 143
    Cairo · 151
    Canada · 33, 68, 127, 144
    China · 13, 17, 20, 34, 41, 78, 83, 101, 140, 143- 144, 147
    Egypt · 26, 47, 57, 87, 151- 152, 162
    Euphrates · 40, 41, 58, 150
    Geneva · 152
    Iceland · 83, 86, 87, 121
    Indian Ocean · 16, 17
    Iran · 155, 159, 171
    India · 34, 101, 104, 127, 140, 143
    Iraq · 11, 150-151, 171
    Japan · 13, 73- 74, 76, 88, 125- 127, 138, 139, 146, 177
    Jordan · 87, 150-153, 162, 164
    Kosovo · 84, 121
    Lebanon · 87, 150- 153, 162, 165, 169
    Libya · 87
    Liechtenstein · 87, 121
    Mecca · 36, 37
    Mexico · 33, 127
    Morocco · 69, 87, 121, 159
    North Africa · 57, 83
    North Korea · 171
    Norway · 83, 86-87, 121, 153, 154
    Riyadh · *See* Israel:Middle East
    Russia · 40, 83, 86- 87, 121, 140, 143- 144, 163
    Russian Federation · 136
    Saudi Arabia · 150
    Singapore · 144
    Soviet Union · 18, 57-58, 63, 65, 73-74, 88, 93, 99- 101, 113, 141, 147-148, 150- 151, 157-159
    Switzerland · 86, 121
    Syria · 26, 87, 150- 153, 155, 159, 162, 167
    Taiwan · 144
    Tokyo · 19
    Tunisia · 87
    Turkey · 83, 87, 12
    USSR · 83
Natural Disasters · 16, 74, 90, 174
    Earthquake · 13, 17, 37, 40
    Earthquakes · 16, 23, 41, 172-174
    Famines · 16, 23, 172
    Haiti earthquake · 13, 16
    Hurricane · 13, 17, 139
    Hurricane Katrina · 17
    Hurricanes · 16
    Pestilences · 16, 172
    Sichuan Province · 17
    Tornadoes · 16
    Tsunami · 16-17
New World Order · 17, 21, 59, 72, 74-75, 88, 139
    Barcelona Declaration · 87
    European Economic Space · 86
    European Free Trade Association · 86, 127
    Global currency · 143, 174
    Globalization · 67
        Earth Summit · 68, 69
    Mediterranean Free Trade Area (EMFTA) · 87
    New monetary world order · 145
    The Eastern Partnership · 87
    The European Bank for Reconstruction and Development · 139

P

Political Ideologies
  Anti-Federalist League · 79
  Anti-fascist · 50
  Christian Democratic · 49, 50, 51
  Christian democracy · 51
  Communism · 48, 50, 66, 75, 88, 148, 150
  Communist · 99, 133, 138, 148, 150
  Federalism · 59, 67
  Fascism · 50, 173
  Green parties · 56
  Mother Earth · 56, 60
  Nationalism · 63, 66, 75
  Socialism · 51
  Socialist · 49
  Totalitarianism · 60
Political Ideology: Federalism
  Altiero Spinelli · 62
  Democratic World Federalists · 60
  European federalism · 64
  European federation · 51, 59, 61,71
  Federal Union · 60, 61, 64
  Federal Union Manifesto · 59
  Joan-Marc Simon · See Commentators
  Lionel Robbins · 60
  Pax Universalis · 66
  Sovereign state · 60
  The Federalist Debate · See European Publications
  The Round Table · 59
  World Community · 63
  World Federalist Association · 60
  World Federalists · 60- 61, 66
  World federation · 60-61, 63, 67, 69, 71-72
Political Union · 11, 34, 74- 76, 78, 80- 81, 89, 104, 113, 116
  Avant garde · 116
  Political core · 116-119, 146, 173
  European Political Cooperation (EPC) · 79
  European Single Act · 65
Prophetic Terms
  144,000 witnesses · 42-43, 121
  70 weeks · 16
  Antichious Euphrates · 36
  Armageddon · 15, 23, 30, 40- 41, 45, 58, 147-148, 176
  As Was the Time of Noah · 15
  Covenant of Death · 39, 162, 166-167
  Covenant with death · 39, 168
  Elijah and Elisha · 42, 108
  Eternal life · 175- 176, 178
  False prophet · 9, 24, 35, 40, 44, 49
  Four beasts · 26
  Fourth beast · 26- 28, 117
  Four horsemen · 39
  Great Tribulation · 15-16, 43
  Great Whore · 45, 47- 48
  Latter days · 37, 57, 88
  Little horn · 91- 92, 94, 117
  Lot · 16- 18, 20, 43, 172
  Moses and Elijah · 42
  Noah · 16- 17, 20, 43, 172, 177
  Number of his name · 98, 123, 131
  Rapture · 16, 43
  Second Coming · 19, 21, 23
  Seven heads · 27
  Seven years · 16, 43, 95, 108
  Seven-year · 15, 23, 94, 95
  Ten horns · 27, 48, 91, 93- 94, 96- 97, 117
  The Day of the Lord · 40
  Tower of Babel · 72
  The mark · 11, 41, 98, 123- 125, 129, 131-132
  The Tower of Babel · 53
  Tribulation · 15-16, 18- 19, 21, 23, 35, 36-37, 39, 41-44, 56, 89-90, 93, 95, 117, 119, 123- 125, 129-131, 147, 149, 155, 166, 171- 174, 177- 178
  Two witnesses · 42, 44
Publications/Various
  Associated Press · 96
  Kesknadal · 101
  National Geographic News · 16
  National Review · 137
  New World Encyclopedia · 20
  New York Times · 138, 144, 157, 171
  Newsweek · 172
  See Change · 52
  The American Free Press · 100
  The Economist · 17, 67, 69, 76, 79, 93, 118, 146
  United Press International · 53

Wall Street Journal · 141
Wikipedia · 17, 20, 54, 101
World Press Review · 99

R

Religion/Churches
- Anglicans · 52
- Al-Aqsa Mosque · 36, 37
- Baptists · 52
- Catholic Church · 9, 39, 47- 48, 50, 52- 54, 59
- Holy See · 54
- Ishtar · 46
- Islamic fundamentalism · 17, 75, 177
- Jezebel · 47
- Judeo-Christian · 54, 89
- Keith Clements · 52
- Lutherans · 52
- Methodists · 52
- Ortho Pope Benedict XVI · 54
- Orthodox · 38, 52
- Monsignor Pierre Raffin · 51
- Muslim · 154
- Pope Pius XII · 50
- The Holy See · 52
- United Methodist News Service · 51
- Vatican · 39, 50, 52-53, 121
- World Wide Council of Churches. · 67

T

Technology
- Adaptive Brain Interface (ABI) · 129
- Bio implants · 129, 174
- CODEST · 127
- Committee for Scientific and Technical Research · 127
- Committee for the European Development for Science and Technology · 127
- Coreu · 79
- CREST · 127
- ESPRIT · 127- 129
- European Nervous System · 132
- European Strategic Programme for Research and Development in Information Technology · 127- 128
- European Technology Community · 127
- Gabriele Taonconi · 132
- Industrial Research and Development Advisory Committee · 127
- IRDAK · 127
- Professor Pierre Rabi Schong · 132
- Radio-frequency identification (RFID) · 132
- Smart cards · 132
- Verichip Corporation · 132

Theologians
- Alan Franklin · 13
- Dr. Ian Paisley · 53
- Dwight Pentecost · 26, 29, 45, 102
- Gaebelein · 26, 102
- Ian Paisley · 55
- Johann Karl Friedrich Keil · 102
- Scofield · 45
- Walvoord · 102, 151

Think-Tanks
- Academy of Political Science · 137
- Federal Trust for Education and Research · 61, 125
- Harvard Center for International Affairs · 21
- Herzliya Conference Institute of Policy and Strategy · *See* Israel
- Institute for International Economics · 78, 142
- Institute Français Des Relations Internationales · 139
- Notre Europe · 115
- The Belmont European Policy Centre · 66, 93, 100
- The Center for Contemporary Arab studies · 149
- The Centre For European Policy Studies · 96, 160
- The Century Foundation · 167
- The European Policy Centre· 115
- The European Union Institute for Security Studies · 85
- The European Union Satellite Centre · 85
- The Federalist Trust · *See* Political Ideologies, *See* Political Ideologies

The Peterson Institute · 142
World Policy Institute · 138

U

United States/US · 11- 13, 16-17,19, 33, 63, 65- 66, 71, 73- 78, 94, 99, 102, 105, 116, 133- 134, 136- 148, 150,153-157, 159- 162, 164 -166, 171- 174, 177
    Alan Greenspan · 143- 144
    Annapolis, Md · *See* Israel:Middle East
    Atlanta Georgia · 144
    Bonn Declaration · 136
    CIA · 146
    Dennis Blair · 141
    European Security Architecture · 136
    Federal Reserve Bank · 144
    GDP · 33, 134, 139, 142, 144-145
    NATO · 65, 73, 83- 84, 136, 167
        Manfred Worner · 66
    New Orleans · 139
    New York City · 18
    Pentagon · 177
    Science and Technology and Cooperation Agreement · 136
    Trans-Atlantic Declaration · 135, 161
    Transatlantic Economic Council (TEC) · 137
    Transatlantic Economic Integration Framework · 136
    US dollar · 11, 77, 143-144
    US Supreme Court · 105
    Washington · 12, 60, 77, 134, 139, 141, 146, 153, 157, 159- 161
US Presidents & Secretary of States
    George Bush ·21,133- 134, 137, 153, 162, 164, 166
    Henry Kissinger · 155
    Bill Clinton · 135, 154, 160
    James Baker · 134, 153, 156-157
    John Kennedy · 63
    Madeline Albright · 154
    Barack Obama · 140, 147
    Ronald Reagan · 121, 133, 141, 152
    Warren Christopher · 154

W

World Insitutions
    Conference on Security and Cooperation CSCE · 70, 73,159
    General Agreement of Tarrifs and Trade (GATT) · 69
    International Monetary Fund (IMF) · 61, 69-70, 143, 146
    Uruguay Round · 69
    Robert Zoelick · 144
    The World Bank · 61, 69, 144, 146
    Maurice Strong · 68
    United Nations · 60- 61, 68- 71, 97, 103, 127, 136, 143, 146, 151-152, 156, 159, 160, 163-164
        The Stockholm Initiative · 69
    World Trade Organization (WTO) · 69, 97, 136-137

www.ingramcontent.com/pod-product-compliance
Lightning Source LLC
Chambersburg PA
CBHW060953230426
43665CB00015B/2188